EDUCATION IN A COMPETITIVE AND GLOBALIZING WORLD

EDUCATING ZIMBABWE FOR THE 21ST CENTURY

WHAT EVERY EDUCATOR SHOULD KNOW

EDUCATION IN A COMPETITIVE AND GLOBALIZING WORLD

Additional books in this series can be found on Nova's website under the Series tab.

Additional e-books in this series can be found on Nova's website under the e-book tab.

EDUCATION IN A COMPETITIVE AND GLOBALIZING WORLD

EDUCATING ZIMBABWE FOR THE 21ST CENTURY

WHAT EVERY EDUCATOR SHOULD KNOW

MORGAN CHITIYO
JOHN CHAREMA
MOSES B. RUMANO
JONATHAN CHITIYO
AND
GEORGE CHITIYO

New York

Copyright © 2014 by Nova Science Publishers, Inc.

All rights reserved. No part of this book may be reproduced, stored in a retrieval system or transmitted in any form or by any means: electronic, electrostatic, magnetic, tape, mechanical photocopying, recording or otherwise without the written permission of the Publisher.

For permission to use material from this book please contact us:
Telephone 631-231-7269; Fax 631-231-8175
Web Site: http://www.novapublishers.com

NOTICE TO THE READER

The Publisher has taken reasonable care in the preparation of this book, but makes no expressed or implied warranty of any kind and assumes no responsibility for any errors or omissions. No liability is assumed for incidental or consequential damages in connection with or arising out of information contained in this book. The Publisher shall not be liable for any special, consequential, or exemplary damages resulting, in whole or in part, from the readers' use of, or reliance upon, this material. Any parts of this book based on government reports are so indicated and copyright is claimed for those parts to the extent applicable to compilations of such works.

Independent verification should be sought for any data, advice or recommendations contained in this book. In addition, no responsibility is assumed by the publisher for any injury and/or damage to persons or property arising from any methods, products, instructions, ideas or otherwise contained in this publication.

This publication is designed to provide accurate and authoritative information with regard to the subject matter covered herein. It is sold with the clear understanding that the Publisher is not engaged in rendering legal or any other professional services. If legal or any other expert assistance is required, the services of a competent person should be sought. FROM A DECLARATION OF PARTICIPANTS JOINTLY ADOPTED BY A COMMITTEE OF THE AMERICAN BAR ASSOCIATION AND A COMMITTEE OF PUBLISHERS.

Additional color graphics may be available in the e-book version of this book.

Library of Congress Cataloging-in-Publication Data

ISBN: 978-1-63117-078-2

Published by Nova Science Publishers, Inc. † New York

CONTENTS

Foreword vii
Dzingai Mutumbuka

Acknowledgments ix

About the Authors xi

Chapter 1 The Zimbabwean Education System: A Historical Overview 1
Moses Rumano

Chapter 2 The Current Structure and Focus of Education in Zimbabwe 19
Moses Rumano

Chapter 3 Early Childhood Education 31
John Charema

Chapter 4 Special Education in Zimbabwe: Historical and Legal Foundations 45
Morgan Chitiyo

Chapter 5 Students with Disabilities and Their Educational Needs 55
Morgan Chitiyo

Chapter 6 Inclusive Education 65
Morgan Chitiyo

Chapter 7 Origins, Theories and Background of Counselor Education in Zimbabwe 75
John Charema

Chapter 8 Teacher Preparation in Zimbabwe 97
Moses Rumano

Chapter 9 The Role of Counselor Education Today 111
John Charema

Chapter 10 Assessment in Education 119
George Chitiyo

Chapter 11 Research in Education 133
George Chitiyo

Chapter 12	Overcoming Current Challenges and Preparing Students for the 21st Century *Jonathan Chitiyo*	**145**
References		**159**
Authors' Contact Information		**171**
Index		**173**

FOREWORD

In the two dozen years that I have lived outside my country I have had the opportunity to travel extensively across the world on business and pleasure. During these travels I met and conversed with a large cross section of Zimbabweans in the diaspora ranging from chief executives of large corporations, professionals in virtually every sector down to itinerant cross border traders and domestic help. The common thread amongst all these diverse persons is their abiding patriotism. It is common knowledge that through their remittance – currently estimated at $1.6 billion dollars a year – the diaspora played a critical role in providing for their loved ones during the days of hyperinflation.

This book, written by five academics based in Botswana and North America, is an example of how the diaspora remains committed to assisting their country. It critically analyses the education system before and after independence to explain why at independence the government undertook reforms to democratize education thereby laying the foundations of what became one of the success stories of independence. They go on to explain how changes in the macro economy negatively impacted what was once one of the best systems of education in Africa.

They conclude by offering some ideas about how to construct the system to respond to the needs of the 21st century. The book is therefore, an excellent resource for anyone interested in the evolution of Zimbabwe's education including policy makers, researchers, teachers and historians.

Honorable Dr. Dzingai Mutumbuka
Former Minister of Education (1981-1989)
Current Chair of the Association for the Development of Education in Africa

ACKNOWLEDGMENTS

First, I give thanks to God for allowing me yet another opportunity to do what I enjoy most – writing. Secondly, I would like to thank my wife, Plaxedes, for her continued support and our two boys, Simbarashe and Tinashe, who have taught me a new meaning of being a teacher. You are the best teachers, boys! To my parents, Abel and Rosemary, all I can say is your formula works. To my siblings, Margaret, Marylou, George, and Jonathan, thanks for being there all the way. To my buddies, Chaidamoyo G. Dzenga and Darlington M. Changara, I can't repay the debt. To the co-authors of this book, this was a rewarding experience. To Dr. Dzingai Mutumbuka, your suggestions and guidance were invaluable. Finally, I am grateful to my mentors, Mr. Claud Chimwaza, Dr. Walter L. Helton, and Dr. John J. Wheeler, who believed in me, showed me the way and never doubted me. You, gentlemen, are my heroes!
Morgan Chitiyo

I give all the praise to God who gave wisdom and knowledge to all the authors. I would like to acknowledge Dr. Morgan Chitiyo for all the hard work he did in coordinating the whole project. To my colleagues, Dr. Moses Rumano, Dr. George Chitiyo and Mr. Jonathan Chitiyo, I appreciate your support, professionalism and advice on this project.
John Charema

First, I give all the glory to God for His divine provisions. I would like to acknowledge the assistance that I got from Malone University Library staff and Dr. CT. My colleagues Dr. Charema, Dr. Morgan Chitiyo, Dr. George Chitiyo, and Mr. Jonathan Chitiyo thank you. My wife, Naomi, deserves a pat on the back, our son, Prosper, and our daughter, Ruvarashe were inspirational with their unwavering support and encouragement. Thanks also to Eddy Furumember who is always encouraging me to express my thoughts in print form. Hon. Dr. Mutumbuka, I am very grateful for your helpful insights.
Moses Rumano

First and foremost, I would like to express my deepest appreciation to my family for their continued support and encouragement in my academic career. I would also like to thank my fellow co-authors of this book; it was such a great experience working with you. I learned a lot through the process. I hope this book will make a positive impact on our country's education system.

Jonathan Chitiyo

I am grateful to Drs. David L. Larimore and Dzingai Mutumbuka for dedicating time towards reviewing the chapters dealing with assessment and research in education. I also thank my coauthors Morgan Chitiyo, Moses Rumano, John Charema, and Jonathan Chitiyo for the effort that they devoted towards this project. Through this all, my wife, Rufaro, has always supported me. My friends Michael Meihls, Joshua Zhungu, and Herbert Chikafu have kept encouraging me to do this work. Thank you all.

George Chitiyo

ABOUT THE AUTHORS

Dr. Morgan Chitiyo
Dr. Morgan Chitiyo is a Board Certified Behavior Analyst, Associate Professor, and Director of the Special Education Program at Duquesne University. Dr. Chitiyo is also the editor of the Journal of The International Association of Special Education and serves on the editorial board of the Journal of Research in Special Educational Needs. He has authored or co-authored three books, two book chapters and over 30 refereed research manuscripts published in reputable journals. He has also presented some of his research at several regional, national and international conferences. His research interests include applied behavior analysis, positive behavior supports, autism, and special education issues in developing countries particularly Africa.

Dr. John Charema
Dr. John Charema is Director of Education at Mophato Education Centre in Francistown, Botswana. He received his Ph.D. in Support Guidance and Counseling from the University of Pretoria. He also has a master's degree in Conflict Transformation and Management from Nelson Mandela University and a master's degree in Special Education from the University of Manchester. He has authored two books and co-authored several others. Dr. Charema has several publications in the field of Counseling, Special Needs, Peace Studies and Health and Wellness. He is a consulting editor for several journals and a member of the Board for Learning Disabilities Worldwide as well as the International Association of Special Education. Currently, Dr. Charema also serves as a supervisor for Ph.D. students studying with the Zimbabwe Open University.

Dr. Moses Rumano
Dr. Moses Rumano is an Assistant Professor of Education at Malone University, Canton, Ohio. He received his Ph.D in Educational Administration from Miami University. He has authored a book and a number of refereed research manuscripts published in reputable journals. Dr. Rumano serves as an external consultant for Consultancy Africa Intelligence HIV/AIDS Unit. He has also presented some of his research studies at several regional, national and international conferences. He served as a primary schoolteacher, secondary schoolteacher, and an educational administrator in Zimbabwe. His current research interests are connecting with students from diverse backgrounds, instructional leadership, and democratic education.

Mr. Jonathan Chitiyo

Mr. Jonathan Chitiyo is a Ph.D. student in the Department of Educational Psychology and Special Education at Southern Illinois University Carbondale. His research interests include Special Education program planning and development and school-wide positive behavior support. He has authored and co-authored a few articles, which have been published in peer-reviewed scholarly journals. He also serves as a consulting editor or reviewer for a number of scholarly journals.

Dr. George Chitiyo

Dr. George Chitiyo is an Assistant Professor of Educational Research at Tennessee Technological University. Dr. Chitiyo conducts research mainly in the area of the psychosocial aspects of HIV/AIDS in Southern Africa, as well as economics of health and higher education both in the U.S. and in Zimbabwe. He has authored and co-authored more than 20 publications and made presentations of his research at several national and international fora.

Chapter 1

THE ZIMBABWEAN EDUCATION SYSTEM: A HISTORICAL OVERVIEW

Moses Rumano

Chapter Overview
This chapter provides a historical development of the education system in the then Southern Rhodesia under the colonial settler regime up to the post-independence initiatives taken by the Zimbabwean government. Racial restrictions imposed on the African students in their quest for education are analyzed through three categories of the education system to serve European, Colored, and African students. In this chapter we also discuss the government's socialist endeavors to provide education for all in the country. Educational reforms, successes, and challenges are highlighted.

Key Topics
The historical context of the Zimbabwean education system
Educational policy in the colonial period
Educational foundation laid by the early missionaries
Kerr Commission
Educational reforms in Zimbabwe

Learner Outcomes
Upon completion of this chapter, readers will be able to:

1) Identify the obstacles, barriers, and hurdles faced by African students in their quest for education.
2) Describe the fundamental roles played by the missionaries to plant education in the then Southern Rhodesia.
3) Articulate the government's socialist initiatives to bring educational opportunities to all children in Zimbabwe.
4) Evaluate the successes and challenges encountered by the Zimbabwean government in the provision of education to all children.

INTRODUCTION

Zimbabwe, a former British colony, gained its political independence in 1980 after a protracted and bloody armed struggle. The colonial legacy of inequality manifested its ugly face on the educational landscape in unmistakable ways of racial segregation and discrimination. European settlers, who were the minority ruling class, had the best access to educational opportunities at the expense of the disenfranchised majority African population. The racially motivated discriminatory policies in colonial Zimbabwe led to the establishment of separate and unequal systems of education to cater to the needs of European and African children separately. After ninety years of British settlement in Southern Rhodesia, two distinct systems of education still existed side by side, serving the African and non-African sections of the population. Soon after independence, Zimbabwe embarked on a massive educational reform program to align its educational goals to the aspirations of the majority of the people.

EDUCATIONAL POLICY IN THE COLONIAL PERIOD

In Southern Rhodesia (now Zimbabwe), as in other parts of British Africa, imperial administrators faced the task of devising educational programs especially suited to the needs of the native peoples, now committed to their care (Atkinson, 1972). Almost inescapably, perhaps, they found themselves forced to balance, on one hand, the moral duty to hasten the pace of African development, and on the other hand, the political duty to safeguard the interests of the colonialists on whose initiative the prosperity of the newly-settled territories chiefly depended (Atkinson, 1972). In Southern Rhodesia, the African population, supplemented perhaps with immigrants from surrounding regions, seemed likely to provide a labor force extensive enough to satisfy the colony's needs for unskilled and semi-skilled workers. In addition, Taylor (1970) noted that not only productive industry, but also domestic and personal service, could be supplied at relatively low cost. The educational policy adopted by white settlers in Southern Rhodesia (Zimbabwe), can best be summarized in the principal of Domboshawa School's report for 1935:

> In such a country as Southern Rhodesia…where a higher civilization impinges upon a lower one, we must not forget that the higher civilization as well as the other is affected. The civilized community in contact with the barbarian community must either raise the latter to its own level or it will ultimately itself sink into barbarism (Atkinson, 1972, p. 14).

The interests of the settlers heavily affected the ways in which the natives could exist and make a decent living, therefore there was need to come up with a plan for coexistence between these two groups. Taylor (1970) stated that Lord Lugard's "Dual Policy," a grand design for partnership between Great Britain and the subject peoples, for whose welfare she had assumed responsibility, was meant to benefit the new settlers. Just as Roman imperialism had laid the foundations of modern civilization, and led the barbarian peoples of northern Europe along the path to fuller development, so British colonial administrators were repaying the debt, by "bringing to the dark places of the earth…the torch of culture and progress, while ministering to the material needs of our own civilization" (Taylor, 1970, p. 7). In Southern Rhodesia the relative strength of the settler community, and its unusually high rate of material investment in the country, provided motives of self-interest for resisting anything liable to encourage a rapid advance in African political power. As stated by Atkinson (1972), "Unavoidably, educational policies in Southern Africa (Zimbabwe), would be subjected to very close scrutiny with a view to assessing their possible impact on European interests" (p. 17).

EDUCATIONAL FOUNDATIONS LAID DOWN BY THE EARLY MISSIONARIES

Atkinson (1972) argued that the impact of the missionary endeavor on life in Southern Rhodesia (Zimbabwe) was probably proportionately greater than in the case of any other African colony. Missionaries opened up the first contacts with the local African people more than half a century before European settlers arrived to exploit the economic and strategic potential of the land. The first contacts made by white people with the African inhabitants of Matabeleland and Mashonaland were due to the evangelizing activities of the Christian church. According to Taylor (1970) the missionary societies were responsible for starting the first formal schools for Africans before the turn of the century and ever since have played a dominant role in the educational system. The first mission station was established by the London Missionary Society at Inyati in 1859; a second was opened at Hope Fountain near Bulawayo in 1870 (Taylor, 1970). These were followed by stations established by the Jesuits at Bulawayo in 1879, the Dutch Reformed Church near Fort Victoria in 1891, and the American Board of Foreign Missions at Mount Silinda in 1893 (Kuster, 1999).

Before the end of the century there were ten Christian denominations carrying out their mission work. However, meaningful organized efforts only came after colonization in 1890, particularly after the enactment of the Education Ordinance of 1899 and, while it was mainly concerned with Europeans, Asian, and Colored schools, it did provide for financial assistance to mission schools subject to the schools complying with certain conditions (Mungazi, 1991). According to Taylor (1970):

> The Education Ordinance of 1899 gave birth to the system of grant-aided schools which today still forms the backbone of the whole education system. The effects of the regulations governing the payment of grants, contained in various ordinances during the decade, were such as to cause African education to develop along agricultural and industrial lines. (p. 3)

In 1910, a committee which investigated the whole question of African development and education recommended that the type of education offered should be a combination of religious, industrial and academic training. Nevertheless, the crafts and skills which it was thought would lead the people to improve their lives in their rural environment continued to be emphasized while academic work received attention only as it was required for a proper understanding of the industrial and religious subject matter of the curriculum (Taylor, 1970). Mungazi (1991) remarked that the problems of African education received considerable attention from the newly elected legislature in 1923. On one hand, the missions were complaining that they were receiving insufficient government aid while on the other hand the Government was dissatisfied with the quality of schools and the lack of clear-cut aims in the administration.

In 1935 the Department of Native Education was reformed, but for administrative purposes was attached to the Native Affairs Department (Taylor, 1970). It was about this time that the social impact of urbanization, brought about by an increasing number of Africans moving to towns in search of employment, began to be felt. In terms of education, it meant that greater attention had to be given to academic work and character training to fit the African population for them to cope with the new conditions they were facing. Lastly, it meant that the problem of providing educational facilities for the increasing demand had to be met (Kuster, 1994).

KERR COMMISSION

Taylor (1970) stated that "The ever-increasing pressure on the schools in the immediate post-war years resulted in demands from various organizations, particularly the Federation of African Welfare Societies (renamed the Rhodesian Institute of African Affairs in 1956), for greater government support for schools" (p. 5). African schools were lagging behind in terms of funding, infrastructural development, and student enrollment. In addition, Taylor (1970) noted that they were critical of some aspects of missionary control and urged that the government should take over all schools. Their demands for a full inquiry into the whole educational system led eventually to the appointment in 1951 of a commission under the chairmanship of Dr. Alexander Kerr, former principal of Fort Hare College in South Africa (Mungazi, 1991). The commission recommended that government and mission partnership should continue. Full credit was given to the role that missions had played in the field of education for Africans, as witnessed by the following excerpt from their official report:

> Missionary enterprises not only bore the whole burden of the earliest attempts at Native education, but has also continued down to the present time to contribute voluntarily to this service a vast amount in personnel, money and self-sacrificing moral, spiritual, physical and intellectual benefit it has been given, or by the European of this country from whom it lifts a load of personal responsibility and perhaps heavier taxation…(Taylor, 1970, p. 6)

The curriculum for African students included a lot of vocational or industrial oriented training, which sheds light on how Africans were considered as a potential source of cheap labor. The emphasis that was placed on industrial education marked the official policy on how the colonial government wanted to use the Africans as their laborers. For all intents and purposes, the curriculum for African students was to produce an obedient, cheap, and reliable labor force (Atkinson, 1972). There was no great interest in giving them quality instruction in reading, writing, and arithmetic, commonly known as the three Rs. In addition, as pointed out by Mungazi (1991), though a further provision in the Ordinance of 1903 required African pupils to be taught to speak and understand English language, this was intended to have a purely functional use only. As the inspector of schools explained:

Injustice arises from the fact that natives and whites are mutually unintelligible, and this be made to disappear gradually if understanding the English language was insisted on; moreover, there was not much advantage to be gained by teaching natives to read and write their own language; when they come into town they have to give up their own language to a considerable extent and talk "Kitchen Kaffir", which missionaries as a rule condemn. It was not intended that there should be any instruction in the reading and writing of English. (Atkinson, 1972, p. 91)

So far, indeed, the initiative for the development of African education, as pointed by Mungazi (1991), rested almost entirely in the hands of the missionary authorities. European opinion, in seeking a further advance by the government in the development of European education, had shown little concern with the position of African schools, except in so far as they might provide a challenge to European workmanship. According to Atkinson (1972), "meanwhile, the government, for its part, showed no enthusiasm for any policies which would imply much heavier financial investment in African education" (p. 91).

EDUCATIONAL REFORMS IN NEW ZIMBABWE

The Zimbabwean educational reforms should be understood in the larger context of the racially motivated colonial education system. During the colonial era, a restriction of access to education for African children by the government was one of the contentious issues that fuelled the struggle for independence by the determined people of Zimbabwe. According to Sokwanele (2013) the newly inaugurated government had to fulfill its promise through the provision of quality education to all its citizens who had suffered under the yoke of the oppressive white minority government. Education was highly regarded as the government wanted to empower its citizens in order to actively participate in the dispensation of new democracy and contribute towards economic development. There was universal access to free education for all Zimbabwean students after independence. To correct the racial inequality planted in the education system, the government opened new schools to all its citizens. However, not all aspiring students were able to seize the opportunity to advance with their education due to a number of challenges that, among others, included shortage of schools, qualified manpower, and limited funding.

In addition, towards the end of the liberation war, several schools were closed down or destroyed, which brought the overall enrollment of students to an all-time low level (Sokwanele, 2013). However, the enrollment drastically increased in 1980 after war hostilities ended due to a Lancaster House brokered ceasefire agreement that subsequently ushered in political independence. The people's enthusiasm to enroll in schools was shown by the rising figures, a trend that has been a perennial feature of the Zimbabwean education system. To illustrate the astronomical rise in enrollment after independence, Sokwanele (2013) pointed out that in 1980, 1,310,315 children were enrolled in schools. Many of them were in primary school with only 74,321 students enrolled in secondary school. The quest for education was shown by a huge and unprecedented enrollment of students to 424,514, an increase of 47.9% from the previous year. In Zimbabwe, 1980 was a watershed point as far as education was concerned. Since the war had ended, many parents and guardians enrolled their children – who otherwise would not have obtained an education – in schools. Also, some of the war collaborators and returning refugees enrolled in schools. With the newly acquired independence, age was not a limiting factor to enroll in school for any Zimbabwean citizen who was interested in advancing their education.

Zvobgo (1999) stated that, "the colonial rule created conditions of semi-slavery which rendered the indigenous people aliens in their own land" (p. vi). Throughout the many decades of colonial rule in Africa, a situation was created through which the colonialists exercised complete control over all aspects of African life. In his analysis Zvobgo (1999) noted that the end of colonial rule in Africa during the second half of the 20th century marked the transition from white minority oppressive rule and domination of black people to a democratically elected black government. This new dispensation of political governance opened new opportunities for reconciliation, social, and economic advancement of black people in Zimbabwe. For several decades Blacks were considered second class citizens in their native country due to lack of freedom and educational opportunities. In rural areas and the farming communities there were very few schools, which were usually in deplorable conditions.

After independence, a number of educational reforms were initiated to reflect the needs of a newly liberated country. These reforms can be divided into three main groups namely, planning and efficiency reforms, quality reform, and relevant curricular reforms. However, Riddel (1998) argued that from a critical point of view, no significant boundaries can be found in these three major reforms as they sought to make education accessible. Dzvimbo (1989) observed that after independence, the Zimbabwean education system witnessed phenomenal growth and development comparable to none in the entire continent. Black Zimbabweans had previously been systematically denied the universal human right to education in their own country. Racially segregated schools had been established to perpetually oppress the African students. Intentional and deliberate discriminatory policies were instituted to underfund and marginalize the African education system. The colonial education system instilled and reinforced an inferiority complex among the African students.

According to Taylor (1970), in 1975 the Rhodesian government was generously spending R$287 (Rhodesian dollars) per student at the primary level and R$493 per student at the secondary level for European, Asian, and Colored education. Unfortunately during the same period, government expenditure for African education was R$23.3 per student at the primary level and R$188 per student at the secondary level (p. 45). Dzvimbo (1989) reiterated that the disparity in funding of the education system led to perpetual control of the African students. For example, Taylor (1970) noted that in 1970 the Rhodesian government enacted a ruthless policy that only permitted 12.5% of African primary students to proceed to secondary education. Only 37.5% of the African students were able to advance to two years of inferior vocational secondary education (Dzvimbo, 1989). One does not need to be a statistician to calculate that half of the student population was left out in the cold even though they had passed the public exit examination at the end of primary schooling. Dzvimbo (1989) stated that this discriminatory policy reduced government grants by 5% to mission-led and council schools that were in charge of the majority of the African primary schools.

In sharp contrast, European students were guaranteed seven years of uninterrupted free primary education and four years of free and quality secondary education. After independence the government embarked on a large expansion of its education to cater for the needs of many African students who were in need of education. Free and compulsory primary education led to a substantial enrollment of students. According to Zvobgo (1999) there was a rapid increase of primary schools from 240 schools in 1979 to 873 schools in 1983. At the secondary level, the same expansion was observed in the number of schools from 177 in 1979 to 789 in 1983. Education was envisioned as the greatest equalizer in a new nation that needed qualified manpower across the racial divide.

EDUCATIONAL EXPANSION IN POST-INDEPENDENCE ZIMBABWE

According to Zvogbo (1999), the educational reforms and policies that were taken by the Zimbabwean government were deeply rooted in the history of colonialism and black oppression, the basic elements of which were racial segregation, brutal economic exploitation and political repression. State policy and facilities were specifically designed to advantage whites. Primary school education for whites was compulsory and free. This was not so for Africans; while only 12.5% of the African school going age was in secondary school, virtually all whites had access to secondary education. At independence in 1980, Zimbabwe had only 3,161 primary schools in three categories, Group A school (only for the white students), Group B schools (for Colored students), and Group C (for African students) with a total enrollment of 1,235,994 pupils. In the secondary school sector there were only 218 schools with a total enrolment of 22,201 pupils (Zvogbo, 1999). Access to education by African children, both at primary and secondary school levels was, as can be seen from the above statistics, highly restricted particularly at the secondary level where a majority of the primary graduates were not catered for at all. Bouncing with the zeal to transform the status quo, the new government had to adopt strategies to increase access to education at all levels in order to fulfill the wish of the African majority.

In addition, Zvobgo (1999) noted that the following measures were taken to address the expansion of primary and secondary school development: reconstructing and opening schools that had been either damaged or destroyed during the war of independence, building new schools particularly in rural areas neglected during the colonial era. Introduction of double sessions (commonly known as hot-seating) in both primary and secondary schools, particularly in former Group B and Group C schools was introduced in order to accommodate as many students as possible.

According to Zvobgo (1999), day secondary schools were introduced that could house some selected primary schools to cater for the increased demand for secondary school places. There was a deliberate policy to relax age restrictions to allow children and in some cases young adults who had been denied opportunity in the colonial era to realize their academic aspirations. The government made an aggressive initiative to abolish school fees at primary school level in order to provide the much-needed opportunity to all students whose parents or guardians could afford to pay for the educational expenses. Evening classes at both primary and secondary levels were introduced mostly in urban areas to give the working adults an opportunity to proceed with their education. The colonial zoning system that prevented African children from attending school in European suburban schools was repealed. Drastic comprehensive measures were wholesomely introduced in the educational sector to provide the much-needed social and economic development to many African children who were denied access to education.

SUCCESSES AND CHALLENGES OF THE EDUCATIONAL REFORMS

The 1980 educational reforms and policies cited above achieved some significant results such as access to education by the previously disadvantaged Africans. In the formal sector, total primary school enrolment rose from 1,235,994 in 1980 to 1,934,614 in 1982, a 56.5% rise in just two years of independence. In the secondary school sector, Form one enrolment rose from 22,201 in 1980 to 110,725 in 1982, a rise of over 80% (Zvobgo, 1986). This monumental increase in access to education continued for the entire first decade of independence. Furthermore, Kanyongo (2005) pointed out that the government policies achieved successes in racial and gender equality, increased the supply of educated manpower, and improved the country's literacy rate. The major highlights of the achievements were captured in the speech delivered by the then Minister of Education, Dr. Mutumbuka in 1984, when he stated:

> Primary education has been made free. Schools at primary and secondary level have more than trebled. The process is still afoot. Our socialist commitment to the removal of all forms of injustice has found expression in the removal of all barriers on the road to knowledge from primary to higher education, and abolishing all social restrictions in admission to educational establishments... (Zvobgo, 1999, p. 115)

The educational reforms and policies not only came with great achievements but some challenges were experienced as well. The result of this educational policy was that schools were inundated with children. The system was quickly expanded to create room for all children of school-going age regardless of their academic or vocational inclinations. Zvobgo (1999) admitted that the implementation of this socialist policy raised several problems. Forged in the heat of the liberation war, the policy pronouncements were over-ambitious in terms of the range of reforms they intended to cover. The resources at the disposal of government were not adequate to finance the party's ambitious socialist ideological agenda. Secondly, the lack of adequate funds meant that civil servants had great difficulty and tremendous frustration in implementing the reforms. A highly excited and expectant black population flooded the education system until pressure on resources became a reality, which forced the government to borrow from other countries. In addition, Zvobgo (1999) conceded that the political mood in the early years of independence did not give policy formulators and implementers much room to rationally examine and debate policies of the ruling party that were imposed on national government.

Some aspects of the educational agenda were resisted by civil servants who opposed change. Most civil servants had served under the colonial regime and were apprehensive of new revolutionary policies. Maphosa, Kujinga, and Chingarande (2007) commented that the educational reforms and policies could not come without some consequences. A number of problems arose, which included the following: overcrowding in schools, shortage of qualified teachers, inadequate teaching space, and perennial shortage of resources such as textbooks, laboratory equipment, and an overstretched budget. Consequently, a decline in the quality of education was noted – a feature which continues to haunt the education sector to date.

NATIONAL POLICIES THAT INFLUENCED THE EDUCATION SYSTEM

Some of the national policies adopted by the government in the 1990s and beyond have contributed to the erosion of the much celebrated post-independence educational achievements. The Economic Structural Adjustment Program (ESAP), the unbudgeted payment of veterans of the liberation war, the military involvement in the Democratic Republic of Congo, the fast-track land reform program, and the most recent Operation Murambatsvina historically stand out. A concoction of these factors contributed to the economic meltdown that finally pushed many professionals, especially school-teachers and healthcare workers, to look for better economic opportunities outside the country. We will briefly look at each of these factors next; but, a more detailed discussion of their impact on the education system is presented in Chapter 12.

The Economic Structural Adjustment Program (ESAP)

According to Boafo-Arthur (1991) the adoption of ESAP in the early 1990s, led to retrenchment of many workers, trade liberalization, devaluation of the Zimbabwean dollar, subsidy withdrawal, and an introduction and/or increase in user fees across many sectors including education and health. Basic social services like health and education became unaffordable to many retrenched workers. These economic reforms engendered an economic disaster, which worsened the HIV/AIDS devastation especially among the most productive population in the country.

Upon gaining political independence, Zimbabwe made commendable efforts in terms of developing its public infrastructure and provision of social services. The literacy rate significantly improved, average life expectancy went up, and childhood mortality rates considerably dropped, giving the much needed hope for prosperity and social stability. However, these developments were soon to be reversed by the harsh economic conditions ushered in by the economic structural reforms, which were prescribed by the World Bank and the International Fund. Research indicates that such reforms have failed dismally in Zimbabwe and other Africa countries (Saunders, 1996). Ghana and Zimbabwe experienced extreme poverty after they had adopted these economic reforms and the quality of education deteriorated following the government's introduction of user-fees; the user-fees ended the free universal education that was introduced after independence (Saunders, 1996). Many students from poor families were denied the opportunity to access education at the time when the school-age population was growing.

The Unbudgeted Payment of War Veterans

The sacrifice and contributions made by veterans and collaborators of the liberation war of the 1970s cannot be overemphasized. No right thinking and patriotic Zimbabwean can deny their selfless contribution. However, the unbudgeted pay-outs given to the war veterans in the late 1990s led to the crashing of the Zimbabwean dollar by over 50% almost overnight. According to Shoko (2013), after a series of street protests and demonstrations, the war veterans were each given Z$50,000 in gratuities and Z$2,000 every month by the government in 1997. Many economic and political analysts believe that the move signalled Zimbabwe's economic collapse. Soon after making these huge pay-outs the government became involved in the 1998 war in the Democratic Republic of Congo, to rescue that country's then president, the late Laurent Kabila. Because of the war, Kabila's government owed millions of dollars to Zimbabwe for military equipment and supplies (Shoko, 2013). Several millions of dollars that should have been used for economic development were diverted to support this war. Faced with a very limited budget, the government had to cut its educational expenditure, which further eroded the educational gains made in the 1980s. In addition, the devaluation of the Zimbabwean dollar made it difficult for many parents to afford their children's education. The buying power of the Zimbabwean dollar was weakened by rising inflation, which further limited the affordability of social services by many families.

The Land Reform

The land question was one of the main reasons leading to the liberation war of the 1970s. The need for comprehensive land reform in Zimbabwe was quite imperative considering how the indigenous people had been displaced and deprived of access to productive land for several decades. However, the manner in which the land reform was carried out brought more challenges than the intended benefits. Following the defeat of a referendum plebiscite in February 2000, the government-backed war veterans started the chaotic land reform by marching into and forcibly taking white-owned farmlands. Critics of the land reform program argue that the unplanned land reform had serious detrimental effect on the Zimbabwean economy. The direct and indirect effects of the land reform program on education are discussed in detail in Chapter 12.

ASPECTS OF CURRICULA REFORMS

The main reason that prompted the expansion of the school system was the need to provide universal free and quality education to all Zimbabweans. However, the government had to come up with some feasible checks and balances to ensure that quality education was offered in all schools (Sokwanele, 2013). A national curriculum was designed in an effort to ensure that all students accessed quality education. However, not all racial groups were impressed with this new radical curriculum move that marked a point of departure from the traditional colonial way of running schools. While secondary education for the European, Colored, and Asian students was free and compulsory, African students had to pay school fees. But beyond that, it had been determined that only half of the African students going to secondary education could pursue an academic curriculum while the other half would be trained in vocational schools to acquire the much needed agricultural and building practical skills. Apart from the discrimination in terms of enrollment, the view that African students were being offered an inferior and less challenging secondary education by being denied academic subjects gained traction. Zvobgo (1999) commented that before independence there were some vocational programs for the European students though their numbers were limited.

The introduction of the F2 vocational schools for African students was resented as it became a symbol of inequality between the races. However, the government had embraced equality as a guiding principle to correct the historical imbalance; therefore, the F2 schools closed their doors. Gradually, the policy of converting these F2 schools was implemented and by the end of 1982 they had become fully fledged academic schools (Sokwanele, 2013). All Zimbabwean students in all schools were thus following the same academic curricula and sat for the same national examinations from the University of Cambridge. While the idea of a national curriculum, which culminated in the Cambridge final examinations, was welcomed, it had its own flaws. Many African students did not have access to good schools; there was a critical shortage of qualified teachers and lack of learning and teaching resources affected the academic performance of many African students. According to Sokwanele (2013):

> It was immediately obvious that the majority of pupils would be severely stressed simply in pursuing academic courses, including pure mathematics which was a compulsory subject. But to expect that all children learn and achieve at the same pace contradicted all knowledge accumulated over years of study of educational practice around the world. It was clear that many children – perhaps the majority – were being set up to fail in secondary schools. (p. 3)

As the government was designing a national curriculum for secondary schools, it noted that science curricula could not be identical in all schools. Rural secondary schools did not have laboratories and electricity. An improvised and innovative new curriculum called "Zimscience" was developed, along with a science kit for experimentation. In the former white schools specific science subjects such as Biology, Physics and Chemistry were offered. These core science subjects prepared students to proceed to Advanced Level unlike their rural counterparts who studied Zimscience. The History and Geography curricula had to be redesigned in order to reflect the new Zimbabwean experience. By and large, all the newly built rural schools were poorly equipped, underfunded and offered little choice to students. A half-hearted attempt by the government to introduce a socialist and Cuban modeled "Education with Production" in the mid-1980s died a natural death after facing stiff resistance from teachers, students and parents (Sokwanele, 2013).

One of the curricular changes made to the education system related to the entry qualification to secondary education. To open up educational opportunities to all students the government made an automatic progression from grade seven to form one starting in 1981. All grade seven students had to take national examinations; however, entrance to secondary school was not determined by passing grades since all students were expected to enroll in secondary school. Chivore (1990) observed that some of the failing grade seven graduates repeated in order to raise their grades though it was not a requirement. Some of the parents who had high expectations for their failing grade seven children required them to repeat in order to acquire the basic knowledge before proceeding to secondary schools. However, the majority of students proceeded to high school despite failing grade seven examinations. The academic challenges that were encountered by the students who had failed grade seven prompted teachers, especially in rural schools to request some children to repeat grades.

The government initiative of automatic progression from primary to secondary school without passing or meeting the minimum standard has remained a permanent feature of the

Zimbabwean education system up to this day (Zvobgo, 1999). The only disadvantage of this automatic promotion to secondary school is that many ill-prepared students either drop out or fail the national secondary examinations. Students who lack the basic literacy and computational skills fall behind in their academic work and eventually give up. Teachers become depressed when their students fail. Zvobgo (1999) remarked that the dedicated and determined teachers struggle with huge classes that have low performing students, which slow down academic progress. The frustrated teachers usually pass on the failing students to the next level and the trend continues up to the end of high school. Automatic promotion and equal curriculum brought short lived joy and fantasy to the education system that inherited racially divided schools.

The cardinal points of Zimbabwe's educational renewal were enunciated by government soon after independence based on a pragmatic curriculum theory and change that rested on a number of salient guidelines. It was considered important that there be a deliberate move towards science and technology in order to discourage the persistence of underdevelopmental trends. Given the new political order, the mass-oriented policies of government, and the Zimbabwean milieu – its traditions, history, level of development, and basic needs – aims and aspirations had to take priority (Zvobgo, 1999). It was important in this regard that Zimbabwe's physical resources, both potential and existing, should be exploited to yield maximum benefit for the society in the interest of development and the satisfaction of its individual and collective needs. Thus, the curricula at all levels of education had to match the Zimbabwean identity and help to build the diversity of culture and background.

In relation to these policy guidelines, Zvobgo (1999) noted that it was considered important that education, like life itself, is a basic human right and government must ensure its accessibility by all. There was deliberate emphasis placed on the importance of education in development and the integration of education in development projects has resulted in a reformed and expanded curriculum. As a preamble to detailed content and pedagogical input at the primary, secondary, tertiary, and non-formal levels, it is useful to outline concrete developmental needs identified on the basis of resources, both available and to be produced.

Curricula Reforms as an Instrument for Rural Development

At the center of the curriculum reform movement has been the need to make education an instrument of rural development and regeneration (Maphosa, Kujinga, & Chingarande, 2007). Even twenty years before independence, arduous attempts at rural development were envisaged under the policy of community development. This failed because of the political climate in which the settler regime began by expropriating land and imposing chiefs as agents of indirect rule (Zvobgo, 1999). The pre-independence attempt is alluded to here only as evidence that rural development was not considered a prized goal for a long period of time in the history of Zimbabwe.

MAKING PRIMARY SCHOOL CURRICULUM RELEVANT

In an effort to reform the primary school curricula, two major considerations were made. The first was to make provisions for the grade seven graduates who could not proceed with education and acquire basic employment skills with which to enter the world of production. This was important because unless the school gives the child knowledge and skills on which to fall back, it would be difficult for the primary school-leaver to secure employment on the competitive labor market. For this reason, Zvobgo (1999) argued that the structure and content of the curricula was designed with a practical bias right across the board. Mathematics and Science assumed a new and more practical role and needed more emphasis in the school because they were considered fundamental and essential for development.

Another consideration was to provide the child with a strong background for secondary education by ensuring that concepts and skills taught in each grade were built upon those taught in previous ones. A spiral-oriented curriculum was produced in order to help students understand concepts in a less frustrating way. More practical subjects were added to the curriculum to produce the best candidates that could easily function in their environment and beyond. Textbooks were written in order to reflect the new environment and the dispensation of democracy in a free country. In both primary and secondary curricula, changes were enacted that sought to make students more productive.

Primary Education (Kindergarten – 7)

The national focus of the Zimbabwean education system is to promote national unity, sustainable economic and social improvement through a constant supply of highly trained and skilled human resources (Curriculum Development Unit [CDU], 1983). The primary education runs from grade zero through grade seven. According to CDU (1983), prior to first grade, children are enrolled in early childhood education and care (pre-school). However, not all six-year old students start school at the same time. Depending on the location some students in the farming communities may start later. While primary education is mainly free, some parents pay levies in the form of building development fund and sports fees if they live in the school districts that require extra funding. The curriculum is centrally planned by the Ministry of Education, Sports and Culture's CDU. There are a number of subjects that are offered such as Mathematics, English, Shona, Ndebele (local languages), Social Studies, Environmental Science, and Religious and Moral Education (from a Judeo-Christian background). Apart from these examinable subjects, the following subjects are also offered at the primary school, Art and Craft, Home Economics, Music, Sports, and Physical Education.

The average teacher student ratio is one to 35. Most teachers in primary schools hold a diploma in education, though many of the primary school teachers are proceeding to get a bachelor's degree. In the most rural and remote parts of the country, there are a number of untrained teachers.

Since independence, primary education has been free and compulsory to all children, irrespective of race, gender or ethnicity and is guided by the policy of impinged progress; grade seven public examination results do not affect progression of the students to secondary education. However, it is important to state that some of the most competitive high schools in the country, such as private and mission schools, have very high expectations from grade seven candidates; therefore, students with low grades will not have automatic entry into such schools.

Grade Seven Examinations

The grade seven examinations take place at the end of primary education. The average age of students taking this examination is 13 years with the common range being 13 to 15 years. Grade seven candidates are tested in five subject areas: Mathematics, English, Shona or Ndebele, and General Paper (composed of environmental science, social studies, and religious and moral education). It is national policy that grade seven candidates do not pay examination fees to take these examinations. Grade seven candidates get separate result for each subject in the form of units on a nine-point grading scale, from one to nine. A score of one is the highest possible grade and nine being the lowest. The best performing students will have a total of four units (one point in each subject excluding General Paper) and the worst results will have a total of 36 units (nine points in each subject).

Grade seven examinations basically serve as a measure of students' level of academic achievement at the end of primary school. Many prestigious high schools use grade seven results to choose their potential form one students. However, many rural and government secondary schools do not have strict entry requirements since they accommodate all grade seven graduates. The government policy on compulsory education ensures that no students can be denied admission for any reason.

SECONDARY EDUCATION (FORMS 1–4)

According to Zvobgo (1999), the dominant feature of secondary school curricula is the infusion of practice based on theory and empirical treatment. The secondary education system is built upon primary education. For reasons of coordinating planning, the Secondary Education Development Unit (SEDU) and the Primary Education Development Unit (PEDU) were combined in 1982 to form the current Curriculum Development Unit (Zvobgo, 1999). The CDU, housed in the Ministry of Education, Sports and Culture has the prerogative to design the national secondary curriculum.

Parents and guardians have a wide choice of high school selection, from mission boarding schools to prestigious private schools. There are parochial private boarding schools, and government-run day and boarding schools. Parents who have the financial ability to pay for their children's school fees send them to expensive boarding schools because most of them provide better education. A majority of students in Zimbabwe attend day secondary schools since they are more affordable. However, many day-schools do not perform at as high academic level as the expensive private schools.

Ordinary Level (O-Level)

Secondary education comprises a four-year (O-Level) cycle where the official entry age is 13 years, and a two-year Advanced Level (A-Level) cycle. The O-Level cycle covers a wide curriculum and different schools offer different subjects depending on the availability of human and financial resources. However, there are core subjects that should be taken by all students such as: Mathematics, English, Science, Shona or Ndebele, Geography, and History. It is government policy that each secondary school student should take a minimum of eight subjects. At the end of the four-cycle, students take the Zimbabwe General Certificate of Education Ordinary Level (ZGCE-O) examinations. A student should pass at least five subjects, including Mathematics, English, and Science. All students who meet this requirement may choose to proceed to A-Level or go to any of the following: teachers' training colleges, technical colleges, agricultural colleges, polytechnic, or nurses' training colleges among other options.

ZGCE O-Level Examinations

The Zimbabwe General Certificate of Education Ordinary Level examinations are administered at the end of form four. Students pay examination fees to take these examinations. These examinations serve a number of purposes. Firstly, they certify students' level of competencies and academic achievement. Secondly, they are used for selection to proceed to Advanced Level, and finally the examination results are used for employment purposes and admission to other institutions of higher learning. The grades used in the final examinations are as follows: A, B, C, D, E, and U – with A being the best grade possible and U (Unclassified) being the lowest. Grades are assigned for each subject, with C being the minimum passing grade. In order for a candidate to be considered successful at Ordinary Level, they should have obtained a minimum of five Cs including English.

ADVANCE LEVEL (LOWER SIX – UPPER SIX))

Advancement to A-Level is based on the Zimbabwe General Certificate Education Ordinary (ZGCEO) performance. Students who wish to proceed with their studies to A-Level need to prove their academic competence at the Ordinary level examinations. In many secondary schools, A-Level students select a minimum of three subjects. Students usually choose the subjects that closely match their future careers and aspirations. To illustrate this point, a student who wants to be a medical doctor, has to take subjects such as Biology, Chemistry, Physics, and Mathematics. Similarly, if one wants to venture into business studies, they can take subjects such as Mathematics, Accounting, Management of Business, and Economics.

ZGCE A-Level Examinations

The Zimbabwe General Certificate Education Advanced Level Examination (ZGCE) is the final public examination taken at the end of secondary school. Results for these examinations determine the future of the students. All universities and institutions of higher learning in them country base their selection on these results. Some prospective employers hire advanced level graduates based on their grades. The letter grade system used is as follows: A, B, C, D, E, F (fail), and O. The O symbol indicates that the candidate's level of academic performance is equivalent to Ordinary Level standard.

HIGHER AND TERTIARY EDUCATION

Tertiary education in Zimbabwe covers all universities, technical colleges, polytechnic colleges, teachers' training colleges, and other vocational skills training centers. The mission statement of the Ministry of Higher and Tertiary Education is "to provide an effective system for the production of patriotic and competent high level manpower through the provision and accreditation of higher and tertiary education programs and institutions for sustainability and global competitiveness" (Ministry of Higher and Tertiary Education, 2013, p. 1). The Curriculum Development Unit is responsible for the coordination, development, and review of vocational and technical curricula. This unit is also tasked to monitor training programs in vocational and technical institutions, and registers non-government vocational and technical training institutions.

According to Kariwo (2007), "higher education in Zimbabwe is going through a series of crises. It is characterized by under-funding and rapidly growing student enrollments. In the past few years, student protests have been frequent. Some of the demonstrations held in the past were very violent" (p. 12). Underfunding of the institutions of higher learning has often been cited as the trigger of such protests. In addition, Kariwo (2007) stated that a lot of valuable property is destroyed each time students engage in violent demonstrations especially at the University of Zimbabwe campus. At least a couple of demonstrations at the University of Zimbabwe led to the closure of the institution for lengthy periods during the 1990s. Apart from student demonstrations at most of the state universities, experienced faculty have been leaving for well-paying regional and overseas universities. Many of the lecturers who leave these institutions of higher education often cite poor working conditions and low remuneration packages. The once reputable and prestigious University of Zimbabwe, is finding it difficult to keep its infrastructure intact, let alone recruit and retain experienced lecturers and staff. Some of the challenges encountered by this oldest institution of higher education include shortage of books, underfunding, and lack of teaching/learning materials among others. Financial constraints have resulted in low standards, for example, failure of the university to subscribe to periodicals and journals on a regular basis has limited the research capacity of faculty members and students (Kariwo, 2007).

Universities and colleges are trying to play their role in preparing youths for employment and national development. Given the fact that human resource development has been the broad aim of educational policy, a great deal of importance was given to the technical and vocational training at independence. The 1981 National Manpower Survey was an attempt to determine, rationally, Zimbabwe's human resource situation and requirements in order to facilitate national rehabilitation, reconstruction and development. Its objectives were, among others, to assess the size and characteristics of the national professional, skilled and semi-skilled workforce and to determine the potential of professional skilled and semi-skilled Zimbabweans (Zvobgo, 1999).

In spite of the above challenges there has been significant increase in enrollment in all technical and vocational areas since independence – a 16% increase from 3,469 in 1980 to 9,261 in 1990 (Zvobgo, 1999). The following is a list of all primary teachers' training colleges in Zimbabwe: Bondolfi, Seke, Morgester, Nyadire, Morgan, United College of Education, Masvingo, and Marymount. The Ministry of Higher and Tertiary Education's website lists the following technical, polytechnic, and industrial training colleges; Bulawayo Polytechnic, Gweru Polytechnic, Harare Polytechnic, Joshua Mqabuko Nkomo in Gwanda, Kushinga Phikelela Polytechnic in Marondera, Kwekwe Polytechnic, Masvingo Polytechnic, and Mutare Polytechnic. Prior to independence in 1980, the University of Rhodesia (now University of Zimbabwe) was the only university in the country. The following universities have since been added to the list of universities in the country: The National University of Science and Technology, Catholic University in Zimbabwe, Midlands State University, Zimbabwe Open University, Lupane State University, Great Zimbabwe University (formerly Masvingo State University), Solusi University, Africa University, Chinhoyi University of Technology, Bindura University of Science Education, Women's University in Africa, Gwanda State University, Zimbabwe Ezekiel Guti University, and Reformed Church University.

According to Kariwo (2007) there is rapid effort to expand higher and tertiary education in Zimbabwe. This expansion was necessitated by the high demand of higher education by many students who were historically denied the opportunity to access higher education. In support, Zvobgo (1999) noted that by 1996, the number of students enrolled in higher and tertiary institutions rose significantly. Kariwo (2007) pointed out that the only university that was established in 1956 (the University of Zimbabwe) was over-stretched in terms of its capacity to enroll all qualifying students. The National University of Science and Technology opened its doors to students in Bulawayo, in 1991. This university has a strong bias in science and technology courses, providing the much needed human development in technological areas to the country. The expansion of higher education took root in Zimbabwe from the 1990s. Many qualified students are now joining institutions of higher learning. As universities have increased in number, so have the challenges that the government has to grapple with in order to provide a viable higher education to its citizenry. Some of these challenges are discussed in Chapter 12.

CONCLUSION

Since the attainment of independence, Zimbabwe has made significant strides towards increasing access and educational opportunities to all its citizens. The ambitious objectives to introduce radical socialist changes in the educational sector brought forthwith desirable results to a new nation. Many primary and secondary schools were opened to cater for the needs of many African students who were denied this basic human right to have access to education for a very long time. The early missionary effort to provide a quality education to African students was the foundation on which the new government built. However, not only successes were brought about but challenges, failures and frustrations as well. In many primary and secondary schools, the perennial problem of inadequate resources continues to haunt the nation to this date. Many colleges, polytechnics, and universities are now available to aspiring students across Zimbabwe. In spite of these big projects, lack of infrastructural development, over crowdedness, unqualified teaching personnel, among other challenges, are some of the issues that the government has to deal with. In higher and tertiary institutions, underfunding continues to be one of the greatest challenges that the government has to deal with. Some of the policies adopted by the government reversed the gains previously achieved in the education sector. These problem needs to be addressed accordingly if the country is to provide quality higher education to its population.

Reflection Questions

1) What initiatives do you think the new Zimbabwean government should have taken soon after independence to promote the development of education?
2) Given the historical challenges that were encountered by African students in Zimbabwe, what do you think is the role of the international community to address those challenges?
3) How can higher and tertiary institutions in Zimbabwe adequately achieve their goal of providing quality education to the Zimbabwean citizenry? How can the challenges they are facing be addressed?

Chapter 2

THE CURRENT STRUCTURE AND FOCUS OF EDUCATION IN ZIMBABWE

Moses Rumano

Chapter Overview

This chapter provides an overview of the current structure of the Zimbabwean education system from primary to secondary through tertiary education, outlining the elements of each of these levels. The goals of the education sector are also discussed as well as issues facing tertiary education.

Key Topics

Primary school (grades 1 to 7)
Secondary school (forms 1 to 4) curriculum
High school (forms 5 to 6) curriculum
The country's educational goals
Governmental involvement in higher and tertiary education
Vocational education
Critical issues facing higher and tertiary education

Learner Outcomes

Upon completion of this chapter, readers will be able to:

- Identify the current structure of the Zimbabwean education system.
- Analyze the specific roles played by the primary, secondary, and higher and tertiary education.
- Recognize the social, economic, and logistical challenges that are encountered by the government of Zimbabwe in the implementation of its educational goals.
- Evaluate the successes and challenges that are encountered by the students and the government at higher and tertiary education.

Introduction

Zimbabwe's education system consists of seven years of primary school, four years of secondary school, and two years of high school. After students have successfully completed secondary education, they have the opportunity to enroll in higher and tertiary institutions. However, not all post-secondary students succeed in going to technical or college due to various reasons. Students who cannot go to college or university join the long list of job seekers armed with their high school certificates. The primary and secondary Zimbabwe school calendar runs from January to December, with three terms each three months long. The three terms are separated by one month holidays. One advantage of having school all year round is that students can easily connect what they learned in the preceding term to the new material. The Zimbabwean higher and tertiary education is composed of teachers' training colleges, polytechnics, technical, industrial training centres, nurses' training colleges, and universities. The main purpose of the Ministry of Higher and Tertiary Education is to adequately prepare students for careers or further education.

Primary School (Grades 1 to 7)

Primary school starts at age six; children applying for grade one enrolment are supposed to have turned six before August of the previous year (Ministry of Education, Sports, and Culture, 2011). Primary education is a seven-year curriculum and typically caters for children from age six to 13 years. Since the attainment of independence in 1980, the government has come up with a national policy that promotes automatic promotion of students from one grade to the next in an effort to make education accessible to all students. However, there are special circumstances under which students can repeat a class. Parents or guardians can request their children to repeat a grade when their academic competency is below the expected standard. The primary school structure was discussed in detail in Chapter One.

Secondary School (Forms 1 to 4) Curriculum

The major subjects offered at the secondary school level include: English, Shona, Ndebele, French, Portuguese, Spanish, Mathematics, Science, Geography, History, Economics, Biology, Chemistry, Physics, Food and Nutrition, Fashion and Fabrics, and Computing Science. These subjects are supposed to serve the interests of the country well. After students have demonstrated their abilities through public examinations in these subjects, they can pursue their preferred careers and professions. Apart from taking these subjects, students have a wide range of extracurricular activities to choose from such as, music, soccer, netball, athletics, swimming, rugby, cricket, and tennis, among others.

By passing ordinary level examinations, a candidate has the option of either proceeding to advanced level, join a college, or seek employment. Advanced level education is designed to prepare students for university education (Ministry of Education, Sports, and Culture, 2011). All council and government secondary schools enroll both boys and girls, while some selective church schools enroll either boys only or girls only. In all the ten provinces in

Zimbabwe secondary boarding schools are more popular because of their academic reputation and better pass rates in the national examinations. In some remote rural areas where cultural practices look down upon the role of women in the society, few girls advance with their education beyond high school. In such cases boys are usually given the opportunity to proceed with their education at the expense of their female counterparts. However, such gender biased preferences are becoming less common.

Secondary education is not free in Zimbabwe. The type of school – that is, government, private, rural, or urban – determines how much students have to pay. In general, private and mission boarding schools are relatively more expensive than day-schools since they provide room and board to students. Although the government intended to have free education for all students at independence, the economic realities on the ground have dictated that school fees should be paid in order for the schools to function. Most of the rural and urban secondary schools are in a deplorable state due to lack of maintenance because of underfunding.

A significant number of brilliant grade seven candidates compete for few places in prestigious private and mission day and boarding schools. These selective secondary schools seek to enroll academically talented students only as a way to maintain their high reputation. Good grade seven results make it possible for the students to join good secondary schools of their choice. It is not uncommon for many secondary schools to require an interview or a placement test before students can be admitted. Secondary education has two levels, forms one to four commonly known as Ordinary level and forms five to six that is referred to as Advanced level. In the past, form two students used to take a public exit examination called Zimbabwe Junior Certificate (ZJC) Examination. However, the ZJC was phased out in 2001. Although the public examination was abolished, the same core subjects such as Mathematics, Science, Geography, English, History, Shona/Ndebele, French, Spanish, and practical subjects are still offered (See Figure 2.1).

The academic performance of students in forms one and two determines the subjects that they will choose to study at forms three to four and subsequently at advanced level. Subject areas assigned at form three to four are based on the results from forms one and two report cards. Students are required to study subject areas that best reflect their academic ability for both ordinary and advanced levels respectively. Students attending schools in rural and high density urban areas do not have as many subject options as their counterparts in private or mission schools. There are limited subjects offered to secondary school students in these poor schools due to lack of resources and manpower. However, in the elite private schools students have the option to take up to 12 or 13 subjects at ordinary level. The Zimbabwe Central Statistical Office, (2000) pointed out that from the early 1990s up until April 2002, GCE ordinary level examinations were set and marked by the Zimbabwe Examinations Council (ZIMSEC) in conjunction with the University of Cambridge International Examination (GCE) system. See the grading system from Chapter 1. From November 2002 up to date, ordinary and advanced level examinations are administered under the ZIMSEC guidelines without the collaboration of the University of Cambridge Local Examinations Syndicate (Zimbabwe Central Statistical Office, 2000).

The Ministry of Education, Sports, and Culture has a policy that ordinary level candidates can only receive a passing ZIMSEC ordinary level GCE certificate after passing at least five subjects including English language with a grade of "C" or better. At ordinary level, English, Science, and Mathematics are considered the core subjects. Entrance to advanced level programs is quite selective and competitive. Many aspiring students cannot make it unless they have the required high grades. Those who cannot enroll due to weak passes either enter the informal trading sector, join the formal work force, or proceed to a technical school or teachers' college. However, the school leavers have very limited possibilities of securing a decent job considering that Zimbabwe's rate of unemployment is currently surpassing 80%. Only the best performing students at ordinary level can join advanced level education.

Sciences	Liberal Arts	Commercial Subjects	Languages	Arts	Practical Subjects
Biology Physics Chemistry Integrated Science Mathematics	English Literature Religious Education Geography History	Accounts Commerce Economics Computer Studies	English Shona Ndebele French Portuguese Spanish German Latin	Art Music	Woodwork Building Metalwork Agriculture Technical Drawing Fashion & Fabrics, Food Nutrition

Figure 2.1. Subjects Currently Offered by ZIMSEC "O" Level Examinations.

HIGH SCHOOL (FORMS 5 TO 6) CURRICULUM

A detailed discussion about advanced level is presented in Chapter One. For a list of subjects offered at this level see Figure 2.2.

Arts/Humanities	Commercial Subjects	Sciences	Technical Subjects
English Literature Geography Shona Language/literature Ndebele Language/literature Divinity History French Art Music Latin German	Management of Business/Business Studies Economics Accounts	Biology Chemistry Computing Physics Mathematics Further Mathematics Pure Mathematics Applied Mathematics Statistics	Technical Graphics Computer Science

Figure 2.2. Advanced Level Subjects Currently Offered in Zimbabwe.

THE COUNTRY'S EDUCATIONAL GOALS

The country's goals and objectives for the education and training sector are clearly expressed in the mission statement of the Ministry of Education Sport and Culture (MOESC) which states that:

> We are committed to the provision of good quality basic, secondary and continuing education to all children and adults through schools, other learning centers and multi-media approaches so as to produce individuals with potential to contribute towards development. In quest for efficiency and effectiveness, the Ministry cherishes in its clients and employees the values of: critical thinking, innovativeness, self-discipline, self-

actualization, consultation and involvement, team work, transparency, professionalism and the role these play in development. (Ministry of Education Sport and Culture, 2000, p. 1)

The goals of the Ministry of Higher Education and Technology (MHET) as stated in the mission statement are:

> To provide, regulate and facilitate tertiary education and training through the planning, development and implementation of effective policies, the provision of resources and management of institutions in order to meet the human resources requirements of the economy and equip individuals to realize their full potential. (Ministry of Higher Education and Technology, 2000, p. 2)

According to the Ministry of Higher Education and Technology (2000), many qualified students proceed to colleges, universities, and technical training institutions. The oldest institution of higher learning in the country is the University of Zimbabwe, formerly known as the University College of Salisbury, which was established in 1956. Before that period, all the aspiring college students had to go outside the country, which limited the opportunities of many students who deserved higher education. To show the commitment of the government to open up higher education opportunities to all its citizens, by 2001, there were 11 universities in the country, including both those that are state-run and those that are privately owned. Some colleges were transformed into universities in order to provide the much needed higher education to all qualifying students. This massive expansion of higher and tertiary education in Zimbabwe has come with both successes and challenges. Some of the achievements made by the government in higher and tertiary education include access to education by the majority of qualifying students, and creation of employment opportunities for both staff and lecturers. However, the rapid expansion of higher and tertiary education has exposed some of the weaknesses in funding and lack of infrastructural development among others.

On average, university students spend between three and five years in college, while in technical and colleges the years of study range from one to three years. The entry qualifications to enroll at a university are five Ordinary level passes including English, and at least two Advanced level passes. Admission into a university or college is highly competitive in Zimbabwe; therefore, prospective college or university students need high passes. The Ministry of Higher Education and Technology (2000) stated that in 1997 the total number of students enrolled in higher and tertiary institutions was 46,495. This figure indicates that many students are now able to access higher education, which presumably will alleviate poverty levels and subsequently raise the standard of living in the country. There are several fields of study for both undergraduate and graduate students, which include social sciences, arts and humanities, several science disciplines, veterinary science, and medicine. Technical and teacher training colleges offer diplomas in various areas of study and specialization.

The Significance of Millennium Development Goals (MDGs)

The Zimbabwe Millennium Development Goals Progress Report (2012) acknowledges that the Millennium Development Goals (MDGs) have become the major guiding framework and gold standard for development throughout the world. Zimbabwe is not an exception since it adopted the United Nations Millennium Declaration in 2000. Being a signatory, Zimbabwe is expected to uphold its pledge to mitigate the effects and origins of extreme poverty and hunger through marked improvement in key sectors such as education, health, employment and social services. Goal 2 of the MDG seeks to achieve universal primary education which was once attained in the first decade after the attainment of independence. Economic growth, human development, and poverty reduction can only become possible through quality education. Throughout the world, education is recognized as a fundamental and universal human right. Zimbabwe faces a daunting task to ensure that by 2015 all Zimbabwean children will be able to complete primary education. High poverty levels, financial constraints, lack of interest in school, among other challenges, compromise efforts to accomplish this goal.

The Zimbabwe Millennium Development Goals Progress Report (2012) noted that there were no official published records to show primary school completion rates beyond 2009. However, the circumstances on the ground, such as student drop out, poor attendance in some schools, and early marriages, among other factors, indicate that it may not be possible to meet the MDG target of 100% completion rates by 2015. The hope to achieve this ambitious goal is based on the effective implementation of the recently developed MDGs Accelerated Action Plan (AAP), which seeks to ensure that by 2015 all Zimbabwean children will be able to complete primary education. The Government of National Unity that was inaugurated in 2009 stabilized the macro-economic environment which had crumbled in years prior. The Political stability following the formation of the Government of National Unity brought much relief to the entire country as efforts to rebuild the broken infrastructure were started. The political and economic stability enabled many children to complete their primary education. In 2009 the primary school completion rate rose to 82.4%, up from 68.2% in 2005. Girls in urban schools had a higher rate of completion than those attending rural schools (Zimbabwe Millennium Development Goals Progress Report, 2012).

The Introduction of the Basic Education Assistance Module (BEAM)

A number of social and economic challenges led to the formation of BEAM in 2001 as a key component of the government-sponsored Enhanced Social Protection Program (ESPP). Smith, Chiroro, & Musker (2012) noted that at the height of the economic collapse in 2000, the Government, in conjunction with the World Bank, UNICEF and other development partners (such as the European Commission, the Department of International Development (DFID), the Australian Agency for International Development (AusAID), the New Zealand Agency for International Development (NZAid), and German Development Bank (KfW)) created the ESPP as a comprehensive social intervention mechanism to protect the poor and vulnerable children from the vagaries of extreme poverty.

The main purpose of BEAM is to provide quality education to orphans and vulnerable children living in abject poverty. According to Smith, Chiroro and Musker (2012) BEAM is now one of the four pillars of the overarching National Action Plan (NAP), intended to reduce household poverty through cash transfers, and to improve access to child social services. Due to economic challenges such as hyperinflation, unemployment, non-availability of goods and services experienced in 2008, the government of Zimbabwe could not afford to fund this initiative. BEAM was re-launched in 2009 with the assistance of donor agencies. Since then, significant financial contributions have been channeled to the orphaned and vulnerable children through payment of tuition fees and levies. Many primary and secondary school students' examination fees are paid through BEAM, giving much relief to the needy families. BEAM has made it possible for several hundreds of students to access quality education.

The effectiveness of BEAM can be measured by its ability to reach out to all poor and vulnerable children across the country (Smith, Chiroro, & Musker, 2012). One does not need to be a political scientist in order to appreciate the relevance of this social intervention in a country that has high unemployment rates. This program has been consistent in serving both boys and girls who qualify as poor and vulnerable. To determine who should be enrolled in this program, a community selection committee vets all possible beneficiaries. Through BEAM, school attendance has improved nationally and drop-out rates have declined. Since the inception of BEAM, schools have recorded an improvement in the public examination pass rates.

Literacy Rates

Zimbabwe has a very high literacy rate – the highest in Africa. The Statistics from the Zimbabwe Millennium Development Goals Progress Report (2012) stated that among 15- to 24-year-olds, the literacy rate increased from 91% in 2009 to slightly above 99% in 2011. This high percentage indicates a strong rebound from the decline that occurred during the political and economic turbulent period from 2000 to 2008. Since the formation of the Government of National Unity, concerted effort has been made to improve access to quality education through numerous interventions launched by the government in conjunction with the United Nations agencies and international donors.

GOVERNMENTAL INVOLVEMENT IN HIGHER AND TERTIARY EDUCATION

The Ministry of Higher and Tertiary Education (2013) vision statement reads, "...to guarantee Zimbabwe as a regional leader in the creative use of new and existing knowledge, skills, attitudes and resources through the local mobilisation and provision of quality higher and tertiary education" (p. 1). In this endeavour, Zimbabwe now has 12 teachers' colleges, 16 polytechnics, four industrial training centres, and 12 universities. The government has a substantial role in crafting functional policies, provides funding, establishes programs of study, determines the curricula, and monitors the academic standards (Republic of Zimbabwe Ministry of Higher and Tertiary Education, 2009). It is the prerogative of the government to approve and establish schools and colleges and to decide what is taught. Governance of the universities is done through university councils, senates and faculty boards. The University of Zimbabwe has traditionally monitored the quality of higher education throughout the country and approves syllabi for colleges and polytechnics. As the oldest institution of higher learning in the country, it has the expertise and human capacity to check the academic standards of all colleges affiliated to it.

The University of Zimbabwe and the Associate College Center, a teachers' association started in 1950, monitors and supervises teacher education programs (Ministry of Higher Education and Technology, 2000). Universities have various roles in the daily running of the institutions such as, coming up with research agendas, supervision, and extension of courses. Many universities are well connected to both the private the public sectors of the country. Some committees are set up to reach out to the private sector in an effort to collaborate on research.

Universities assign teaching loads to lecturers through selection boards chaired by the administrators that include the vice-chancellor the dean, and the department chairperson. Many universities in Zimbabwe provide comprehensive graduate studies in various areas. In order to be admitted into a master's program one should have an undergraduate degree in a specified area of study. Admission into a doctoral program is very competitive and requires an earned master's in a particular area of specialization. On average, the completion of master's degrees takes between one to three years, while doctoral degree programs take a minimum of two to three years to complete.

VOCATIONAL EDUCATION

Apart from colleges and universities, polytechnics and technical institutions play a major role in the provision of quality higher education in the country. The need for vocational education was underscored by the stagnant economy's inability to absorb new workers since the 1980s. Due to a high rate of unemployment, the need to impart and expand technical and vocational oriented skills is of paramount importance. With this need in mind, subjects such as accounting and management of business were introduced in secondary schools. Few selected secondary schools also introduced different specialties such as automotive, electrical, mechanical, or production engineering, among others.

All technical and polytechnic colleges' main purpose is to provide the graduates with effective job skills. The government introduced these technically-oriented colleges in order to create a trained workforce comprising of individuals eager to revive the economy through business entrepreneurship. Remarkable growth and demand for higher and tertiary education in Zimbabwe has resulted in an increase in the number of universities from one before independence to 12 as of 2013. The flagship institution, the University of Zimbabwe, offers a number of fields of study for both undergraduate and graduate students, which include social sciences, arts and humanities, law, several science disciplines, veterinary science, and medicine. To cater to the needs of the students interested in majoring in science and technology, the government launched the National University of Science and Technology (NUST), located in Bulawayo, the second largest city. This university houses some of the country's best and vibrant science and engineering programs. Some of the general university degree programs such as Bachelor of Arts and Bachelor of Science are three years long with the possibility of an additional honors year. Many of the specialist degree programs take four years to complete.

MAJOR CHALLENGES FACING HIGHER AND TERTIARY EDUCATION

Zimbabwe has experienced an unprecedented economic meltdown over the last decade leading to serious social and macroeconomic malfunctions characterized by hyperinflation, perennial foreign currency shortage, and an accumulation of public debt, and reduced industrial capacity. According to the University World News (2010):

> Following the new fees and currency regime, the 2009 first school term and academic year saw huge dropouts and students forced to defer. Tuition fees ranged from between US$400 to US$1,200 per semester while the average salary in Zimbabwe is set at US$100 per month. During June 2010, hundreds of students were prohibited from sitting exams after failing to pay tuition fees. A further challenge to the teaching and learning quality at Zimbabwean academic institutions is the severe staff shortages. In March 2010, university lecturer salaries were increased to $800 per month; however, they remain well below the regional average which is set at $2,000 per month. (p. 6)

Since the 1990s, the government has been struggling to adequately fund all the institutions of higher learning in the country. The Zimbabwe Independent Newspaper, (2010) reported that institutions that normally received research funds from businesses and the donor community dried up. This lack of funding severely affected the standard and quality of education in colleges and universities. Without financial resources from the private sector many universities could not afford to buy up-to-date teaching and learning materials, equipment and resources. Higher and tertiary education requires up-to-date technology that enhances well focused research and enriches curricula.

Due to lack of private and government funding, most of the educational infrastructure, facilities and equipment are dilapidated and in dire need of renovation. It is common knowledge that effective learning and research take place in conducive and supporting environments. The challenges that students face on a daily basis in all the institutions of higher education need not be overemphasized. Students are not only affected by the lack of materials and infrastructure, but also being taught by inexperienced lecturers due to the brain drain of the past decade (Makuto & Maponga, 2009). Highly skilled and experienced professionals from Zimbabwean universities, colleges, polytechnics and schools left the country in search of greener pastures. The vacuum left by these experienced professionals has been felt throughout higher and tertiary education.

To fill the vacant positions in higher education, some inexperienced professionals were hired to teach and supervise some programs that were only manned by highly qualified and experienced personnel. Heavy workloads, low staff salaries, deteriorating conditions of service, and emigration of professionals have crippled the once vibrant higher education sector and the economy in general. There is therefore, need to look at increasing remuneration and incentives in an effort to retain the best qualified personnel in the country. The government has to engage the private sector, the donor community, and the international community in an effort to revive the vibrancy of the once thriving higher and tertiary education.

PHYSICAL RESOURCE GAPS

The CARA/IOM Zimbabwe Higher Education Initiative 'Consultation Findings' (2010) reported that laboratories did not have adequate and up-to-date technical equipment. Without the necessary equipment, no proper experiments and research can be successfully carried out. Students' abilities and innovation will be compromised and incapacitated. For example, the most recent findings on the impact of deteriorating standards in higher education pointed out that students based at the National University of Science and Technology, in Bulawayo, had to travel more than 400 kilometers to Harare in order to witness laser technology in action. Some of the complex challenges besieging higher and tertiary institutions include water and sanitation problems thereby threatening students and staff health. Some of the lacking materials and equipment include overhead projectors, office furniture and equipment for staff offices; also, regular power cuts at universities stifle any significant progress.

In addition, the Ministry of Higher and Tertiary Education (2009) noted that lack of office equipment for lecturers hinders the effectiveness of teaching and learning. To further compound to the perennial challenges faced by higher and tertiary institutions, the quality of many students coming from the ailing secondary school system negatively affects the academic standards. Students enrolling at the university system therefore, need remediation support in order to meet the required standard. This crucial need for student support is not currently being met due to lack of manpower.

SHORTAGE OF FUNDING

The University World News (2010) reported that student fees were the largest source of income, yet students were often unable to meet payments thereby affecting institutions' financial stability to function properly. Without sound financial support, there has been a marked decline in student social welfare. Lack of student financial support has resulted in some students being forced to drop out of their studies, defeating the government's ambitious policy of making education accessible to all qualifying students. To alleviate some of the challenges that are encountered in higher institutions of learning, the Ministry of Higher and Tertiary Education has since formed the Brain Drain and Human Capital Mobilization Committee whose mandate is to deal with the issue of skills shortages brought about by the brain drain in the country (Jongwe, 2009). The committee is tasked to explore various ways in which the brain drain can be turned into a brain gain. The main goal of the committee is to retain more professionals in the country while reaping the benefits of expatriate Zimbabweans. At independence in 1980, such similar shortages of teaching staff were resolved by bringing in expatriate teachers but today Zimbabwe does not have the financial capacity to hire more teachers. The problem of inadequate teaching staff has resulted in heavy teaching loads in some universities with some lecturers having to teach all year without a break. These challenges are further discussed in Chapter 12.

CONCLUSION

The Zimbabwean education system is composed of primary, secondary, higher and tertiary education. The main goal of the education system is to provide good quality basic, secondary and continuing education to all children and adults through schools, other learning centers and multi-media approaches so as to produce individuals with potential to contribute towards national development. The education system aims to produce citizens who are well qualified for various professions and generally, who are good citizens. There are a number of challenges that are currently affecting the Zimbabwean education, largely, the lack of funding. The lack of funding has adversely affected the quality of education over the past several years, starting in the early 1990s. The introduction of the BEAM has brought much relief to many poor and vulnerable children through payment of school fees and levies. To further compound to the challenges faced by higher and tertiary institutions, the quality of students coming from the ailing school system is having a negative impact on the university sector. Another challenge faced by the Zimbabwean education is the problem of inadequate teaching staff due to brain drain, a perennial problem from primary level through higher and tertiary.

Reflection Questions

1) What possible changes can be made to the current primary and secondary education structures in Zimbabwe?
2) Zimbabwe is currently experiencing a high rate of unemployment. How can its education system empower its citizens to be employers instead of employees?
3) How can higher education in Zimbabwe sustain high academic standards in the face of funding problems?
4) How relevant is the higher education and technology curriculum to the current social and economic problems?

Chapter 3

EARLY CHILDHOOD EDUCATION

John Charema

Overview

This chapter focuses on early childhood education, the types of services, facilities available, and the skills to be acquired during the important formative years. A discussion is pursued on policy and legislation, the benefits of early education, suitable activities to engage children and choosing the appropriate services. The chapter highlights all major aspects in early childhood education, the challenges that governments face and the benefits of the programs.

Key Topics
Definition of early childhood education
Policy and legislation
The benefits of early childhood education
From here to primary school
- Physical development
- Social development
- Emotional development
- Intellectual/Cognitive development
- Creative and problem solving skills

Parental and family involvement
Early childhood education programs
- How to choose an appropriate service

Learner Outcomes
After reading this chapter learners should be able to:

- Articulate and state the importance of early childhood education
- Explain the benefits of early childhood education
- Outline skills gained during early childhood education
- Describe activities and materials used to develop the required skills
- Identify features that characterize an appropriate program

INTRODUCTION

While UNESCO (n.d.) defines early childhood education as the period from birth to eight years, this chapter focuses on three to five year olds. Indeed a time of remarkable brain growth, these years form the basis and foundation for subsequent learning and development. Early childhood education (also referred to as early childhood learning and early learning) involves the informal and in some cases formal teaching of young children by people outside the family or in settings outside the home. Research is quite clear and established that there is correlation between quality early childhood experiences and positive performance in primary school (UNESCO, 2002). Early childhood education is considered a critical stage which supersedes later educational programs that seek to enhance a child's performance. Investing in early childhood education builds sound educational foundation that can withstand most of the challenges that children meet in their day-to-day learning. Community and support services for parents with young children are becoming an integral part of early childhood programs within a broader context of their (children's) physical, social and cognitive development.

What is Early Childhood Education?

Early childhood education refers to the education provided to children under the "formal" school going age. The same also refers to the formal teaching of young children by people outside the family or in settings outside the home. "Early childhood" is usually defined as the time before the age of "normal" schooling which is the age of five in most nations, Zimbabwe included. Such education is provided in a variety of services set up in different environments. This is common practice particularly in Zimbabwe and many other African countries. Most of these are set up within schools, in specially built centers or settings outside the home. Some of these centers are homes modified to suit the purpose of the service provided. Usually the services are grouped under either (i) day care center, (ii) nursery (iii) play center, or (iv) pre-school.

In these centers, children are taught a variety of gross and fine motor skills. However, the goal of these educational settings is to meet the needs of all the three to five year olds. In some cases this is achieved with voluntary participation by people from the local community and universal programs that positively promote healthy, emotional, physical and cognitive outcomes for children. The nature of the service delivery is mostly characterized by indoor activities that culminate with out-door physical activities. Basically early education is provided at the concrete operational stage with children using a lot of concrete educational materials such as toys, both electronic and non-electronic, building blocks, pictures, balls, ropes and many other related materials. They engage in a variety of activities that benefit them in a number of ways including stimulating their minds, developing their social and emotional beings, their cognitive and psychological capacity, their gross and fine motor skills, and their coordination and balance. For early education to succeed, young children should be provided with a safe, secure, comfortable and loving environment in which they can learn and thrive under the care of well-trained adults. It is the responsibility of both parents and service providers to ensure that children have access to affordable and beneficial programs whether private or public. Some of these centers are set up by the government or community and are run by the community through the use of volunteers, while others are run as private enterprises.

Policy and Legislation

As indicated in the two cited documents, in 2005 the government of Zimbabwe drafted a policy for primary schools to establish classes of Early Childhood Development (ECD) under the Early Childhood Education and Care (ECEC) program (Mywage.org/Zimbabwe; Portfolio Committee Report, 2010). Under this program, it was mandatory for all infants to attend preschool one year or two before "official" school entry. The aim of the government was for pre-schools to educate children, provide care for them and foster their development mentally, socially, emotionally, psychologically and physically.

Working parents welcomed the policy since it gave their children a chance to receive meaningful guided development and preparation for "formal" school. However, private childcare centers in Zimbabwe were and continue to be unaffordable for the ordinary parent in the low-income bracket. The involvement and support by government provides positive initiative for children to gain access into the important programs of early childhood education. Cited challenges at the time included shortage of trained ECD teachers, inadequate play and arts materials, as well as lack of appropriate sanitary facilities, and nutrition challenges.

Challenges were also encountered in the registration of early childhood education centres. Most of the centres were and are still not registered. It is the Ministry of Education policy that all centres should be registered in order to ensure that children receive their education in an appropriate environment equipped with suitable facilities that meet the expected healthy standards. Licensed early childhood services are bound to meet the standards and provide educational services that are monitored through the Ministry of Education. Such service providers should have trained personnel and be well equipped with a variety of suitable materials for children to use. Sound foundation and educational background is formed in the child's formative years which are critical for all round development.

Most countries have pre-school education policies in place, what is lagging behind is the implementation of the programs, mostly due to limited resources. As pointed out by Nyanga (2009), the government of Kenya assumed responsibility for pre-school education in 1980 and has since streamlined the pre-school programs. The training of pre-school teachers, the preparation and development of the curricula, and the preparation of teaching materials are now undertaken by the government. Like many other African countries the development of pre-school units in Kenya and the cost of teachers' services have, on the other hand, continued to be met by the local communities and non-governmental agencies. To enhance the development of pre-school education, the government of Kenya in collaboration with the Van Leer Foundation, established the National Center for Early Childhood Education (NACECE), mainly to train trainers of early education teachers. Zimbabwe is experiencing the same. The training of early childhood education teachers and the provision of learning materials to these centers are still hampered by financial constraints and limited resources.

The Benefits of Early Childhood Education (I Am Ready to Play)

In most early childhood education programs, the philosophy is that children learn through play with the guidance and support of adults. However, these adults sometimes disturb instead of facilitate play. Given time, space and freedom, children are experts at play. Miller (1982) asserts that in early forms of play, the child acts without any awareness of rules. It is simply pleasurable motor activity, often spontaneous in nature. As they play, children develop an understanding of their experiences, and further craft their self-identities, expand their mental horizons and shape their future. Like adults, children use their past experiences to make sense of the present and use the present to predict the future. Through play children establish dimensions, meanings, values and implications of different actions. Reifel and Brown (2001) purport that play is extremely robust and remarkably fragile in the sense that it is universal, and that youngsters always manage to play, no matter how poor or desperate their backgrounds may be. The backdrop that underpins this discussion is under the auspices of the United Nations Convention on the Rights of Children. UNESCO (2002) advocates for Early Childhood Care and Education (ECCE) programs that attend to health, nutrition, security and learning and which provide for children's holistic development. The two arms create weighty responsibilities which rest upon the shoulders of adults who shape, and more often than they realize, control children's play.

There is increasing recognition, awareness and knowledge that the first few years of a child's life are a particularly fundamental and sensitive period in the process of development, laying a foundation in childhood and beyond for cognitive functioning as well as behavioral, social, physical health and self-regulatory capacities (Charema, 2012; Karoly, Kilburn, & Cannon, 2005). Yet many children face various challenges and stressors during these years that can hamper their healthy development. Karoly et al. (2005) go on to explain that interventions in early childhood programs are designed to mitigate the factors that place children at risk of poor outcomes. Such programs provide supports for the parents, other guardians, the children themselves, or the family as a whole. These supports systems are likely to be in the form of learning activities or other structured experiences that affect a child directly or that have indirect effects through training parents or otherwise enhancing the care giving environment (Karoly et al., 2005). It is worth mentioning that while most research findings (Child Forum, 2010; Brewer, 1998; Reifel & Brown, 2001) suggest that early benefits in terms of cognition or school achievement may eventually fade, emerging evidence (e.g., Parker-Rees & William, 2006) suggest that early education can bring about longer-lasting and substantial gains.

The growth of early childhood development programs in countries around the world both developed and developing, attest to the increasing recognition of the importance of promoting the physical, social, and psychological development of infants and young children at developmental risk, due to the direct and indirect effects of poverty. According to the UC Berkeley Parent Handbook (2012), Early Childhood Education is no longer viewed merely as a preparatory stage assisting the child's transition to formal schooling. The Parent Handbook posits that services and support for parents with young children is becoming an integral part of early childhood services and policy, placing Early Childhood Education within a broader context of social development and gender equity. This is a clear indication that the divide between early childhood education and care persists, but integrated approaches to the child's care, development and learning are gaining ground. It has been noted through research studies

(Child Forum, 2010; Ramey, 2013; UNESCO, 2002), that from the moment a child engages in an early education program, the focus on achievement begins. When children are well prepared, their early achievements lead to more successes in school, but when they are not prepared, a lifelong struggle can begin (Ramey, 2013).

Early childhood education often focuses on children learning through play, based on the research and philosophy of Jean Piaget, first published in 1920 (Donaldson, 1978). This belief is centered on the "power of play." It is perceived that children learn more efficiently and gain more knowledge through play-based activities. These include, but are not limited to, social games, dramatic play, art, music and movement and many other related play games. The play theory stimulates children's natural curiosity and endowed social fabrics to "make believe" acquiring knowledge and assuming responsibility through role play. Scholars attribute play to surplus energy, relaxation, recapitulation, cognitive functioning, or instinct (Reifel & Brown, 2001). Support for play has additionally gained momentum as a result of effort to fortify scientific theories of learning. Play which can be described as "the work of children" contributes towards children's general growth, cognitive, social, emotional and physical growth.

Pre-school education and kindergarten covers learning from three to five years of age. The terms "day care" and "child care" do not convey the educational aspects, although many childcare centers use more educational approaches (Parker-Rees & Willam, 2006). The distinction experienced over years in many countries, Zimbabwe included, between childcare centers and kindergartens have disappeared due to personnel employed to work in these institutions of education. Many countries require teachers in early childhood facilities to have a teaching qualification. Therefore, as children learn and develop a variety of skills in their pre-school centers, they are guided by professionals who are well knowledgeable about the activities that develop the required skills.

There is strong evidence to suggest that early childhood education can have some great benefits for children, but the quality of that education must be assessed to see what kind of benefits it actually provides. The quality of education offered in different child education centers is determined by the quality of teachers and facilities in these centers. The major aspect is for children to have guided purposeful play since they spend most of their time in daycare settings, if this is not provided to benefit children, perhaps the best is to advise parents to engage a teacher aid, and supply them and the child with play materials to use while at home. Maturity and individual differences are factors to consider since not all children benefit the same from early education.

There are a number of claims towards the benefits of early childhood education. It is proclaimed that early childhood education provides most children with a sound educational background to their learning during their elementary years. Research suggests that children who attend preschool do better at number work, reading and social skills than children who do not attend (Brewer, 1998; Ramey, 2013). The authors go on to suggest that children who attend early childhood education programs are likely to develop increased cognitive skills at the beginning of school, relate better to other students, which can increase their social skill, and are more socially competent in their preschool, kindergarten and school-age years. Such children are likely to be better socialized and can work easily with other children. A study from the Massachusetts Institute of Technology (MIT) (2005) says that early childhood education boosts the economy by providing jobs to people employed in these centers who in-turn pay taxes. The same MIT study states that there is better job preparedness and ability to meet future labor demands in children who attend and receive an early childhood education.

From Here to Primary School

The best foundation one can give to a pre-school child prior to a formal school education is to enrol the child in a preschool so that the child can learn and develop independence, which further enhances the development of thinking and problem solving skills (Child Forum, 2010; Ramey, 2013). The growing demand for quality early education is fuelled by parents who want their children to have an early head start and get off on the right foot so they can be successful in life and at work. The popularity of early childhood care and education is also attributed to a changing view that given the right material under skilful guides, infants are competent individuals. At this level, among other skills, children learn self-control and self-assertion.

Things the home can carry on to do to encourage young children to develop independence, which are taught at early childhood education learning centres include making their own breakfast, tidying up their own toys after play, carrying their own bags, and learning to dress and undress without help. If early education is to adequately prepare children for primary school, programmes should be consistent with research findings and the importance of play in the early years of learning. The aim is to develop in children, the five different developmental domains which all relate to each other. They can be referred to as the SPICE of life: social, physical, intellectual, creative and problem solving and emotional, skills (Child Forum, 2010). These can be achieved through the use of a variety of activities with the use of relevant games and learning materials.

PHYSICAL DEVELOPMENT

For physical development of gross and fine motor skills, children need to be afforded the opportunity to engage in physical play. To begin with, there should be adequate materials for children to use both outdoors and indoors in order to facilitate play. This includes multipurpose equipment with the following: tree huts, steps, slides, rocking boats, tunnels, swings, that encourage climbing, jumping, running, balancing, swinging, crawling, drawing, writing in the sand and many other related activities. It is important to emphasize that play should always be graded according to children's age groups.

For indoor activities, children should be provided with toys, rubber foams, yarn, pairs of scissors for cutting, rubber balls for throwing and catching, painting brushes and materials, clay to manipulate, beads for stringing, sewing cards, pegs and peg boards and many others. On the open sports field children can be given the opportunity to run up and down, play with balls, use jump ropes and hula-hoops for experimenting and developing movement and control.

SOCIAL DEVELOPMENT

Social development refers mostly to the ability to form attachments, play with others, cooperate, share, and create lasting relationships (http://en.wikipediaorg/wikiEarly childhood education). This also concerns the child's identity, relationships with others, and understanding of his/her and other children's place within a social environment. Puppets can be utilized through role-play for children to develop or model some of the necessary social skills such as appropriate techniques for joining a social group for play or conversation, and receiving visitors at home and in the classroom. As their social development progresses children become capable of successful interactions with others. Ideally they develop pro-social behaviors such as helping, cooperating, learning to control aggression and also develop a positive concept of themselves. Basically the key factor at this stage is to develop socially acceptable behavior in order to relate well with others.

EMOTIONAL DEVELOPMENT

Emotional development involves self-awareness, self-confidence and the ability to cope with and understand feelings as indicated in (http://en.wikipediaorg/wikiEarly childhood education). Typically, this is observed as children interact with others and evolve from expressing undifferentiated responses to emotions to being able to express their emotions in socially acceptable ways and to control their impulses. With more and more experiences, children become more capable of understanding how others feel, react, and develop a sense of right and wrong. Children need to be allowed to express and share their emotions which could be in the form of humor, anger or excitement in order to appreciate real life situations. However, this should always be done in a controlled manner. Emotional development in children can be achieved through a variety of activities. They can be allowed to dramatize situations in which anger or frustration is handled appropriately without necessarily hitting or shouting at other children. The use of puppets can be used effectively to help children practice emotional control by giving appropriate responses to emotional outburst through the use of positive language. In their play groups, the teacher or children can ask one another what makes them angry, what do they feel like doing when angry? Answers could be; when I am denied what I want or something that I really like to do, when I lose in a race or game, when I am not given what I want, or when I do not get my way. May be the next thing would be to ask children how they show their anger, and ask them to act, say it or indicate by body language. Activities to model appropriate behavior can be engaged through puppet play in groups.

INTELLECTUAL/COGNITIVE DEVELOPMENT

Cognitive development occurs when children will be learning to make sense of how living and non-living objects relate to the physical world. Their intellectual development grows gradually in proportion to their chronological ages. This is well detailed in Jean Piaget's stages of development, which are relevant but not necessarily part of our current discussion. A variety of play activities with the use of toys, puzzles, role play story-telling, make believe stories, attaching incidences to pictures as well as most activities given in different situations of life, naturally develop and enhance cognitive . One cannot separate cognitive development from other developments since they are all interwoven.

CREATIVE AND PROBLEM SOLVING SKILLS

For developing thinking and problem solving skills, children can be provided with puzzles to practice on, and harder ones are added as their skills develop. As suggested in (Child Forum, 2010), children can be asked questions in groups with situations discussions to find possible solutions and answers, for instance how chicks, birds and other insects like butterflies grow inside eggs and tiny cocoons, or why certain food staffs fill the pot when boiled such as beans, rice, macaroni, from as little as half the pot? Why does water increase when mother boils green vegetables, different types of meat or vegetables from the fridge? Why is that when something is rotten it smells and we can quickly identify the smell? Some questions will challenge children to think and in their groups discuss possible solutions with an adult's guidance. Children need to be supported to remain on task in order to practice and improve their concentration for success. Help can be given for children to expand their knowledge through practical hands-on activities and experiences. Children need to be provided with lots of play-based learning opportunities through, drama, adult role play, fun, and to be exposed to a broad range of activities. This can be done through role plays on what happens in the community, through travel to different places, shopping in different towns, going on bush and mountain walks, watching different types of buildings being constructed, what happens at matches be it soccer, cricket, tennis, net ball, hockey and the like (Child Forum, 2010). They also need to be encouraged to make many decisions and to provide many possible solutions or explanations to problems. During play, children should be allowed to engage in activities and experiences of their own choice. They can be asked why they choose such activities.

It is unfortunate that in some pre-schools, play time has been replaced by skill drills and an over emphasis on activities intended to enhance children's emerging literacy and both gross and fine motor skills (Brewer, 1998). Brewer explains that the prevailing rigid and academic mindset can be explained by the persistence of fundamental beliefs that continue to influence authorities. For most educators, the enshrined ethos that children should be disciplined and controlled, seem to have given birth to the conviction that play appears chaotic and undisciplined and further undermines the school's primary purpose which is to bring order and control in children's lives. Educational accountability and the so-called quality education have pressured early childhood educators to narrowly focus on academic skills rather than social aspects of life. It is of paramount importance that early childhood educators are cognizant that the decisions they make about prohibiting, permitting, condoning or encouraging play have a profound effect on children's day-to-day lives. Children spend most of their waking hours at different settings and in most cases in centers away from home.

For children to develop a sense of independence, teachers can organize and provide for activities such as dress up corners where children can assume a variety of roles using simple costumes such as over size clothes, aprons, hats, sun glasses, shoes and many others ensuring correct dressing. There should be a plenty of popular play materials so that children are not disadvantaged by having to wait long for their turn and that fewer arguments arise among children. As children mature, teachers should help them work out approaches to turn-taking, sharing play materials by using a waiting list or a timer. With the use of a variety of play materials, under knowledgeable guidance, development takes place in an orderly process of moving from an undifferentiated movements and reactions to finely differentiated controlled movements and specific responses. When most of the (SPICE) aspects of life are developed, not always fully, the child is reasonably ready for "formal" school.

Parental and Family Involvement

Parental involvement is one of the key factors that both researchers and early childhood educators view as an integral part of the early childhood education process (Charema, 2012). Often educators refer to parents as the child's "first and best teacher". Many researchers (Justice, 2007; Karoly et al., 2005; Ramey, 2013) have reported strong relationships between parent-child interactions and children's cognitive and socio-emotional development. An early childhood centre can provide only a fraction of all thata child needs – which is why parents and everyone in the community also play a role in children's early learning. Parental and family encouragement in a child's education plays a very important part in boosting the child's morale and confidence. Children from well to do families with a variety of resources whose parents are likely to recognise the importance of supporting their child's early learning at home are likely to get a lot of support. This would give them an additional advantage in their general education from primary school all the way to high school. While such parents' homes may be well-resourced, what their children benefit socially, emotionally and mentally through interaction with other children cannot be substituted by anything. In the early years of a child's development research (Child Forum, 2010; Brewer, 1998; Ramey, 2013) show that the family is one of the most influential forces on the child's learning. The part played by siblings, play mates, parents, and members of the extended family cannot be under estimated. With time such family members significantly influence a child's attitudes, thinking, physical well-being, social skills and behaviours for future successes or failures. Although it is believed that with a well-resourced home, children are not really disadvantaged if they do not have early childhood education prior to starting school, however, there would be some gaps socially and emotionally which they could cover by attending early childhood classes. In some cases if the home environment is richer educationally and can provide the child with a greater range and variety of learning experiences the child may be disadvantaged if they attend a poorly resourced and equipped early childhood programme. There is need for an opportunity to participate in the community outside of the centre building for outdoor activities. It is very important for parents to stay engaged in their child's learning process even if they are getting most of their education from a daycare, home-school, pre-school and any other related service provider. The knowledge and experience gained from a parent will be more appreciated and remembered by a child than if any other person taught them, especially at an early age (Child Forum, 2010; Reifel & Brown, 2001). Early childhood education is crucial to child development and children should be carefully entrusted into the hands of someone trusted to benefit the child.

Early childhood education should teach the child about self in relation to other children. This is a crucial part of the child's ability to determine how they should function in relation to other people. They also learn to appreciate the importance of having other people in their company and working in groups. Early care must emphasize links to family, home culture and home language by uniquely caring for each child (Charema, 2012). Parents should provide their children with nutritious meals, show a nurturing attitude, give them attention, affection and encouragement so that they develop fully in a healthy manner. If part or all of the above is lacking, children may experience developmental deficits. There is a false belief that more hours of formal education for a very young child confers greater benefits than a balance between formal education and family time. A systematic, international review, (UNESCO, 2002) suggests that the benefits of early childhood education come from the experience of play participation which greatly adds to child development outcomes, especially with the support of parents and family experiences.

Early Childhood Education Programs

In general early childhood education refers to a diverse range of child programs, from daycare, play center, transition to preschool and others (www.wisegeek.com). The documents explains that the quality of preschool programs can be very beneficial to children if well-resourced and are run by professional people. Children can learn social and interpersonal skills that can only be learned with other children around. During play they learn to adapt to different school settings where they will be transitioning from activity to another. If the early childhood education program is well resourced and the learning experiences provided for children exceed in quality what can be provided for at home then the child will be advantaged in terms of benefits. In later high school years some of the academic benefits are likely to wash out but not totally. There is also a school of thought that the benefits of getting a good head start are far lasting for they are likely to make a young adult more resilient and able to cope with life's pressures and challenges (www.wisegeek.com). But if the quality of the early childhood education program is lower than that of the quality of the child's home learning environment, then the child is likely to benefit less by participating in a formal early childhood education program. However, by the mere factor of mixing and interacting with other children, every child benefits in one way or another. Family background factors, including parents' education level and home learning environment have a much greater influence on children's development and achievement. It is every parent and every child's wish to experience a quality service from an early childhood program at least better or equivalent to the quality of their home setting.

Information from (www.wisegeek.com), explains that not all early childhood programs are equally beneficial, and their value can vary depending on funding, learning materials, play facilities, the teacher-to-child ratio, and teacher qualifications and experiences. Among others some of the long-term benefits of early childhood education in quality preschools include but are not limited to greater parental involvement, fewer referrals to special education or remedial services, higher grades, better social skills, and a greater ability to focus. Some studies (Ramey, 2013; UNESCO, 2002) also show that children attending preschool are more likely to graduate and pursue higher education, and be well integrated socially as an adult. These children may also be less likely to commit illegal acts, and tend to earn more money.

Many research studies (Child forum, 2010; Ramey, 2013; UNESCO, 2002) on young children living in deprived environments and from low-income families whose parents do not have high school or college qualifications have shown that these children can be given an educational head start and are more likely to succeed at high school and engage in less crime. They even benefit more if they are placed in a conducive high-quality and well-funded organised early childhood program with qualified teachers, in small group sizes and high adult-child ratios right from an early age. The benefits can wash out in later years due to the effects of later school experiences, on-going problems associated with poverty, and the community children live in. However, where families are involved in the early childhood program, the benefits of attending the program for the child seem to be more enduring and greater.

How to Choose an Appropriate Service

When selecting an appropriate early childhood education program for your child, it is better to start by writing down first your reasons for wanting to use a service then match these reasons to what the different early childhood services in your area provide (Child Forum, 2010). Actually it is important to make sure that a service benefits your child physically, socially and educationally, therefore the service should provide a developmentally rich environment that does not hamper the development of the child. Service centres should have programs that cover the whole development of a child as indicated under the heading (From here to Primary School) together with a number of activities that develop those skills. If a service centre does not have adequate resources and qualified personnel, then it might not be the best one to consider for your child. It is important to note that the responsibility of staff and providers of early childhood education services is to work in partnership with parents and to serve children and families. Also it should extend on what parents can provide for their children. For example, the home environment of parents should influence the choice of an early childhood service that provides opportunity for contact with urban or farm and native animals. Other aspects to consider would be outdoor physical play, painting, constructing items, water and sand play.

A review of literature offers some guidelines of features that are associated with better developmental outcomes for children (Child Forum, 2010; www.wisegeek.com; MIT Study Report, 2005). Six main features appear to be associated with more effective early child education and development:

- Programs with better-trained caregivers appear to be more effective due to the knowledge they have on child development and activities to engage children for better outcomes.
- In the context of any pre-school, play center or day care center, there is evidence to suggest that programs are more successful when they have smaller child-to-staff ratios.
- There is some evidence that more intensive programs are associated with better outcomes, but only if the activities are varied, with particular emphasis on directed play.

- Early childhood intervention programs have been shown to yield benefits at a later stage in academic achievement, behavior, educational progression and attainment, delinquency and crime, labor market success, among other domains.
- Well-designed early childhood interventions with clear objectives and well-organized activities have been found to generate positive results for the children.
- Programs that are designed for different age groups with related activities and resources to use seem to yield better results in developing the whole child better than programs that involve all pre-school age groups.

Conclusion

Early childhood education benefits children, their families, and their communities. From improved academic outcomes to the economic savings to schools and governments, the benefits of high-quality early childhood education are irrefutable. The positive correlation between quality early childhood experience and performance in primary school is well established. Research has also shown that investment in the early years outperforms other public policy options in terms of savings on benefits for the unemployed and benefit on taxes from the employed. For children from poor families, Early childhood is a time-bound opportunity to break the cycle of poverty. Some of the long-term benefits of early childhood education in quality pre-schools include greater parental involvement, fewer referrals to special education or remedial services, higher grades, better social skills, and a greater ability to focus. Such programs help in strengthening the care environment, building the capacity of vulnerable parents, families and communities to care for their children. There is bound to be successful transitions of young children from their home environment to daycare, preschool and school. The early care and education industry is vitally important economically and would provide employment on a larger scale than the ailing industrial sector in Zimbabwe and most African countries. Some of the benefits include social inclusion and respect for diversity thereby promoting equal opportunities and skills that will help children to live in diverse societies. Children attending pre-school are more likely to graduate and pursue higher education and be well integrated socially as adults. These children may also be less likely to commit illegal acts, criminal offences and tend to earn reasonably good money to afford them a decent living that form part of useful members of the society.

This chapter has given an overview of Early Childhood Education and its importance. The policy and legislation under consideration have been discussed. The benefits of the program to the children, family, schools, the government and the country as a whole have been enumerated. Activities and materials used to enhance children's development and skill acquisition have been discussed and examples have been given. The chapter has also demonstrated the importance of having trained teachers, adequate facilities and relevant materials in pre-schools. Parents have been guided in choosing an appropriate program for their children. The chapter emphasized early education as a must for every country that is geared for development.

Reflection Questions

1) Define Early Childhood Education and using your own words describe its importance of cancelled
2) Explain how the following institutions benefit from early childhood education: (a) the family, (b) the primary school, (c) the government (d) the country
3) Why is it important to require pre-schools to be registered and why should parents and the family be involved in early childhood education?
4) Is it necessary to have trained teachers in pre-schools? Why?
5) Children like to play. What do you think is the role of play in pre-schools?
6) What do you think the government should do to improve early childhood education in the country?

Chapter 4

SPECIAL EDUCATION IN ZIMBABWE: HISTORICAL AND LEGAL FOUNDATIONS

Morgan Chitiyo

Overview
This chapter provides an introduction to the development of special education in Zimbabwe. It provides an historical overview of special education before, during, and after the colonial era. The chapter also highlights the work of some individuals who contributed to the development of special education in the country and concludes with a discussion of the legal foundations of special education in the country.

Key Topics
Special education defined
The need for special education
History of special education
Special education laws and policies
Current status of special education

Learner Outcomes
Upon completion of this chapter, readers will be able to:

- Define special education
- Articulate the need for special education in Zimbabwe
- Describe the historical development of special education in the country
- Describe how the work of Mr. Jairos Jiri and Mrs. Margarreta Hugo contributed to the development of special education
- Identify and describe the laws and policies that govern special education in Zimbabwe
- Describe the current state of special education

INTRODUCTION

Special education in Zimbabwe is still quite rudimentary. This is in spite of the country having rapidly developed its education system, following the attainment of political independence from Britain in 1980, resulting in the country having one of the highest literacy rates on the African continent. In this chapter we will discuss the historical development of special education in the country. We will highlight the contributions made by specific individuals towards this cause. We will also discuss special education laws and policies that guide special education in the country.

WHAT IS SPECIAL EDUCATION?

Special education can be defined as instruction that is specially designed to meet the individual needs of exceptional students (Hallahan & Kauffman, 2006). By exceptional students, we refer to students who are either gifted or who have disabilities that interfere with their ability to benefit from the general education curriculum. Such students would require individualized supports in the form of special learning materials (e.g., Braille, hearing aids, or magnifying glasses), curricula and instructional modifications (e.g., differentiated instruction, functional curriculum goals or adapted assessments), behavioral supports (e.g., positive behavior interventions) or related services (e.g., physiotherapy, speech therapy or counseling). These supports should be considered part of the student's educational program depending on the student's particular needs.

Even though special education encompasses both students who are gifted and those with disabilities, in this text we will focus on students who have disabling conditions and, therefore, struggle to access the general education curriculum on account of those conditions. Examples of such disabling conditions would be sensory disabilities (i.e., hearing impairment or visual impairment), physical disabilities (e.g., Spina Bifida, Cerebral Palsy), intellectual or cognitive disabilities (previously referred to as mental retardation), developmental disabilities (e.g., autism), and learning disabilities. Students who have health conditions (e.g., Asthma, AIDS) that affect their learning would also qualify for special education. Because these conditions can seriously affect students' learning, educators have to tailor their instruction to meet the students' unique educational needs.

Another group of students who may also be candidates for special education are at-risk students. These are students who, because of certain conditions (i.e., environmental, biological, or developmental) have a greater than usual chance of developing disability (Heward, 2009). Conditions that can put children at-risk include severe malnutrition, war/conflict, disease, extreme poverty, birth complications, and developmental delays. Even though they may not yet be identified as having specific disabilities, at-risk students may experience significant challenges in their learning – a result of their exposure to the conditions. Just like their peers with disabilities, such students may require specialized instruction in order to facilitate their learning and possibly prevent them from developing disability.

We will discuss different types of disabilities and their educational implications in the next chapter. But, before we do that we will look at the concept of disability in the historical context of Zimbabwe.

THE NEED FOR SPECIAL EDUCATION IN ZIMBABWE

In 1981, the government conducted a national disability survey and reported that there were 54,900 children with disabilities in the country (Csapo, 1986). Almost two decades later, UNICEF (1998) found that there were 150,000 children with disabilities in the country while the Zimbabwe Central Statistics Office (1997) reported documenting 218,421 people with disabilities. Because these statistics appear low, Chimedza (2001) cautions that this could be influenced by cultural factors which determine what is considered a disability in Zimbabwean society. Also, children with other health conditions (such as asthma, epilepsy and AIDS) may have been left out as these conditions are less likely to be identified as disabilities in Zimbabwean culture. However, children with such conditions could be classified as having disabilities and would, therefore, be in need of special education if their condition interferes with their learning.

According to the 1981 national disability survey a majority of the people with disabilities (53%) were children (birth through 15 years of age). In addition to this number, about 200,000 children between the ages birth through 14 years were reported to be living with HIV (UNAIDS, 2011). Apart from the children who may be infected with HIV, many children have been orphaned by the disease. In fact, Zimbabwe has one of the highest numbers of children orphaned by HIV/AIDS. According to UNAIDS (2011) there were about one million children orphaned by HIV/AIDS in Zimbabwe. Many of these children may also be candidates for special education as they may suffer from conditions such as emotional behavioral disorders or post-traumatic stress disorders – effects of watching the usually long illnesses and the eventual death of their parent(s).

Furthermore, there are many children who, today, may be classified as at-risk in Zimbabwe. Over the past decade the country has experienced devastating socio-economic and political crises characterized by violence, conflict, hunger, severe deprivation and extreme poverty. The impact of these crises on the wellbeing of children can never be overemphasized (this subject is further discussed in Chapter 12). Many children have been victimized, tortured, abused, and traumatized. Also, the crumbling health delivery system could not afford decent maternal health and childcare for most women and their infants, respectively. Although there is no immediately available data to support this, that the last decade has left indelible scars on the lives of most children across the country cannot be contested. Unfortunately, the formal education system fails to address the needs of these children (Chitiyo, Changara & Chitiyo, 2008; Pridmore & Yates, 2005).

According to Pridmore and Yates (2005) regular schools are failing to meet the educational needs of children with disabilities resulting in many affected children failing to access the national curriculum or to develop basic literacy and numeracy or functional skills. Special education is, therefore, necessary. Because it is specialized and individualized to meet the children's unique needs, special education is well placed to promote positive educational and adult outcomes among the many children who are challenged by disability.

HISTORICAL PERSPECTIVE

Traditionally, in Zimbabwe, individuals with disabilities were looked at with suspicion; because people did not understand why some individuals were born with or would develop disabilities, they came up with different explanations to account for such occurrences. These explanations were mostly related to the spiritual or metaphysical – that is, witchcraft or curse from God or ancestral spirits (Hapanyengwi, 2009). For others, having a disability was simply a misfortune or bad luck. How people view disability is important because it influences how they treat people with disabilities. If people ascribe disability to supernatural forces they are likely to seek supernatural solutions such as witchcraft; education may not be seen as a viable intervention for remediation. For example, because people interpreted disability as a curse from the numinous or as a sign that one had fallen out of favor with the ancestors, parents of children with disabilities would consult traditional healers – *n'anga* – for cleansing and possibly remediation.

Although the general inclination towards disability and the societal outcomes for people with disabilities appeared to be negative, researchers such as Devlieger (1999) argue that this wasn't always the case. Based on a study of African linguistic anthropology – Shona proverbs in this case – Devlieger found that some Shona proverbs discouraged people from looking at people with disabilities scornfully while others actually commended them. However, in spite of this sometimes favorable disposition, having a disability in pre-colonial Zimbabwe was generally characterized with unfavorable consequences ranging from derision, neglect and sometimes infanticide.

Special Education before Independence

Prior to the colonial era, education in Zimbabwe was not formal. Knowledge was passed on from one generation to another in an informal way, which has been referred to as indigenous knowledge systems (see Mapara, 2009). According to Hammersmith (2007), knowledge under the indigenous knowledge systems emanated from the "… complex kinship systems of relationships among people, animals, the earth, the cosmos, etc. …" (p. 2). Older generations would pass to younger generations knowledge about different aspects of community life such as agriculture, medicine, security, botany, zoology, craft skills and linguistics (Mapara, 2009). Under this system of education individuals with disabilities were accommodated to the extent that they could contribute to the society; as such, the degree to which an individual participated varied based on what they were perceived to be capable of contributing (Kabzems & Chimedza, 2002).

Formal education was introduced during the colonial era. However, the formal education system that was introduced was very exclusionary such that only a few "outstanding" blacks were enrolled in school. For children with disabilities, formal education was a product of the pioneering work of Christian missionaries and other philanthropists who felt a moral obligation to help. Such work can be traced back to the 1920s with the establishment of education for children with visual impairment at Chivi Mission by Mrs. Margarreta Hugo of the Dutch Reformed Church of South Africa in 1927 (Zindi, 1997). As enrollment grew, the school was moved from Chivi to Capota near Masvingo in 1939. The Capota Mission School for the blind still operates to this day.

The years following Mrs. Hugo's groundbreaking work saw a proliferation of similar works of philanthropy dedicated to individuals with disabilities. For example, in the 1940s, a man named Jairos Jiri started creating facilities for individuals with disabilities. Mr. Jiri strongly believed in rehabilitation and therefore, started workshops where individuals with various disabilities would be trained in skills such as leatherwork, basketry, music, and woodwork, among others (Farquhar, 1987). The centers' and institutions' focus was not initially academic curricula; the individuals were taught a variety of functional skills so that they could contribute to and become productive members of the society. Mr. Jiri's work would eventually earn him posthumous recognition as a national hero from the government of Zimbabwe. Today, the Jairos Jiri Association, his legacy to Zimbabwe, runs a few centers around the country.

There is no doubt that Mrs. Hugo and Mr. Jiri's work contributed immensely to the development of special education in the country. Mr. Jiri's work in particular challenged the traditional belief system that relegated people with disabilities to the fringes of society as beggars and vagrants. Through his work, Mr. Jiri demonstrated that individuals with disabilities had the capacity to learn and could, thus, be equipped with skills to become contributing members of the society. In short, these philanthropists changed attitudes – a particularly important development in a society so characterized by superstition, mistrust, and indifference to the welfare of individuals with disabilities.

Special Education after Independence

The attainment of political independence from Britain in 1980 ushered in a new era in the lives of many indigenous black people who had hitherto been denied access to education through the colonial educational system. In the first decade following independence the new government passed laws and ordinances promoting educational opportunity for all Zimbabwean children as described in Chapter one. The Education Act of 1987 was the most important of these laws declaring that all children, regardless of their race, tribe, place of origin, national or ethnic origin, political opinions, color, creed or gender, had a right to a school education.

Though not directly related to special education, these laws and ordinances had notable impact on the education of children with disabilities. According to Peresuh and Barcham (1998) the government's policy of universal primary education was an important step in promoting the education of children with disabilities as evidenced by the sudden increase in their school enrollment in the years following its enactment.

As stated earlier, the curriculum for individuals with disabilities, up until 1980, comprised mostly of functional skills. With government getting more involved in their education individuals with disabilities started accessing the academic curricula at independence.

This was particularly true for individuals with physical or sensory disabilities. They could now access the general education curriculum with special supports provided via special schools, self-contained special education classrooms or resource rooms.

Today, there are several schools serving children with disabilities around the country. Some of the schools are run by private organizations such as churches. The schools mostly follow the concept of integration via resource rooms, self-contained integration units, and special classes (Chimedza, 2008).

Integration is when students with disabilities are placed together with their peers without disabilities for educational purposes whenever possible. It differs from the concept of inclusion in the sense that with inclusion all services and supports for children with disabilities are usually provided in the general education environment; with integration the said children can be pulled out and would only mix with their peers without disabilities when they are considered ready to do so. Figure 4.1 provides a description of different forms of integration in Zimbabwe. Most of these programs are for children with mild disabilities such as sensory disabilities. Educational services for children with severe disabilities are still quite limited (Baeza, 2002).

Many students with moderate/severe disabilities either attend the regular schools where they would receive all their instruction in self-contained special classes or attend special schools with boarding facilities. The curricula for children with disabilities vary depending on the severity or type of disability. Many students with sensory disabilities or mild disabilities participate in the general education curriculum while those with moderate/severe disabilities participate in a functional curriculum which focuses on life skills.

Even though Zimbabwe is a signatory to the 1994 Salamanca Statement and Framework for Action on Special Needs Education, which calls on countries to endorse the inclusive education approach for children with disabilities the approach is only practiced to a very limited extent in the country. Many highly qualified special education professionals would be needed to provide the necessary support to the students with disabilities in the general education classrooms. The country does not currently have the capacity to successfully promote full inclusion of all students with disabilities. Some of the limitations are lack of personnel, underdeveloped infrastructure, lack of resources and unfavorable attitudes towards inclusion in some communities (Charema, 2010). Hence the country tries to promote inclusion by using different forms of integration as discussed earlier.

In order to promote quality of education for children with disabilities the government, through the Ministry of Education and Culture, established a department of School Psychological Services and Special Education. The major function of this department is to support schools in order to enhance the quality of educational services provided to students with disabilities.

This includes providing professional development, guidance, and technical assistance to school-teachers in support of the countries' policy of inclusion. However, the effectiveness of this department has been severely compromised because of limited funding.

Even though many children with disabilities can now attend school there is still no guarantee that they will receive an appropriate education – one that addresses individual student needs. One of the main reasons for this is the lack of a specific legal framework providing the assurance for the fulfillment of this governmental obligation. Another main reason, related to the first one, is lack of resources such as qualified special education professionals. Whatever the reasons may be, we strongly believe that a cogent legal framework is the bedrock for any successful special education program. We will, therefore, look at the legal foundation for special education in the country next.

Resource Rooms
These are support units designed to provide support needed to promote the success of students with disabilities who will be participating in the general education classroom. They are mostly used for students with visual or hearing impairments who will be learning alongside their peers without disabilities; they would go to the resource rooms to receive support on how to use braille or sign language and reinforcement of concept taught in the classroom.

Integration Units
Integration units are more exclusionary than resource rooms. Instead of receiving academic instruction in the general education classroom, students with disabilities would receive their instruction in these units and only participate with their peers without disabilities during extra-curricular activities.

Integration

Special Classes
These are self-contained special education units where students with disabilities receive all their instruction separate from their peers without disabilities. Special classes are considered more transient than integration units. Students are assessed frequently and once they meet certain criteria they are usually moved back into the general education classroom. They are appropriate for all types of disabilities.

Figure 4.1. Forms of Integration.

SPECIAL EDUCATION LAW

Even though the government of Zimbabwe started taking the education of individuals with disabilities seriously following the country's independence, there is still no direct legislation guiding the provision of special education services up to this day. Instead, there are several policy statements which were designed to guide educators in terms of decision-making. This is in addition to the Education Act of 1987, which provides for universal education for all children.

Despite being the most important law in providing educational access for children with disabilities, the Education Act of 1987 does not guarantee that the education would be appropriate for the children. In fact, there is no legal instrument to ensure that children with disabilities receive appropriate education. For students who need special and individualized support such as assistive technology, the Zimbabwe Policy Statement on Special Education states that these would be made available based on the availability of funds (Peresuh & Barcham, 1998). This condition exonerates the government from its responsibility to ensure every child gets the necessary devices for an appropriate education.

Another important policy that guides the provision of special education is the policy of integration which was introduced in 1987 to ensure that children with disabilities had equal opportunities in the regular schools (Ministry of Education and Culture, 1987). In addition, Policy Circular 36/1990 recommended special schools and regular schools for students with severe/profound disabilities and those with mild/moderate disabilities, respectively (Chitiyo, 2008; Oakland, Mpofu, Glasgow, & Jumel, 2003). Policy Circular 36/1990 provided for the placement of children with disabilities in special classes, resource rooms, and special schools (Ministry of Education and Culture, 1990). A major weakness of these policies is that they do not stipulate how placement decisions are made (Chitiyo, 2008). As a result, Oakland et al. (2003) argue that children may end up being placed in available options regardless of whether their needs will be met there. Such a situation would compromise the successful delivery of special education. Where a child with disabilities should be educated should depend on their unique educational needs and not on the availability of services. If a child needs special educational services, those services should be considered an inalienable part of their education. This includes the type of placement that is deemed necessary for the child to access education.

There are certainly a variety of policies in the country that guide the provision of education to children with disabilities. However, these policies do not obviate the need for comprehensive special education law to the same effect. Policies do not have the same legal authority as laws and so would not be considered binding to the government. Even more important is governmental commitment to the provision of appropriate education for children who are challenged by disability. An appropriate education would address each learner's unique educational needs and promote their development to become independent and contributing members of society. We therefore strongly urge educators and policy makers to come up with specific and comprehensive special education legislation that will guide the special education process encompassing all aspects from defining who is eligible for special education services to assessment and identification, placement decisions, curriculum issues, preparation of teachers, and funding. Unless such legal framework is put in place, receiving an appropriate education will continue to be an elusive goal for most children with exceptional needs.

CONCLUSION

In this chapter we have defined special education and discussed the need for its development in Zimbabwe. We have also discussed the historical development of special education in the country starting with the pre-colonial era, moving on to the colonial and post-colonial times. We identified some individuals who made notable contributions to the development of special education in the country and described their contributions. Finally, we discussed the legal foundations of special education in the country highlighting the need for comprehensive laws designed to guide the education of children who are challenged by disabilities.

Reflection Questions

1) Define the term special education and using examples, discuss what is meant by at-risk learners.
2) Identify factors that put children at-risk for special education.
3) Explain why special education is needed in Zimbabwe.
4) Describe how people with disabilities where treated in pre-colonial Zimbabwe.
5) Describe the contributions of Mrs. Margarreta Hugo and Mr. Jairos Jiri in the development of special education in the country.
6) Identify the laws and policies governing special education in the country and describe why such laws are important for individuals with disabilities.

Chapter 5

STUDENTS WITH DISABILITIES AND THEIR EDUCATIONAL NEEDS

Morgan Chitiyo

Overview
In this chapter we explore different disabilities and their characteristics. We will also look at how the disabilities interfere with the learning capabilities of the affected children. This is particularly important because we believe educators should understand their students' needs first as a precursor to designing appropriate educational interventions that address these needs.

Key Topics
Specific disabilities
Specific learning needs of students with disabilities

Learner Outcomes
Upon completion of this chapter, readers will be able to:

1) Identify different types of disabilities
2) Describe the cognitive, social, behavioral, and learning characteristics of students with disabilities
3) Describe the learning needs of students with disabilities

INTRODUCTION

One of the reasons educators fail to provide appropriate education for students with disabilities is because of the educators' lack of understanding of the educational needs of the students. In order to provide appropriate and meaningful education, it is imperative that educators first seek to understand their students in terms of how they learn as well as any factors that may interfere with their learning. Disability is one of the factors that significantly influence students' learning. Different disabilities affect individual students differently. However, researchers have observed some characteristics that tend to be most common across students with disabilities.

We will be discussing these characteristics in this chapter. But, one should bear in mind that every child is unique and may be uniquely affected by their disability. As educators, we should desist from making general assumptions about students based on disability labels.

INTRODUCING MILD DISABILITIES

Mild disabilities refers to a group of disabilities for which the affected students would require fewer supports (compared to students with moderate/severe disabilities) in order to benefit from their education (Raymond, 2008).

The term should not be construed to refer to less serious conditions because even though mild, the disabilities may still, and often do, seriously affect students learning. Generally, the term is thought to encompass disabilities such as learning disabilities, mild intellectual disabilities (i.e., mental retardation), emotional or behavioral disorders, attention deficit hyperactivity disorders (ADHD), autism, communication disorders and sensory disorders. We will briefly look at these disabilities next.

Learning Disabilities

Learning disabilities refers to a group of disorders that interfere with an individual's ability to acquire and use certain skills such as speaking, writing, reading, reasoning or doing mathematical computations. These deficits stem from a neurological disorder which affects the brain. Since the affected skills are fundamental to the learning process, learning disabilities negatively affect an individual's academic performance. Some students may display a variety of reading problems (dyslexia). Others may have difficulty understanding and manipulating numbers (dyscalculia). Still, others may have difficulty with the physical aspect of the writing process resulting in failure to produce legible handwriting (dysgraphia). These disorders are briefly described in Figure 5.1.

Several factors have been implicated as possible causes of learning disabilities. These include brain damage or dysfunction, genetics, biochemical abnormalities, and environmental factors (e.g., severe malnutrition, or exposure to toxins such as lead or mercury). Whatever the cause, educators should understand that learning problems are not always volitional on the part of the student. Acknowledgement of this verity is a prerequisite for effective teaching.

Intellectual Disabilities

Previously referred to as mental retardation, intellectual disability refers to a developmental disorder that significantly affects an individual's present levels of functioning in terms of intellectual growth and daily functioning (Beirne-Smith, Patton & Kim, 2006). Individuals with intellectual disability usually display significantly below average intellectual functioning alongside deficits in daily functioning skills. The level of an individual's intellectual functioning is measured by their performance on formal intelligence tests; IQ tests are currently the primary measure of intelligence and if one scores about 70-75 (i.e., two standard deviations below the mean) or below they are considered to have significant sub-average intellectual functioning. Functional skill limitations could be in the area of conceptual skills (e.g., problem solving, being able to analyze situations) social skills (e.g., interpersonal relationships), or practical skills (e.g., personal care, mobility, occupational skills) (Heward, 2009).

Several possible causes of intellectual disabilities have been discussed in the literature. The causes can be either biological or environmental. Biological causes include neurochemical imbalance, brain injury (before, during or after birth), and genetics, among others. Environmental factors include malnutrition, child abuse, and lack of prenatal care, among several others. However, in many cases of intellectual disability, the cause is not known.

Dysgraphia
Refers to a condition where an individual struggles with the physical aspect of the writing process. The individual fails to form letters or numbers when writing making their handwriting difficult to read or illegible.

Dyscalculia
Individuals with dyscalculia have difficulty understanding and manipulating numbers and mathematical symbols and/or signs.

Dyslexia
Refers to a reading disorder affecting an individual's ability to read fluently or comprehend what they read. Indicators of dyslexia include poor phonemic awareness, poor sound blending, and poor pronunciation.

Dyspraxia
This is a disorder that generally affects the development of fine motor skills. Individuals with this condition usually have difficulty with organization skills; they may struggle with following or remembering directions and are usually slow in completing tasks that require fine motor skills such as writing.

Figure 5.1. Specific Learning Disabilities.

Emotional or Behavioral Disorders

Quite often children exhibit behavior that deviate from familial, school or societal norms. Such behavior could be either inward oriented (i.e., internalizing) or outward oriented (i.e., externalizing) (Friend, 2006). Internalizing behavior includes behaviors such as depression, anxiety, social isolation/aloofness, or different types of phobias. Externalizing behavior, on the other hand, includes behaviors such as aggression, bullying, defiance, non-compliance and stealing. Because most children exhibit some of these behaviors at some point in their lives and also because every society may have a different standard for what is considered acceptable or unacceptable behavior it is difficult to come up with a universal definition of this disability category. Nevertheless, it is generally agreed that when children exhibit behavior that is so extreme that it's not just slightly different from the usual, so chronic that it is not just transient, and is unacceptable based on social or cultural expectations they may be said to have an emotional or behavioral disorder (Hallahan and Kauffman, 2006).

The impact of emotional and behavioral disorders on children's learning cannot be exaggerated. In fact, teachers often consider children with emotional or behavioral disorders more difficult to teach than students with the other types of disabilities (Gunter, Countinho and Cade, 2002). Fortunately, researchers have identified effective strategies that can make teaching such students quite a rewarding experience. We will discuss some of these strategies in a subsequent chapter.

As numerous as the emotional or behavioral disorders are, so are the possible causes. The causes can be divided into two categories – environmental and biological. Examples of biological causes include genetics, temperament and brain injury while environmental causes include parenting style, exposure to violent environments, child abuse, or school disciplinary style, among others. Knowing what causes the disorders can assist educators in designing prevention strategies.

Attention Deficit Hyperactivity Disorder (ADHD)

ADHD is an increasingly common disorder that affects an individual's ability to pay attention. It can manifest as hyperactivity, inattention, impulsivity or a combination of any of these conditions. Hyperactivity is a condition where an individual struggles to sit still; they are always on the go, and act as if they are driven by a motor. Impulsivity is characterized by quick actions undertaken without forethought or reflection on the consequences of the actions. The last one –inattention–is characterized by an individual's failure to keep their focus on one thing; a students who is inattentive may listen to the teacher briefly and then get easily distracted by extraneous stimuli. Students with these attention deficits are often not able to learn effectively; whereas they may be physically present, they may not be mentally available to engage the learning tasks. The educational consequences for such students can be devastating. The good news is that there are a variety of evidence-based interventions that educators can use to help such students overcome these challenges and become successful learners.

Researchers have identified several possible causes of ADHD. The causes can be classified into five broad categories, i.e., organic causes, birth complications, intellectual developmental causes, psychological issues, and environmental factors (Raymond, 2008).

Autism Spectrum Disorders (ASD)

ASD is a spectrum of developmental disorders affecting communication and social interaction and often characterized by stereotypy (i.e., repetitive or ritualistic behavior). Today autism is conceptualized as a spectrum of disorders ranging from very severe to mild forms. On the severe end of the spectrum (i.e., low functioning autism) are a group of individuals who have extensive impairment in all areas of development; such individuals either have limited or no language at all. High functioning autism, on the other end, is primarily characterized by social skills deficits; individuals with this condition have language but exhibit difficulties understanding and using the basic elements of social interaction.

To date, there is no known cause for ASD. However, research suggests that genetics plays an important part. Even so, research has not succeeded yet in isolating the exact genetic factor responsible for the condition. But educators can still make a difference in the lives of children with autism; research-based interventions based on applied behavior analysis have proven quite successful in improving educational outcomes for children with autism.

Sensory Disabilities

Students with sensory disabilities are those with hearing impairments and/or visual impairments. Visual impairment or blindness refers to loss of vision which could either be partial or total vision loss. The condition is usually defined in terms of one's visual acuity (i.e., being able to discriminate among visual stimuli) or field of vision (i.e., the area that one can see in front of them without moving their head). Using a Snellen chart normal vision is considered to be 20/20 in terms of visual acuity. Having 20/20 vision means that you can see at 20 feet what a person with normal vision can see at 20 feet. The greater the second number, the worse one's vision is, e.g., if your vision is 20/100 it means you will have to stand at 20 feet to see what a person with normal vision would see at 100 feet. The educational needs of students with visual impairments vary depending on the severity of their vision loss as well as when the loss of vision occurred (at birth or after).

Any disease or condition that damages the visual system (e.g., glaucoma, cataracts, diabetes, and trachoma) can cause blindness. In west and central Africa a worm that breeds in rivers has been found to cause blindness. Prematurity and albinism are also risk-factors for blindness (Mcleskey, Rosenberg & Westling, 2013). There are several other possible causes of visual impairment.

Just like visual impairment, hearing impairment may also be partial or total hearing loss. In educational terms, hearing loss is considered disabling to the extent that it interferes with a child's learning. It is defined based on the sound volume that is required to hear; normal hearing is considered to be the ability to hear 0-15 decibels (dB) (Mcleskey, Rosenberg & Westling, 2013). A person is considered *hard of hearing* if they have a hearing loss in the 20-70 dB range and *deaf* if their hearing loss is 70-90 or greater (Turnbull, Turnbull, Wehmeyer, & Shogren, 2013). The impact of hearing loss on individual children depends on the severity of the hearing loss and also the age of onset. Just like with visual impairment, a person who is born without hearing would have different educational needs compared to a person who loses their vision after acquisition of language, for example.

The causes of hearing loss include genetics, infectious diseases, and developmental abnormalities. Environmental factors such as accidents, loud noises, and trauma can also cause hearing loss. In many cases the causes are still unknown.

Communication Disorders

Children who have speech and language disorders, often characterized by difficulty with articulation, fluency, and voice quality, are said to have communication disorders (Raymond, 2008).

Language disorders affect a child's ability to use (expressive language) and understand (receptive language) spoken language while speech disorders affect a child's ability to verbally transmit messages. While some students may speak too rapidly (stuttering), others may speak with a hoarse voice making it difficult to understand what they say. Still, others may have difficulty understanding language. Whatever the case, communication disorders can have quite devastating effects on a child's learning.

Communication disorders can be caused by congenital malformations, injury, brain damage, drugs, cleft palate and environmental toxins, among others (Gargiulo, 2012). They can also be linked to other disabilities such as hearing loss.

Physical Disabilities

Physical disabilities refer to a group of disorders that affect gross and fine motor control (Friend, 2006). Students with physical disabilities usually have difficulty with movement because of impaired ability to use their legs or arms. Some may have difficulty writing or sitting in a chair because of loss of muscular control. Cerebral palsy, spina bifida, muscular dystrophy or spinal cord injuries are examples of physical disabilities. See Figure 5.2 for a brief description of these disorders.

Cerebral Palsy

A group of non-progressive neurological disorders affecting voluntary movement or posture; it is caused by brain damage and is classified topographically according to the affected part(s) of the body (i.e., paraplegia, monoplegia, quadriplegia, etc.).

Spina Bifida

This is a congenital malformation of the spinal cord; it is a result of the spinal cord not being properly closed at birth. At times this may result in the spinal cord protruding through the uncovered opening. Conditions associated with spina bifida include bulging spine, loss of skin sensation, or hydrocephalus.

Muscular Dystrophy

This is an inherited condition which is characterized by progressive atrophying of the body's muscles. Children affected by this disorder usually have difficulty getting to their feet, falling easily, unusual gait, protruding stomach, among others.

Figure 5.2. Physical Disabilities.

HEALTH IMPAIRMENTS

'Health impairments' is a term used to refer to any health condition that affects a child ability to learn. It includes conditions such as epilepsy, asthma, diabetes, and HIV/AIDS, among others. Such conditions affect a student's vitality, strength, or alertness. With the prevalence rate of HIV/AIDS so high in the country, there may be a large population of children affected by this disease. Educators need to be aware of the implications of these disorders on the psychosocial and physical well-being of children in order to make judicious instructional decisions that promote positive learning outcomes.

SPECIFIC LEARNING NEEDS

The disabilities we have identified, and others, can significantly affect students' learning. Educators need to understand the nature of these disabilities and how they may interfere with students' learning. We will discuss characteristics of the disabilities next in order to help you understand the instructional implications for you as an educator. We will look at academic learning characteristics, behavioral/social skills, cognitive characteristics, communication skills and functional skills. However, in doing this we are not suggesting that all students with disabilities are alike. On the contrary, we acknowledge and recognize the uniqueness of each individual child and suggest that you do the same. In presenting these characteristics, our goal is to encourage you to appreciate how disability may impact children's learning and therefore incite you to explore effective instructional strategies that are designed to address the myriad needs – with the ultimate goal of promoting educational success for every student.

Cognitive Needs

The term cognitive refers to a variety of thinking skills (Henley, Ramsey & Algozzine, 2006). This includes skills such as memory, reasoning, attention, analyzing, and meta-cognition, among others. Students with disabilities may display deficits when it comes to some or all of these skills.

A student who has attention deficits may have difficulty coming to attention; that is, it may be quite difficult for the classroom teacher to capture their attention, which is a pre-requirement if students are going to successfully participate in the learning process. Another student may have difficulty focusing on relevant stimuli long enough to successfully learn (sustained attention) – a condition often referred to as short attention span. Some students may struggle to focus on relevant stimuli in the presence of distractions (selective attention), which could be audio, visual or physical. These attention deficits can be quite debilitating for some learners. To be effective, teachers need to identify appropriate instructional strategies that are designed to address such challenges. Anticipatory sets, for example, could help students who struggle coming to attention while frequent breaks and minimizing distractions could help students with sustained and selective attention deficits, respectively.

Memory deficits can also hinder students' success in learning. Memory refers to the ability to store and retrieve information (Cagne, 1985). To be effective learners, children need to be able to store information for both short (minutes to hours) and long (days to years) periods of time. Students who cannot store information for a short while (i.e., short term memory deficits) may find it difficult to process cognitive tasks that involve multiple steps (e.g., long division in mathematics or reading long passages for comprehension). On the other hand, students who cannot store information or retrieve information that has been stored in the long term may struggle to learn since learning involves relating new experiences to old experiences. Students with memory deficits may take longer to process information compared to their peers without memory deficits. However, there are a variety of instructional strategies that have been demonstrated to be effective in promoting learning among students with these deficits. These strategies will be discussed in a subsequent chapter.

Meta-cognition is a process of regulating one's own thinking processes and it involves self-questioning, organizing information, and use of environmental cues (Henley, Ramsey & Algozzine, 2006). Effective learners display good thinking and learning skills; they know how to think through problems and select effective strategies to solve problems (Chitiyo, 2013). Some learners, especially those with disabilities, exhibit deficits in their ability to self-question, self-monitor, self-organize and solve problems. Such learners just do not know how to learn. While some teachers may be frustrated, disappointed, and at times give-up on these learners, it is important to recognize that meta-cognitive strategies can be successfully taught to students. In other words, students can be successfully taught how to learn. Teachers should know that taking time to train their students on meta-cognitive skills can make a big difference in the students' learning.

Social/Behavioral Needs

Children with disabilities often exhibit a variety of behavioral needs. Some of them may display behavioral deficits while others may display behavioral excesses or both. Behavioral deficits may be in the form of social skills deficiencies for example failure to establish or maintain social relationships or violation of social norms (Chitiyo, 2013; Meese, 2001). Behavioral excesses, on the other hand, are behaviors that occur too frequently such as tantrums, compulsions, or self-stimulation, among others. Whatever the nature of the behavior, problem behaviors can seriously interfere with learning. In fact, problem behavior is one of the most serious concerns among schoolteachers (O'Shea & Drayden, 2008). Problem behaviors that have been identified as most common in Zimbabwean schools include violence, truancy, bullying, insubordination, and theft (Chitiyo et al., in press). A lot of instructional time is lost while teachers attend to students' problem behavior because students cannot engage in problem behavior and learn at the same time. In other words, there is a direct link between problem behavior and academic achievement because the more students exhibit problem behavior the less time they engage in academic tasks.

Because problem behavior can be related to disability, it is important for teachers to understand the nature of problem behavior among their students. How teachers manage problem behavior can either escalate or eliminate problem behavior. Teachers are, therefore, urged to be vigilant in identifying proactive strategies that prevent problem behavior from occurring in their classrooms while equipping their students with appropriate social skills and behaviors that promote learning. Strategies such as Positive Behavior Interventions and

Supports now have an increasingly strong evidence-base documenting their effectiveness in managing problem behavior in school settings.

Academic Learning Needs

Motivation
Motivation is an important component in the learning process. According to Raymond (2001) motivation can be defined as "force or drive from either intrinsic or extrinsic sources that leads an individual to act a certain way" (p.398). Intrinsic motivation is the internal push to undertake and accomplish something without seeking external rewards. It is considered more influential in promoting learning than its counterpart, extrinsic motivation. Extrinsic motivation is relying on outside rewards to accomplish a goal and research suggests that it rarely promotes learning. Unfortunately, many students with disabilities tend to be more extrinsically than intrinsically motivated. Since extrinsic motivation rarely promotes learning, teachers need to identify ways to foster intrinsic motivation among their students. Strategies such as providing choices or relating the instructional content to students' lives and experiences help to foster intrinsic motivation among students.

Locus of Control
Locus of control refers to how individuals view the connection between their actions and any outcomes that may be achieved (Raymond, 2001). Individuals who have an external locus of control attribute outcomes to external factors such as fate, chance, or luck. Success for such individuals may be explained as a result of being lucky. Individuals who have an internal locus of control, on the other hand, tend to view outcomes in terms of their own efforts i.e., there is a connection between results attained and effort expended. The latter tend to be more in control of their learning than the former. Regrettably, learners with disabilities often exhibit an external locus of control. They fail to see the connection between their effort and outcomes. As a result they may not bother to put effort because to them it would not make a difference. Teachers of such students have a responsibility to help the students to value their own effort and realize how it may be connected to outcomes.

Stages of Learning
Learning occurs in four stages – acquisition, fluency, generalization and maintenance. During the first stage of acquisition, the teacher's primary focus is to promote accuracy in responding. Once a student can perform a skill accurately, the teacher should move to the next stage of fluency whose goal is to promote an acceptable rate of performance. If the teacher is satisfied with the student's rate of performance they can move to the third and fourth stages of generalization and maintenance. Generalization focuses on making sure the student can perform the skill under different circumstances than those in the instructional setting while maintenance targets sustained performance of the skill over time. Success across all four stages is necessary for a student to be considered as having attained mastery. Understanding these four stages is important for school-teachers because students differ in how they progress through the stages.

Students with disabilities may require more opportunities to learn before they can meet the goals at each stage. Some may require more rehearsal and practice before acquisition is attained. Others may require more practice opportunities to be fluent. Still, others may require systematic instruction targeting generalization for them to be able to perform the skill in settings other than the instructional setting. An effective teacher is one who identifies appropriate interventions for their students taking into consideration whatever learning needs they may have.

CONCLUSION

Students with disabilities, like their peers without disabilities, have the potential to learn. Whether they learn or not depends on how successful their teachers are at recognizing their needs and identifying appropriate instructional strategies designed to promote learning for such students. In this chapter we have explored different types of disabilities and their characteristics. We have looked at the cognitive, social/behavioral, and academic learning needs of students with mild disabilities. We hope that school-teachers will be able to use this knowledge to improve their skills and become more effective in promoting the learning of all students – particularly those with disabilities who have been neglected for a long time.

Reflection Questions

1) Define the term mild disabilities
2) Define each of the following disabilities and identify their characteristics:
    - Learning disabilities
    - Intellectual disabilities
    - Emotional or behavioral disorders
    - ADHD
    - Autism spectrum disorders
    - Sensory disabilities
    - Physical disabilities
    - Communication disorders
3) Describe the cognitive needs of students with mild disabilities
4) Describe the social/behavioral needs of students with mild disabilities
5) Describe the academic learning needs of students with mild disabilities

Chapter 6

INCLUSIVE EDUCATION

Morgan Chitiyo

Overview
In this chapter we will introduce the reader to inclusive educational practices. Practices such as differentiated instruction, universal design for learning and different educational adaptations will be explored. We will also describe positive behavior support and how it promotes effective inclusive education.

Key Topics
Inclusive Education
Mainstreaming
Accommodations
Positive Behavior Supports

Learner Outcomes
Upon completion of this chapter readers will be able to:

1. Differentiate between mainstreaming and inclusion
2. Identify effective inclusive educational practices such as:
    a) Differentiated instruction
    b) Universal Design for Learning
    c) Educational Adaptations
3. Describe effective academic supports for inclusive educational environments
4. Describe positive behavior supports

INTRODUCTION

In June of 1994, representatives of 92 governments and 25 international organizations reaffirmed, through the Salamanca Statement, the right of every child to an acceptable education regardless of their physical, intellectual, social, emotional or linguistic characteristics (UNESCO, 1994). Since then, many countries, including Zimbabwe, have made strides to promote access to education for children with disabilities in inclusive educational settings. In this chapter, we will discuss the concept of inclusive education. Specifically, we will describe different instructional practices that are the bedrock of successful inclusive educational practices. These practices include differentiated instruction, universal design for learning, positive behavior supports and other adaptations that promote learning for all children including children with disabilities.

Defining Inclusion

The term inclusion is defined differently across educational systems. In this text we take McLeskey, Rosenberg and Westling's (2010) perspective that looks at inclusion as a philosophy of "… including students with disabilities as valued members of the school community" (p. 3). Schools that embrace this philosophy would, therefore, target creating meaningful and appropriate curricula that challenge all students, including those with disabilities, to reach their fullest potential. Such curricula would have to adapt to the needs of a diverse student population some of whose characteristics have been discussed in Chapter 5.

Some schools differentiate between full and partial inclusion. Full inclusion is when students with disabilities spend all their school day in the general education classroom receiving instruction alongside their peers without disabilities. With partial inclusion, students with disabilities spend part of the school day in the general education classroom with their peers and the other part in a separate placement outside the general education classroom; the separate placement could be a resource room or a self-contained special education classroom. The extent to which students with disabilities would be pulled out of the general education classroom would depend on their educational needs. For full inclusion to work, general education teachers and their classrooms need to be well-equipped and fully prepared to provide the accommodations and support necessary for the effective learning of students with disabilities. Unfortunately, such resources are not readily available in many developing countries including Zimbabwe, thus, rendering full inclusion an elusive goal.

In Zimbabwe, inclusion takes different forms as described by Mutepfa, Mpofu and Chataika (2007). According to Mutepfa and colleagues, there are four options through which inclusion is practiced in the country. The first one is locational inclusion where students with disabilities attend the general education schools but receive their general education curriculum in a self-contained class or resource room. The second option is inclusion with partial withdrawal; under this option students with disabilities receive part of their instruction in the general education classroom and part of it in a resource room. The third option, referred to as inclusion with clinical remedial instruction, is when students receive all their instruction, including any necessary support, in the general education classroom; this option is synonymous with full inclusion. The last option, known as unplanned inclusion, is when students with disabilities receive all their instruction in the general education classroom by default – meaning students with disabilities may not be identified as such and will, therefore, participate in the general education classroom anyhow (for more detailed description about these options, we refer you to Mutepfa et al., 2007).

Evidently, Zimbabwe has attempted to promote inclusive education. However, the country has experienced severe socio-economic and political upheavals since the turn of the 21st century. One of the victims of these crises has been the country's education system. As discussed in Chapter 12, the once vibrant education system was reduced to a mere shadow of its former self. With minimal resources, a system already failing to provide the most basic services could not be expected to afford the accommodations necessary for successful inclusion. Besides, the Zimbabwe Policy Statement on Special Education "committed the government to procurement of equipment, funds permitting" (Peresuh & Barcham, 1998, p. 79). There is no doubt that over the past tumultuous decade, funds would not permit the government to procure equipment that would be necessary to make the participation of children with disabilities in general educational settings possible.

MAINSTREAMING

Before we discuss the concept of inclusion further, it is necessary to mention mainstreaming. We believe it is necessary to do so because it helps one to understand the concept of inclusion better by pointing out what inclusion is not – especially in the Zimbabwean context where mainstreaming has been a dominant approach. Mainstreaming is when students with disabilities receive their instruction outside of the general education classroom – in a resource room or self-contained special education classroom – but get to intermingle with their peers without disabilities part of the school day for example during extra curricula activities. Unlike with inclusion where students with disabilities have the right to be educated in the general education classroom, mainstreaming does not guarantee a place for the students in the general education classroom; students with disabilities have to earn their way into the general education classroom (Salend, 2005).

CREATING INCLUSIVE EDUCATIONAL CLASSROOMS

Differentiated Instruction

In order for inclusion to work, educators have to be able to differentiate instruction to meet the diverse educational needs of an inclusive classroom. Differentiated instruction is a systematic way to proactively adjust teaching and learning so that the teacher can meet each student where they are and take them to the intended destination of educational success (Adams & Pierce, 2004). As discussed in Chapter 5, students vary in their abilities, interests, readiness to learn, motivation, learning profile and many other characteristics. Successful inclusive classroom teachers understand and appreciate these differences and, therefore, adjust their teaching in response to the diversity. According to Tomlinson (2000), teachers can at least differentiate four classroom elements, that is: content, process, products and learning environment.

Differentiating Content
Content refers to what the students are going to learn; this is usually based on national standards or goals set forth by the relevant educational authorities, for example, the Curriculum Development unit of the Ministry of Education Sports and Culture. Content differentiation therefore involves varying the content that students will learn and how they

will access that knowledge. Because students may be at different learning stages, a teacher may design a variety of tasks based on their students' learning profiles. As described in Chapter 5, some students may still be at the acquisition stage while others are already at the fluency stage, maintenance or even generalization stages. For example, while other students may still be learning to pronounce a list of words correctly (acquisition), others may be learning to read sentences made up of the same words (fluency). Still others may be learning how to read the same words presented in different sentences (generalization). Alternatively a teacher may differentiate their content based on Bloom's taxonomy of learning objectives (i.e., cognitive, psychomotor, affective). However, it is important to remember that content differentiation does not imply lowering performance standards for any of one's students. All students should be held accountable to reasonably high standards.

Differentiating Process

Differentiation can also be applied to the process of learning. Process refers to the activities that students engage in to enable them to learn the content. Process differentiation may be based on student learning styles. Some students may learn best by reading about the topic; others may need some hands-on activities to master the content. Some students may also prefer having a classroom discussion on the topic while others may prefer having an individual research project on the topic. In order to meet the educational needs of all students, an effective teacher should be able to identify the children's different learning styles and consequently adapt their instruction to appeal to those learning differences.

Differentiating Products

Products are the culminating projects that result from the learning process – that is, how students demonstrate what they have learned. Since students may have used different processes to acquire the same knowledge, it is only reasonable that we vary how they demonstrate what they have learned. Thus, teachers can differentiate the products and require students to demonstrate their knowledge via different products. Examples of different products are classroom tests (oral versus written), essays, research reports, drawing pictures, work samples, etc.

Differentiating the Learning Environment

The learning environment is very crucial to the educational success of students. By learning environment we refer to both the physical space as well as the psycho-social atmosphere of the classroom. Teachers should endeavor to create positive learning environments where all students, regardless of their physical, cognitive, and social characteristics, are valued and respected. This means if there is a student who uses a wheelchair or crutches for mobility in the classroom, desks and chairs should be arranged in a way that promotes the student's mobility within that classroom. The physical arrangement of classroom furniture would also be an important consideration for students with visual impairment. Teachers should also maintain positive social interactions among students and between the teacher and students based on mutual respect. Classrooms where intimidation, threats, violence, aggression, bullying, and stereotyping flourish hinder students from freely expressing themselves and therefore prevent the mutual growth and success of all students.

UNIVERSAL DESIGN FOR LEARNING

Universal Design for Learning (UDL) is another strategy that teachers can use to successfully promote inclusion. Universal design is a concept that originated from the field of architecture; according to the concept, when you construct structures such as buildings, you have to make them accessible to all users. UDL was, therefore, "developed to extend the concept of universal design to embrace the diverse ways in which individuals learn" (Dolan & Hall, 2001, p. 1). Teachers have to consider the diverse needs of their students in terms of how they learn. Every student, whether they have a disability or not, brings a unique set of circumstances into the classroom. For example, some students may have attention deficits; others may be slow in terms of their cognitive processing while others may have physical or sensory disabilities. In designing instruction and learning environments for such heterogeneous groups of students, teachers have to consider how to make the curriculum or the environment accessible to all students. UDL can achieve this through the following three principles: multiple means of representation, multiple means of expression, and multiple means of engagement.

Multiple Means of Representation

This principle is designed to give learners a variety of ways of acquiring information and knowledge. In order to appeal to the different ways students perceive information, the curriculum should be represented in different ways. For example, apart from the most commonly used text format, the curriculum could also be represented in Braille or auditory (e.g., books on tape) formats to appeal to a broader range of student needs.

Multiple Means of Expression

This principle requires teachers to give their students various ways to demonstrate mastery of the learned material. Examples of different ways to demonstrate mastery include written or oral exams, oral presentations, or work samples. Giving students different ways to demonstrate their mastery is essential to successful inclusion. It gives every student an appropriate avenue for expression.

Multiple Means of Engagement

This principle is meant to promote flexibility in teaching strategy. Teachers need to vary their teaching strategy in order to motivate and engage all students. If the curriculum is not engaging, students may become bored and less motivated. Examples of strategies that could be used include class discussion, role playing, video tapes guest speakers, etc.

ASSISTIVE TECHNOLOGY

Assistive technology refers to "any item, piece of equipment, or product system – whether bought, modified, or customized – that is used to increase, maintain, or improve the functional capabilities of an individual with a disability" (Salend, 2005, p. 17). The goal of inclusion is to promote the success of students with disabilities in the general education classroom. Assistive technology can promote the participation of students with disabilities in classroom activities that they could otherwise not participate in (McLeskey, Rosenberg & Westling, 2010). Assistive technology can be either high technological devices (e.g., speech recognition devices, battery powered wheelchairs, and touch screens) or low technological devices (e.g., pencil holders, customized grip pens or pencils, and crutches for mobility) (Salend, 2005). Providing students with disabilities with such devices can promote their successful participation in different learning activities in the general education classroom.

ACCOMMODATIONS

Accommodations refer to changes made to the curriculum to promote access for students with disabilities. Unlike modifications which alter instructional content, accommodations do not change the instructional content but focus on helping students with disabilities access the content. Accommodations can be made to how the material is presented, how students respond, timing of instructional tasks or assessments, or the setting where the instructional activities occur. For students with disabilities, teachers may have to repeat instruction or highlight key points to enhance understanding, give students extended time to complete tasks, or give students frequent breaks. While these accommodations may help students with disabilities to reach mastery, they do not alter what students have to learn; instead, they alter how they learn it. It is important not to confuse accommodations with modifications. Not all students with disabilities require curriculum modifications. Many students with disabilities could learn as much as their peers without disabilities if only they were taught differently.

POSITIVE BEHAVIOR SUPPORTS

An outgrowth of applied behavior analysis, positive behavior support (PBIS) is a relatively new technology in behavior management. It is a philosophy of proactively managing problem behavior by emphasizing prevention instead of relying on the traditional reactive and punitive strategies such as physical punishment, school suspensions or expulsions. Through the use of PBIS, schoolteachers can make classrooms or school environments safe and supportive for all students.

PBIS is implemented across three tiers, i.e., primary (school-wide), secondary (setting or group specific) and tertiary (individual students). School-wide PBIS are designed to prevent problem behavior for the whole school. Interventions at this level involve defining specific behavioral expectations for all students, teaching all students what the expectations mean, reinforcing students who meet the expectations, and continuous data collection. A majority of the school population (about 80-85%) usually benefit from school-wide interventions leaving about 1-15% still needing more supports (Sugai et al., 1999).

Secondary interventions are designed for the 1-15% of the school population who still continue to exhibit problem behavior even with the primary interventions in place. Secondary interventions target specific groups of students or specific school-based settings. For example, the school administration may notice that even after implementing primary interventions, some students still exhibit problem behavior in the cafeteria, in the hallways or on the playgrounds. In that case, they have to come up with setting-specific expectations targeting those problematic areas, teach the expectations and provide reinforcement to students meeting the expectations. While most of the targeted students at this level may benefit from the interventions, about 1-5% of the students may still continue to exhibit problem behavior. These are usually students with chronic behavior problems such as students with emotional behavioral disorders. Such students would require individualized behavioral interventions. In order to develop the individualized interventions, teachers have to first conduct functional behavioral assessment (FBA).

FBA is a process used to identify the functions of problem behavior. Identifying the functions of challenging behavior before designing interventions at this level is essential because it helps teachers to identify appropriate replacement behaviors to teach. One of the fundamental assumptions of PBIS is that behavior serves a function (Crone & Horner, 2003). Thus, when children exhibit problem behavior they are trying to communicate something. It may be that they want attention, access to something tangible or escaping from, or avoiding doing something. If the teacher knows the purpose of the problem behavior, they can identify an appropriate behavior that serves the same function as the problem behavior and teach the appropriate behavior.

PBIS has the potential to revolutionize our school systems because it changes the way we perceive problem behavior. Instead of looking at the child as the "problem" that needs "fixing' PBIS looks at settings and instructional factors and tries to change them to promote positive behavior among all children. This approach allows teachers to prevent problem behavior from occurring in the first place instead of reacting after the fact. It also allows teacher to create a positive learning environment which supports the success of all students, including students with emotional or behavioral disorders.

ATTITUDE TOWARDS INCLUSION OF STUDENTS WITH DISABILITIES

One of the obstacles to inclusion is societal attitudes (Campbell, Gilmore & Cuskelly, 2000; Peresuh, Mushoriwa & Chireshe, 2006). Research on attitudes towards disability in Zimbabwe has yielded mixed results. While some researchers have reported negative attitudes towards disability or inclusion of children with disabilities (e.g., Barnart and Kabzems, 1992, Chireshe, 2011; Mandina, 2012), others have reported positive attitudes among schoolteachers (e.g., Mielke, Adamolekun, Ball, & Mundanda, 1997). Chireshe (2011), in particular, looked at the views of in-service special education teacher trainees' views on inclusion and reported that the teacher trainees did not believe that Zimbabwe was ready for inclusion. These findings were corroborated by Mandina (2012) who reported that teacher trainees in Zimbabwe had negative attitudes towards inclusion. These research findings have important implications for proponents of inclusion.

If inclusion is going to be successful, there needs to be a shift in societal attitudes. Teacher attitudes are particularly important because they influence whether teachers embrace inclusion or not (Charema, 2010). In order to promote positive attitudes, among school teachers, towards disability or inclusion of students with disabilities Charema recommends that teachers should be provided with awareness training through both pre-service and in-service professional development, workshops, professional conferences, and through public awareness campaigns through the mass media. Such programs, according to Charema (2007), should focus on "re-culturing of schools to reflect inclusive beliefs and values and enhancement of teacher skills and knowledge to address the learning needs of all students" (p. 92).

The attitudes of students without disabilities are also important in promoting the successful inclusion of students with disabilities. This is particularly important because being accepted and welcomed by their peers can create a positive educational experience for children with disabilities. Besides, students without disabilities can provide academic and social support to their peers with disabilities through cooperative learning activities (Charema, 2010). In societies severely affected by limited availability of resources (such as paraprofessionals) school teachers can therefore, harness this readily available resource for the benefit of all students involved.

However, in order for teachers to ensure effective involvement of students without disabilities in promoting inclusion of their peers with disabilities, it may be necessary to educate the students about disability – introducing them to causes, characteristics, and necessary supports.

CONCLUSION

The push towards inclusive education is getting stronger around the world. Zimbabwe is one of the countries that have made significant strides to promote access to education, in inclusive educational settings, for children with disabilities. As described by Mutepfa and colleagues (2007) the country uses different options to facilitate the participation of children with disabilities in the general education classroom. The extent to which these efforts have been successful is still unknown as there appears to be no research evaluating the outcomes. However, researchers have identified different practices that can promote the success of all students, including students with disabilities, in the general education classroom. These practices include differentiated instruction, universal design for learning, assistive technology, positive behavior supports and other accommodations that promote learning for all children. Effective inclusive classroom teachers need value all their students regardless of their individual characteristics.

The practices described in this chapter are indispensable for successful inclusive classrooms. We encourage every educator to explore these practices further and to make them part of their instructional repertoire.

Reflection Questions

1) Define and distinguish between the following terms:
   - Inclusion
   - Mainstreaming
2) List the advantages and disadvantages of inclusion and mainstreaming
3) According to Mutepfa and colleagues (2007) there are four options through which inclusion is being practiced in Zimbabwe. Describe these four options.
4) Describe how classroom teachers can use each of the following practices to promote successful inclusion:
   - Differentiated Instruction
   - Universal Design for Learning
   - Assistive Technology
   - Accommodations
   - Positive Behavior Supports

Chapter 7

ORIGINS, THEORIES AND BACKGROUND OF COUNSELOR EDUCATION IN ZIMBABWE

John Charema

Chapter Overview
This chapter gives an overview of the origin of counseling in African countries, theories of counseling, the background of counselor education in Zimbabwe and further offers family counseling from an African perspective. Bearing in mind that counseling involves theories and a number of counseling stages, a brief discussion of the process of counseling is given. The role of learning institutions in counseling is also discussed. The author then engages a critical discussion and an explanation of the traditional and western methods of counseling.

Key topics
The origins of counseling
Theories of counseling
Counseling in Zimbabwe
Family counseling
Traditional counseling in Zimbabwe
Western perspectives of counseling in Zimbabwe

Learner Outcomes
After reading this chapter learners should be able to:

- Define counseling and explain what it entails
- Explain the origins of counseling and how it has developed
- Describe and evaluate theories of counseling
- Briefly describe western and traditional counseling
- Identify counseling challenges in Zimbabwean schools

INTRODUCTION

The starting point should be what we understand to be guidance and counseling. Many authors (e.g. Gladding, 1996; McLeod, 2003; 2013; Mearns, Thorne, 2000), take guidance and counseling to be an interactive processes between a person or group and a qualified mental health professional (psychiatrist, psychologist, clinical social worker, school counselor, licensed counselor, or other trained practitioner). Its purpose is the exploration of thoughts, feelings and behavior for the purpose of problem solving or achieving higher levels of functioning. In the same vein (Healey, & Hays, 2011) describes counseling as a general term referring to therapeutic interaction or treatment contracted between a trained professional and a client, patient, family, couple, or group. They go on to explain that the problems addressed are psychological in nature and can vary in terms of their causes, influences, triggers, and potential resolutions. Accurate assessment of these and other variables is dependent on the practitioner's capability and can change or evolve as the practitioner acquires greater experience, knowledge, and insight. Considering the above explanations, it would stand to reason that counseling is a process in which clients learn how to make decisions and formulate new ways of behaving, feeling, and thinking. Counselors focus on the goals their clients wish to achieve. Clients explore their present levels of functioning and the changes that must be made to achieve personal objectives. Thus, counseling involves both choice and change, evolving through distinct stages such as exploration, goal setting, and action. Counseling is often performed face-to-face in confidential sessions between the counselor and client. Typically the process of counseling involves talking with a person in a way that helps that person solve a problem or helps to create conditions that will cause the person to understand and/or improve their behavior, character, values or life circumstances. Professional counseling does not involve giving advice, but directing a client towards discovering solutions to his/her problems.

THE ORIGINS OF COUNSELING

Having known what counseling involves one can say it is a response to economic, social and psychological human needs and therefore existed in the world, from the time of the creation of humanity. However, counseling practices have always differed and continue to do so, from country to country, tribe to tribe and culture to culture. The practice of counseling has its roots and sources underpinned in the structures of individual traditional families. In the African culture, Zimbabwe in particular, church leaders and grandparents and the elders in the community were considered to be sources of wisdom and knowledge and therefore provided counsel and advice to the youth. In the so called primitive societies, no elaborate career guidance programs were developed or needed because occupational limitations were usually determined by two criteria, age and sex (Charema, 2004). It was considered that an individual belonged to a society and every adult was every child's parent in a community. Therefore all individuals could not exercise free will because they were bound by the family, cultural and traditional controls. Philosophers like Plato organized systematic theory and examined the psychology of the individual in all of its ramifications: in moral issues, education, society and its dynamics and religious perspectives. One thing that was very clear is that human beings needed counseling to come to terms with their emotions, spirituality, family and cultural challenges.

While it would be conjectural to identify particular events in the history and development of the counseling profession, two major events within the timeline stand out as milestones in the development of the counseling profession (Healy & Hayes, 2011). Healy and Hayes go on to point out two major reforms: the Mental Health Reforms of the early 20th Century, and the Community Mental Health Centers Act. They cite these two developments as the most important because of their contributions to the shaping of the profession's philosophical values, which include wellness, resiliency, empowerment, advocacy, development and prevention. The relevance of the Mental Health Reforms owes to the efforts of Clifford Beers's "A Mind That Found Itself (1908)", written from the author's personal experience on the deplorable conditions in mental health institutions in the United States of America. Clifford Beers himself was a Yale student who had been hospitalized several times throughout his life for mental illness, and as a result of his experience in hospitals, he advocated for better mental health facilities and reform in the treatment of the mentally ill. Gladding (1996), points out that Clifford's work is largely considered to be the impetus for the mental health movement in the United States, one of the major milestones in the development of the counseling profession. Working with the mentally ill and depressed people brought about counseling in the lime light. It was indeed apparent that humans needed counseling to resolve issues that destroyed self and others. However, as civilization, education and general development progressed, populations grew and religions changed shedding more light on the importance of counseling. It was at this point that psychiatry and psychology registered their presence.

It appears that the history of counseling had its origins, first in anthropology, then in religion, philosophy, and later still in medicine. As pointed out by Bass (2002) anthropology, religion and philosophy asked the same questions that deals with the individual, the family, the society in which the individual lives and the causes and the solutions to the challenges of life. From time to time the members of the community would suffer from the ups and downs of life from which they sought answers and solutions to their problems. For this they would approach the clergy, elders who were considered wise men, relatives or witch doctors. Most of the problems they faced were related to grief due to the loss of family members, frustration of not succeeding in acquiring or doing something of importance in life or guilt related to wrong doing for example killing someone or stealing from others, love-sickness, anxiety, madness, as well as general bad behavior. Christian counseling which was brought by missionaries to Africa gained eminence over the indigenous traditional counseling practiced in different African countries. However, with time counseling theories were developed.

THEORIES OF COUNSELING

Theories of Counseling are estimated to be more than 350 and a number of therapies have been advanced (Amen, 2012). The same author points out that although most of these have received little attention or validation, a core group of about 10 major theories, and fewer than 50 secondary approaches or modifications of the major theories, dominate the counseling profession. Most of these theories are characterized by important ingredients embedded in the concept of how people develop throughout their life span. Typically, this involves a sequence of stages and describes important factors that are likely to influence development. These involve mental health and manifestation of symptoms of unhealthy or disordered emotional functioning either explicitly or implicitly stated. Counselors use this information to help clients set realistic treatment goals, develop and enhance coping skills which brings about satisfaction in their lives. A description of the role of the effective counselor and the desired relationship between client and counselor is considered as a major part of all the theories.

Theories of counseling were initially developed by Anglo European Counselors. Theoretical models for counseling have their origins in the values and beliefs of persons who, in turn, have converted these into a philosophy and a theoretical model for counseling (Brammer, Shostrom & Abrego, 1989). Theory helps to explain what happens in a counseling relationship and assists the counselor in predicting, evaluating, and improving results. It also provides a framework for making systematic observations about counseling and encourages the coherence and production of new ideas. Hence counseling theory can be viewed as a practical means of helping to make sense of the counselor's observations. A theory suggests guidelines that provide signs of success or failure of counseling activities. Essentially the theory becomes a working model to explain what clients may be like and what may be helpful to them, in this case students in learning institutions.

The end result is twofold, counselors reach a deeper and richer understanding of the nature of their client, and their theory is enriched in ways that make it useful in working with future clients. Perhaps most importantly for counselors, is the fact that a theory can directly influence the strategies they use with their clients. If a counselor strictly follows a theory without being flexible, it can affect the counseling procedures that are most applicable with a given client or with a particular presenting problem. Theories can be enhanced by multi-cultural/cultural awareness and considerations. In fact the counselor's failure to recognize the unique cultures of clients from diverse backgrounds is likely to handicap interaction with those clients (McWhirter & McWhirter, 1991). A study by Webb (2000) in New Zealand, where the white settlers did not recognize the cultural differences and what partnership with the Maori people meant, shows that counseling could not make any headway. It is therefore important for counselors to consider the extended background family support networks, coping styles and the cultural context of the client for integration into their theoretical orientation. In this book we have only selected the ten commonly used theories (presented below), which are sometimes referred to as types of therapy with the eleventh one being a combination of all.

- Psychoanalytic Theory
- Individual Psychology Theory
- Client-Centered Therapy
- Behavioral Theory
- Rational Emotive Therapy
- Reality Therapy
- Transactional Analysis
- Existential Counseling
- Gestalt Therapy
- Eclectic Counseling
- Integrated Theories

While our intention is not to fully exploit the details of these theories, an explanation of how they were developed and how they work is given. This is done in view of the fact that counselors who counsel students and parents use any and/or a combination of these.

Psychoanalytic Theory

According to Corey (1986) Freud gave psychology a new look and new horizons. He called attention to psychodynamic factors that motivate behavior, focused on the role of the unconscious and developed most of the first therapeutic procedures for understanding and modifying the structure of one's basic character. He stimulated a great deal of controversy, exploration, and further development of personality theory and laid the foundation on which later psychodynamic systems rest. His theory is a benchmark against which many other theories are measured. The psychoanalytic theory views the structure of personality as separated into three major systems, the id, the ego and superego. Hereditary factors are represented by the id, which functions in the inner world of one's personality and is largely unconscious. It is usually viewed as the original system personality that is inherent and present at birth. It is believed that the id is ruled by the 'pleasure principle', and thus it seeks to avoid tension and pain, seeking instead gratification and pleasure. Corey (1986:304) describes it as 'the spoiled brat of personality'. The ego, which is only viewed as the only rational element of personality, has contact with the world of reality, controls consciousness and provides realistic and logical thinking and planning. If counseling could bring parents and students to this realization, then they would apply logic and reason to solve their problems and to plan ahead for their future.

The superego represents the conscience of the mind and operates on the principle of moral realism. It represents the moral code of the person, usually based on one's perceptions of the moralities and values of society. As a result of its role, the superego provides rewards such as pride and self-love, and punishments, such as feelings of guilt or inferiority, to its owner. When a parent is summoned to school after a child commits an act of misconduct, parents lose pride, self-love, feel punished by the creator and suffer feelings of guilt and inferiority (Allen & Allen, 1979).

As a result of this triangle, (id, the ego and superego) the Psychoanalytic Theory views tension, conflict and anxiety as inevitable in humans and the major goal of counseling is seeking to direct behavior towards reduction of this tension. Since personality conflict is present in all people, nearly everyone can benefit from professional counseling. The Psychoanalytic approach requires insight that relies on openness and self-disclosure. Multi-culturally oriented counselors would be aware that these traits might sometimes be seen as signs of immaturity.

The goals of psychoanalytic theory, according to Wadsworth (1990), aim to provide a climate that helps clients re-experience early family relationships and uncover buried feelings associated with past events that carry over into current behavior. Other reasons are to facilitate insight into the origins of faulty psychological development as well as to stimulate a corrective emotional experience.

The Individual Psychology Theory

This theory is often called Adlerian therapy. It sees the person as a unity, an indivisible whole, and it focuses on the individuality of persons. At the core of this theory is the belief that there exists within a human being an innate drive to overcome inferiorities and develop one's potential and self-actualization. The theory hinges on social interest, which is central to the growth and actualization of the individual and the good of the society. Because social interest is viewed as an innate aptitude, it must be consciously developed over time (LaCombe, 2012). Social interest, also referred to as one's ability to give and take, is accomplished through the life tasks in which all human beings participate. These tasks include work, friendship, and love (Sweeney, 1989). When a person comes for therapy, it is in one or more of these areas that he/she is experiencing incongruence or discomfort. The counseling process then is seen as a means by which the therapist and counselee work together to help the counselee develop awareness as well as healthier attitudes and behavior so as to function fully in society. The Adlerian counseling process involves four stages:

- establishing relationship
- diagnosis
- insight/ interpretation
- reorientation

In the first session the counselor establishes a relationship with the client through an interview in which the client is helped to feel comfortable, accepted, respected and cared about. The client is then encouraged to explain what helped her/him to determine the need for counseling. The counseling process is explained and discussed with the client. The client is then asked to discuss how things are going in each of the life task areas. The diagnostic stage involves the 'life-style interview'. The interpretation phase is the time during which the counselor and client develop insight from the lifestyle interview into the client's problems. The orientation stage is the most critical. The therapist helps the client to move from intellectual insight to reality. With the counselor's support, encouragement and direction, the counselee changes from unhealthy ways of thinking, feeling and behaving to ways more satisfying to him/her and society. Wallace (1986) believes that this theory is most effective in marriage, child and family counseling and less effective in one to one therapy. The Adlerian theory creates a therapeutic relationship that encourages participants to explore their basic life assumptions and to achieve a broader understanding of lifestyles. It helps clients recognize their strengths and their power to change and also encourages them to accept full responsibility for their chosen lifestyle as well as for any changes they want to make.

Client-Centered Therapy

Client-centered (now frequently referred to as 'person centered') counseling is another historically significant and influential theory. This theory was originally developed by Carl Rogers as a reaction against what he considered the basic limitations of psychoanalysis. Due to his major contributions, the approach is referred to as 'Rogerian Counseling'. The approach focuses on the client's responsibility and capacity to discover ways to more fully encounter reality. Therapists concern themselves mainly with the client's perception of self and of the world. Rogers points out that the therapist should be genuine, non-possessive, warm, accepting and have empathy. These aspects constitute the necessary and sufficient conditions for therapeutic effectiveness. The therapist's function is to be immediately present and be accessible to the client and to focus on the here and now experience created by their relationship. The client-centered model is optimistic and positive in its view of humankind. Clients are viewed as being good, possessing the capability of self-understanding, insight, problem solving and decision-making, as well as change and growth. The counselor facilitates the counselee's self-understanding, clarifies and reflects back to the client the expressed feelings and attitudes of the client. The aim is to help the client bring about change in oneself.

The theory provides a safe climate in which members can explore the full range of their feelings. It helps members to become increasingly open to new experiences and develop confidence in themselves and their own judgments. Clients are encouraged to live in the present, develop openness, honesty, and spontaneity. The theory makes it possible for clients to encounter others in the here and now and to use the group as a place to overcome feelings of alienation. It works more effectively on a one to one basis.

Behavioral Theory

Behavioral theory and conditioning can be traced directly from Pavlov's 19th century discoveries, and from further research carried out by Watson, Thorndike and Skinner who developed the theory to its present popularity. The behaviorist views behavior as a set of learned responses to events, experiences or stimuli in a person's life history. For the behaviorist counseling involves the systematic use of a variety of procedures that are intended specifically to change behavior in terms of mutually established goals between a client and a counselor. Behaviorists also believe that stating the goals of counseling in terms of behavior that is observable is more useful than stating the goals that are more broadly defined, such as self-understanding or acceptance of self. Therefore counseling outcomes must be identifiable in terms of overt behavior changes. Counselors utilizing behavioral theory assume that the client's behavior is the result of conditioning. The counselor further assumes that each individual behaves in a predictable way to any given situation or stimulus, depending on what has been learnt (Ivey, et al., 1993). Gilliland, James and Bowman (1989) point out that modern counseling involves the client in the analysis, planning, process and evaluation of his/her behavior management program. The counselor is expected to have training and experience in human behavior modification and also to serve as consultant, teacher, adviser, reinforcer and facilitator. The theory helps group members eliminate maladaptive behaviors and learn new more effective behavioral patterns.

Rational Emotive Theory (RET)

The Rational Emotive theory was developed by Albert Ellis. This theory is based on the assumption that people have the capacity to act in either a rational or irrational manner. Rational behavior is viewed as effective and potentially productive whereas irrational behavior results in unhappiness and non-productivity. Ellis assumes that many types of emotional problems result from irrational patterns of thinking. This irrational pattern may begin early in life and be reinforced by significant events in the individual's life as well as by the general culture and environment. The RET approach to counseling declares that most people in our society have developed many irrational ways of thinking and that these irrational thoughts lead to irrational or inappropriate behavior. Therefore counseling is designed to help people recognize and change these irrational beliefs into more rational ones. The accomplishment of this goal requires an active, confrontational, and authoritative counselor who has the capacity to utilize the whole variety of techniques (Hansen, et al., 1986). The RET therapist does not believe that a personal relationship between the client and counselor is a prerequisite to successful counseling. In fact it is believed that the therapist may frequently challenge and provoke the irrational beliefs of the client. Rational Emotional Therapy can be applied to individual and group therapy, marathon encounter groups, marriage counseling and family therapy.

The goal of this theory is to teach group members that they are responsible for their own disturbances and help them identify and abandon the process of self-indoctrination by which they keep their disturbances alive. It also aims at eliminating the clients' irrational and self-defeating outlook on life and to replace it with a more tolerant and rational one.

Reality Therapy Theory

Reality therapy theory was largely developed by William Glasser (Adler, 1959). Glasser's approach places confidence in the counselee's ability to deal with his or her actions through a realistic or rational process. From a reality therapy standpoint, counseling is simply a special kind of teaching or training that attempts to teach an individual what he should have learnt during normal growth in a short period of his life. However, it appears that Glasser's theory leaves a lot to be desired. If counseling were learnt through a natural growth process, a mechanism would have been built within humans to be able to think logically and resolve their problems during difficult times. This is not normally the case. Nystul (1999) points out that when a client is in a helpless state, he/she needs someone who can listen with full attention, allow the client to go through his/her emotions, acknowledge the client's problems, create a positive environment for the client to think logically and rationally and allow the client time to find solutions to his/her problems. Amen (2012) holds that reality therapy is applicable to individuals with any sort of psychological problem, from mild upset to complete psychotic withdrawal. It works well with behavior and drug-and alcohol–related problems. It has been applied widely in schools, institutions, hospitals, families and business management. It focuses on the present and upon getting people to understand that essentially they choose all their actions in an attempt to fulfill basic needs. When they are unable to do this, they suffer or cause others to suffer. The therapist's task is to lead them towards the better or more responsible choices that are almost always available. Reality therapy does not emphasize the client's past history but emphasizes a major psychological need that is present throughout life, the need for identity. It includes a need for feeling worthy, a sense of uniqueness as well as separateness and distinctiveness. The need for identity is considered to be universal among individuals in all cultures (Corey, 1986). Reality therapy is based on the assumption that a client will assume personal responsibility for his/her well-being. The acceptance of this responsibility, in a sense, helps a person achieve autonomy or a state of maturity by which one relies on one's own internal support. Whereas many of the counseling theories suggest that the counselor should function in a noncommittal way. Reality therapists praise clients when they act responsibly and indicate disapproval when they do not.

The theory helps members toward learning realistic and responsible behavior developing a 'success identity'. Group members are assisted in making value judgments about their behaviors and in deciding on a plan of action for change.

Transactional Analysis (TA)

Transactional analysis is a humanistic approach that assumes a person has the potential to choose and direct or reshape his/her own destiny. Eric Berne developed and popularized this theory in the 1960s. It is designed to help the client renew and evaluate early decisions and to make new, more appropriate choices. Transactional analysis stresses understanding the transactions between people as a way of understanding the different personalities that comprise each of us. The theory places a great deal of emphasis on the ego. The client is assisted in gaining social control of her/his life by learning to use all ego states where appropriate. The ultimate goal of the counselor is to help clients change from inappropriate life positions and behaviors to new and more productive behaviors. An essential technique in TA counseling is the contract that precedes each counseling step. The contract between counselor and counselee is by mutual agreement, in terms of time, when to stop and whether to record the session or not. Once signed the contract becomes binding and legal. The theory can be used with individuals but is more suitable for persons within a group setting. Transactional analysis counselors feel that the group setting facilitates the process of providing feedback to persons about the kind of transactions in which they engage. The counseling group then represents a microcosm of the real world. In this setting the individual group members are able to work on their own objectives, and the counselor acts as a group leader.

The theory assists clients in becoming free of scripts and games in their interactions and also challenges them to reexamine early decisions as well as make new ones based on awareness.

Existential Counseling

Existentialists have the view of human nature and believe that the individual writes their own life story by the choices that they make. This theory was developed by Rollo May and Viktor Frankl. In this theory anxiety is seen as a motivational force that helps the clients to reach their potential. Conversely, anxiety is also seen as the paralyzing force that prevents clients from reaching their full potential. Therefore, through awareness, this anxiety can be helpful in the client living a more fully life. Frankl shares that each person searches for meaning in life, and that while this meaning may change, the meaning never ceases to be. In the school set up students have to realize why they are at school and how education affects their lives. With this therapy the client has to experience achievements, values and reconciliation.

The role of the counselor is to create a unique relationship with the client, focusing on being authentic with the client and entering into a deep personal sharing relationship. The counselor models how to be authentic, helps the client to realize personal potential, and to make decisions with emphasis on mutuality, wholeness and growth. It is not the responsibility of existential counselors to diagnose and assess clients like other models do. The goal is to have the client take responsibility for their life and life decisions. The therapy further aims to develop self-awareness in the client in order to promote potential, freedom, and commitment to better life choices. With time the client is expected to develop an internal frame of reference, with full control of his own life as opposed to the outward control from other people.

The most common technique used in existential counseling is to develop a relationship with the client in this case students. Confrontation is also used to challenge clients to take full control, responsibility and consequences for their actions in live.

Gestalt Counseling Therapy

The Gestalt therapy was developed by Fredrick Perls and is a humanistic approach in which the therapist assists the client towards self-integration (LaCombe, 2012). This helps him/her to learn to utilize his/her energy in appropriate ways, to grow, develop and actualize. The primary focus of this approach is the present, the 'here and now.' The implication being that the past is gone and the future is yet to come. Therefore, only the present is important. Gestalt counseling has as its major objective the integration of the person or "getting it all together". The treatment is finished when the client has achieved the basic requirements. These are: a change in outlook, a technique of adequate self-expression and assimilation, and the ability to extend awareness to the verbal level. In this state a client has reached integration, which facilitates its own development. Thereafter, progress can be left to the counselee. In order to achieve this togetherness the counselor seeks to increase the client's awareness by providing an atmosphere conducive to the discovery of the client's needs or what the client has lost because of environmental demands. The counselor can create the atmosphere in which the client can experience the necessary discovery and growth. From these assumptions we can conclude that the Gestalt therapist has a positive view of the individual's capacity self-direction. Furthermore the client is encouraged to utilize his/her capacity and to take responsibility for his own life. The main goal is to enable members to pay close attention to their moment-to-moment experiences, so they recognize and integrate disowned aspects of themselves.

Eclectic Counseling

The eclectic approach to counseling is one of long standing traditional, and one of equally long-standing controversy. It originally provided a safe middle-of-the-road theory, for counselors who neither desired nor felt capable of functioning as purely directive or non-directive counselors. This approach allows the counselor to construct his/her own theory by drawing on established theories. It has often been suggested that an eclectic counselor can choose the best of all counseling worlds. Others contend that the theory encourages counselors to become theoretical 'jacks of all trades'. Left to the counselor's decision, the approach can develop deficiencies and be open to abuse. The counselor is likely to be influenced by his/her values, views, and beliefs. This can only be avoided by self-study of client-counselor relationships as well as personal therapeutic experiences resulting in increased self-understanding. As observed by Wallace (1986), counselors cannot shelve their responsibility for constructing a personal theory of counseling by turning it into an intellectual game or academic exercise. Their obligation to the clients is far too real for that. We strongly feel that this approach should only be used by highly skilled counselors who are capable of weaving a number of approaches into their counseling practice.

Developing an eclectic approach to therapy requires an enterprising juxtaposition and a genuine confrontation of one's work with the values, thoughts, and research of others. While independence of observation and thought is essential to an eclectic stance, so are understanding and respect for other theorists. Before counselors in search of a personal theory of counseling and psychotherapy can choose the best, they must become fully aware of all that are available. The eclectic approach then is no shortcut to theory formulation. Indeed, when properly travelled, it is one of the most difficult paths to follow.

All the above-mentioned theories are interwoven to such an extent that one cannot compartmentalize one from the others during the process of counseling. They all aim at one goal, that of creating a conducive environment for the client to find solutions to his problems. As pointed out by Colledge (2000), that counseling theories work like a web where one thread pulls the other. However, some differences have been noted, where some theories give the counselor authority and power whilst others try and empower the clients. According to our experiences with counseling students and parents of children with special, most theories work so long as they are applied appropriately. We applied the Client-Centered Therapy and the Individual Psychology Theory and found them helpful. The theories seem to have worked because they allowed parents and students an opportunity to review their situations and workout solutions to their problems. Reality Therapy and Behavioral Theory may produce short lived results in that clients, especially students and parents of children with special needs, may be dependent on the counselor for solutions since there is teaching and conditioning.

Integrated Theory

This theory takes into account a number of aspects from other theories. It borrows from all other theories to enhance its position. Ivey (1987) notes that an integrated knowledge of skills, theory, and practice is essential for culturally intentional counseling and therapy. The culturally intentional therapist knows how to construct a creative decision-making interview and can use micro-skills to attend to and to influence clients in a predicted direction. Important in this process are individual and cultural empathy, client observation skills, assessment of person and environment, and the application of positive techniques of growth and change. Cultural values are central to counseling such that in any society cultural demands have influence on societal norms.

The theory provides organizing principles for counseling and therapy hence the culturally intentional counselor has knowledge of alternative theoretical approaches and treatment modalities. Practice is the integration of skills and theory. Therefore, the culturally intentional counselor or therapist is competent in skills and theory, and is able to apply them to research and practice for client benefit. The main aim of this theory is to provide conditions that maximize self-awareness and reduce blocks to growth. It helps clients discover and use freedom of choice and assume responsibility for their own choices.

APPLICATION OF THEORIES IN COUNSELING

Theories of counseling are usually insight or action-oriented because in general students do not require a highly psychiatric oriented approach. Rather they appreciate the counselor's general style of social behavior and the type of relationship he develops with his client. All counseling theories are based on the 'therapeutic alliance' (Amen, 2012). Person-centered therapy known as Non-directive Psychotherapy, originally advanced by Carl Rogers in 1959, holds the view that at some level of consciousness, patients or clients know what is best for them. Whereas behavioral counseling, unlike the Rogerian approach, is a directive method. Students are advised that they derive reward by making environmental changes, which will produce positive behavioral changes. The client-centered approach views the client as one who is rational, socialized and realistic. The Rogerian theory asserts that the responsibility for the counseling process rests with the client whilst the counselor facilitates rather than directs his /her efforts at insight. The efforts and decisions regarding change of behavior after counseling also remain the responsibility of the client. On the other hand, the action theorists are much more problem-oriented and would try to find the problem, then using various techniques, try to change behavior in the hope that the problem would be alleviated. The counselor is expected to observe that the process from maladjustment to adjustment is a self-regulatory one. The basic philosophy of the counselor is represented by an attitude of respect for the client, for his capacity and right to self-direction and for the worth and significance of each individual. There is the basic assumption in the theory that individuals are capable of changing by themselves in ways they choose without the direction or manipulation of the therapist. The counselor is expected to accept the client as an individual with all his/her conflicts and inconsistencies, bad and good points, being a consistent person with no inherent contradictions between what he/she is and what he/she says. The client must see the counselor as accepting and understanding. In this case the counselor-client relationship will be seen by the client as safe, secure, free from threat and supporting but not supportive.

GROUPS AND COUNSELING

Students can be counseled as a group, as friends and as individuals. It is important to understand that there are advantages and disadvantages with each and every approach. Before getting into the details of group counseling, it is important to understand what 'group' means. To clarify the various labels in group counseling and guidance, including a definition of group, we will use the work of Capuzzi and Gross (1997). They define "group" as 'a number of individuals bound together by a community of interest, purpose or function'. However, within and across the professional disciplines engaged in the study and practice of groups, there are wide variations in definition. To narrow the definition of group for discussion in this study, it should be noted that counseling groups are characterized by interaction. They are functional or goal-oriented groups. Counselors view various group activities as occurring at three levels: the guidance level, the counseling level and the therapy level.

It is almost impossible to go it alone in today's group-oriented, group-dominated and group processed society. In fact today, to be well adjusted in a given society, usually means that the individual has mastered the society's norms of social interaction and of functioning appropriately in groups. The following observations were drawn after a study of the influence and dependence on groups of the individual's functioning in today's society.

Humans are group oriented. People are meant to complement, assist, and enjoy each other. Groups are natural environments for these processes to occur. Humans seek to meet most of their basic and personal social needs through groups, including the need to know and grow mentally. Groups are a most natural and expeditious way to learn. Consequently groups are influential in how a person grows, learns, and develops behavioral patterns and adjustment techniques. Apart from understanding the organization, influences and dynamics of groups, group counseling may be more effective for some people and individuals than individual counseling.

GROUP COUNSELING

More than 100 years ago the psychologist William James in the 1800s wrote "We are not only gregarious animals liking to be in sight of our fellows, but we have an innate propensity to get ourselves noticed, and noticed favorably, by our kind. The most dreadful punishment would be that of being turned loose in society and remaining absolutely unnoticed by all members within one's environment." The importance of human relationships is to meet basic needs and influencing personal developments and adjustments of members of the society. Most relationships are established and maintained in a group setting. For many, daily adjustment problems and developmental needs also have their origins in groups. Since most frequent and common human relationship experiences occur in groups, groups also hold the potential to provide positive developmental and adjustment experiences for many people.

Group counseling is the routine adjustment to developmental experiences provided in a group setting. It focuses on assisting counselors to cope with their day-to-day adjustment and development concerns. Examples might focus on behavior modification, developing personal relationship skills, concerns of human sexuality, values and attitudes, or career decision-making. Gazda et al. (2001) suggest that group counseling can be growth engendering insofar as it provides participation incentives and motivation to make changes that are in the clients' best interest. On the other hand, it is remedial for those persons who have entered into a spiral of self-defeating behavior but who are capable of reversing the spiral with counseling intervention.

GROUP GUIDANCE

Group guidance refers to group activities that focus on providing information or experiences through a planned and/organized group activity (Ivey & Ivey, 1993). These include orientation groups, career exploration groups and classroom guidance. Group guidance is also organized to prevent the development of problems. The content could include educational, vocational, personal or social information, with the goal of providing students with accurate information that will help them make more appropriate plans and life decisions.

GROUP THERAPY

Group therapy provides intense experiences for people with serious adjustment, emotional and developmental needs. Therapy groups are usually distinguished from counseling groups by both the length of time and the experience for those involved. Counselors devote most of their time to help clients learn to recognize and cope with self-defeating behavior and to master developmental tasks (Capuzzi & Gross, 1997). In group therapy students come together, help one another, engage in interaction, share experiences and ideas. The counselor acts as a facilitator.

T-Groups

T-Groups are derivatives of training groups. They present the application of laboratory training methods to group work. T-Groups represent an effort to create a society in miniature in which an environment is created for learning. These are relatively unstructured groups in which the participants become responsible for what they learn and how they learn it. This learning experience frequently includes learning about one's own behavior in groups. A basic assumption appropriate to T-groups is that learning is more effective when the individual establishes authentic relationships with others.

Sensitivity Groups

A sensitivity group is a form of T-group that focuses on personal and interpersonal issues and on the personal growth of the individual. Sensitivity groups emphasize on self-insight, which means that the central focus is not the group and its progress but rather the individual member.

Encounter Groups

Encounter groups are also in the T-group family, but are more therapy oriented. McLeod (2013) defines an encounter group as a group that stresses personal growth through the development and improvement of interpersonal relationships via an experiential group process. Such groups seek to release the potential of the participant in an intensive group. With much freedom and little structure, the individual will gradually feel safe enough to drop some of his defenses and facades, he will relate more directly on the feeling basis with other members of the group, he will change in his personal attitudes and behavior and he will subsequently relate more effectively to others in his everyday life situations. Extended encounter groups are often referred to as marathon groups. The marathon encounter group uses an extended block of time in which massed experience and accompanying fatigue are used to break through the participants' defenses. While encounter groups offer great potential for the group members' increased self-awareness and sensitivity to others, such groups can also create high levels of anxiety and frustration. Therefore if encounter groups are to have maximum potential and minimal risk, highly skilled and experienced counselor leaders must conduct them. Both students and their parents tend to be defensive of their situations at the expense of facing reality and solving their problems. In the same vein group counseling could help break such students and parents' defenses.

Mini-Groups

While two or more people can constitute a group, the term mini-group has become increasingly popular to denote a counseling group that is smaller than usual. A mini-group usually consists of one counselor and a maximum of four clients. Due to the smaller number of participants, the potential exists for certain advantages resulting from the more frequent and direct interaction of its members. LaCombe (2012) indicates that because of the increased dynamics that occur in a group of limited size, members of the mini-group are less able to withdraw or hide and interaction seems to be more complete and responses fuller. Mini-groups may either function as the singular treatment focus or be used in conjunction with individual counseling.

GROUP PROCESS AND GROUP DYNAMICS

Two terms commonly used interchangeably in describing group activities are process and dynamics, (Allen & Sawyer 1984). However, the terms have different meanings when used to describe group-counseling activities. Group process is the continuous ongoing movement towards achievement of its goals, representing the flow of the group from its starting point to its termination. It is a means of describing or identifying the stages through which the group passes. Group dynamics, on the other hand, refers to social forces and interplay operative within the group at any given time. It describes the interaction of a group, which may include a focus on the impact of leadership group roles and membership participation in groups. It is a means of analyzing the interaction between and among the individuals within a group. Group dynamics is also used on occasions to refer to certain group techniques such as role-playing, decision-making, 'rap' sessions, and observation.

IN-GROUP AND OUT-GROUP

These are groups organized or overseen by counselors, but are important in understanding influences on client behaviors. These groups can be based on almost any criteria, such as socio-economic status, athletic or artistic accomplishments in a particular area of ability, racial-cultural origins and many other factors. In-groups are characterized by association largely limited by peers of like characteristics, while out-groups consist of those excluded from in-groups. Such members are non-participants in athletics, drama, and/or have not been invited by participants to become involved in such social clubs. In many counseling situations, it is important for counselors to understand how clients see themselves and others in terms of 'in' or 'out'. Students normally group themselves according to how they perceive their problems. Hegarty (1986) asserts that students who have similar problems tend to group and share their experiences.

SOCIAL NETWORKS

These are not groups in a formal sense: however, social networks result from the choices that individuals make in becoming members of various groups. Counselors may be concerned with how these choices are made and their impact on individuals. Engaging in social network analyses helps to determine how the interconnectedness of certain individuals in a school society can produce interaction patterns influencing others both within and without the network. Social networks are important. Dale (1984) states that students need continuous support during and after counseling until they can cope on their own. This support can be offered by professional counselors, friends, other members of teaching staff, relatives and the family.

Nearly all theories of counseling currently recognize the powerful impact of the therapeutic alliance and offer clinicians ways to collaborate effectively with their clients (LaCombe, 2012). A safe and healing environment and a caring, skilled, and trustworthy counselor are essential to successful treatment. These theories offer strategies and interventions that counselors can use and apply to help people achieve their counseling goals. Examples cited in the theories include; reflections of feelings, modifications of cognitive distortions, and systematic desensitization. Theories also offer information on treatment parameters such as duration and frequency of sessions; whether to use individuals, groups, or family treatment; and benefits of medication and other adjunct services. Identification and location of those people who are most likely to benefit from this treatment approach are achieved.

COUNSELING IN ZIMBABWE

While Zimbabwe was still Rhodesia, counseling was practiced on a small scale mainly for the elite by qualified psychologists most of whom were trained in European countries. A few had qualified from the then University of Rhodesia. Around 1975 the National Guidance and Counseling Association (NGCA), was established (Richards, 2012). This organization was not very active and it served very few people if at all it did. When Zimbabwe obtained independence in 1980, there was a great need for counseling mainly to help ex-freedom fighters and many other people who were psychologically and emotionally affected during the liberation struggle. Others had their parents, children or relatives killed by either freedom fighters or the Rhodesian forces for being allegedly sell outs. The aftermath of the liberation war had people who suffered from stresses, trauma and emotional imbalance. This situation helped to strengthen the National Guidance and Counseling Association of Zimbabwe. More and more organizations took to counseling in order to help war and domestic violence victims as well as those affected by the HIV/AIDS pandemic.

In more recent times several nongovernmental organizations such as the Musasa Project are helping to counsel young women who suffered rape, divorce and the abuse of violent husbands in order to recover and lead normal lives (Mawire, 2011). Abandoned Babies Committee (ABC) invited young women who threatened abortion due to unplanned and unwanted pregnancies, for counseling so that they would not dumb their babies (Mawire, 2011). The committee went further to engage the young ladies into self-help projects. The Ministry of Health and Child Welfare started to have counselors helping parents of children who were born with disabilities, HIV/AIDS patients and those who suffered long term illnesses. The police force and the army also formed family counseling units to help families that experienced discord, abuse and violence. Such services were established in all police and army stations throughout the country. Churches through their pastors and elders offered counseling to their members during marriage and also to those who experienced loss of loved ones or close relatives (Charema & Eloff, 2011). Charema and Eloff go on to point out that Special Schools offered counseling to parents of children with disabilities who suffered denial of the situation, grief, frustrations and depression due to the birth of a child with disabilities in the family and in addition not knowing what to do with the child. All the above mentioned organizations had very few qualified counselors most of whom were trained on the job within their organizations to alleviate the situation.

From 1994 a training counseling organization, CONNECT that was established in Harare, trained counselors in child and general counseling. The organization offered a number of counseling programs at certificate, diploma and advanced diploma level in family therapy. CONNECT was affiliated to Tavistock a counseling organization in London. CONNECT established another training center in Bulawayo and had a mobile training unit. Many counselors were trained through CONNECT and this led to the establishment and strengthening of more counselor training within organizations like those mentioned before. With CONNECT gaining recognition, many school counselors were trained to offer counseling services in schools, which is the subject of the next chapter of this book. In the 1990s many secondary schools set up counseling services to help students who experienced various problems.

Family Counseling

In Zimbabwe and many other African countries, counseling is a day to day thing is every family. However, this type of counseling was and in some cases continues to be one sided top to bottom. The elders have a duty to counsel the young and direct their ways of behaving, the young have no voice but to listen and obey (Charema, 2004). This helped in student behavior and in that schools had strong support from home. With urbanization, more development in African countries and more economic hardships, the family has disintegrated due to migration in search of better living conditions. The family support system has been broken and therefore counselors have to fill in the gap in schools to support students who experience different challenges in different ways in different situations. A family with both parents alive is likely to bring up well groomed and up right children in terms of societal values and moral behavior. Such children are likely to help other students with positive influence and peer-counseling. Therefore parental counseling has its roots in human values as accepted by the society. However, with some homes having single parents and others without parents at all, the challenges of parenting teenagers continues to spiral out of societal expected norms. Unfortunately the school has to deal all the harbored bitterness, and frustrations in teenagers that are exhibited among others through indecorum behavior and substance abuse. This where the counselors play an important role to model these students and redirect their lives in order to make them concentrate on their education and to help them become useful members of the society.

In the African context, particularly in Zimbabwe, students were controlled by family elders in form of uncles, aunts, traditional leaders and in some cases church leaders. Every adult was every child's parent. However, the situation has changed with the coming of children's rights, child abuse, the nuclear family and respect of family and individual privacy. It is not easy to correct any child seen doing wrong because of so many protection acts. However, this is not to say protection acts are bad but society has lost values of human dignity and respect for human life. In some cases the same adults who are supposed to correct and protect the young, physically and sexually abuse them. In some cases they abduct for destruction of life. Educational Institutions have the responsibility through counseling programs to build self-esteem, self-worthiness and acceptable behavior in these students who live in a confused environment where both adults and students abuse drugs and human life.

Traditional Counseling in Zimbabwe

Throughout the ages of human society people have from long way back sought to understand themselves, developing systems and ways of coping with the problems and challenges of life through guidance and counsel (Charema, 2004). Such skills are developed over time and they are passed on from one generation to another. Skills for human survival target health and healing, primarily to resolve and to do away with physical, mental, psychological problems as well as negative social interactions. Most traditional African clients believe that the problems they encounter are caused by outside forces from the community. Traditional practices are sanctioned by the elders and indigenous people in that community.

Traditional cultural values and the extended family have always been esteemed in the Zimbabwean culture. These factors combine to strengthen and bring about counseling success in the traditional pattern. This is similar to what is done in other African countries. Elders and chiefs by virtue of their positions in society also serve as a valuable source of guidance and counseling which is well accepted and appreciated by all in the community. In most cases, these traditional leaders work as a link between ancestors and the living people. The link has traditionally been enhanced through the use of rituals, ceremonies and taboos which served as a means to prepare youth for adulthood or to appease spirits for resolving issues, or for individual healing or progress.

The Zimbabwean society is dominated by the tenets of traditional culture, with approximately 80% of Zimbabweans living in rural areas where traditional customs are strictly adhered to in the community (Charema & Shizha, 2008). Charema and Shizha go on to point out that the community is a strong cultural, social, political and economic institution that enhances social networks and social support provision and coping strategies. Within a community the aunts and uncles played a very important role in marriage counseling which was mostly in the form of advice. Although the advice given was usually subjective, and the advisors expected the advisees to accept and implement the advice as given. This promoted a dependence syndrome on the part of young people in terms of their plans for the future. Whatever, plans the young people had, in most cases they had to have them approved by their elders. If they went ahead with their plans without consulting the elders, they would not get any support particularly if something went wrong. The aunts taught the young girls who were preparing for marriage how to run a home and how to relate to a husband. Young girls were taught and counseled on issues of feeding the family, sickness, illnesses, hygiene and disease in the home. The aunts would then report to the elders - issues that they would have "resolved" and how they would have "resolved" them. In the same way, boys who were getting ready to get married approached their uncles for advice and counsel. The same process was carried out with the young men being taught about women and marriage. Further discussions were carried out on how to run a family, support and provide for family, relate to a wife, relate to in-laws and other relatives. In all cases, young men and women were advised of the channels of communication.

At present Zimbabwe and most sub-Saharan African countries continue to experience changes in the traditional system of counseling and advising due to globalization. With increased migration into urban areas many people in towns have acculturated into the western world view slowly drifting away from their cultural socialization thereby weakening the traditional structure of the society. There is a gradual shift from the extended family unit to the nuclear family unit or the single parent unit. For better facilities and better living conditions, there has been a rapid rate of urbanization with a high unemployment rate compounded by poor economic performances. The infiltration of foreign culture has destroyed the once strong African culture and caused moral decay through modern media (e.g., movies, television shows, , books and magazines).

In the ancient times man seemed to be in control of the economic and social forces of life within his environment. Nevertheless, not all the skills and knowledge passed on can effectively deal with the present challenges of life. Therefore the use of psychology and other forms of counseling have become paramount in helping man to resolve and address the challenges of modern day times.

The Western Perspective of Counseling in Zimbabwe

The indigenous African counselor did not exist in the western practice. If recognized he/she was referred to as a local herbalist, a divinator or at best an advisor whose techniques and procedures were unorthodox and unscientific (Makinde, 1978). Makinde goes on to explain that while in the western society this type of a counselor is an enigma the majority of Africans who live in community settings and even in urban areas continue to regard with respect such an office. From the writer's own experiences in Zimbabwe, relatives and community members, who live in peri-urban and urban areas, still consult indigenous African counselors who reside in towns. However, to do justice to the African counselor and put them in their proper place, western counseling needs to be examined.

Western counseling is normally supposed to be practiced by qualified and certified psychologists or counselors, which is not always the case particularly in Zimbabwe. This is due to inadequate qualified counselors and the existence of traditional counseling (Charema, 2004). In most cases it is the client who seeks the services of a counselor and the services are paid for. A counselor who uses western principles or modern methods of counseling in an African setting must understand both traditional and cultural ethics embedded in the African social being. Western principles when applied with appreciation of the local culture, generally tends to be more effective since they incorporate counseling the individual with all those closely attached to him/her. Borgman (1988) posits that in the Yoruba society in Nigeria, for example people who require counseling are referred to the Babalawa-men who are specially trained for community counseling and divining. Western counseling without knowledge of cultural and community beliefs will not resolve problems associated with family and illnesses that may be believed to be caused by ancestral or spiritual forces. While traditional counseling helps individuals fit into extended families - and communal groups, western counseling attempts to be scientific, in working with individuals whose goal is relative autonomy and healthy personal relationships (Borgman, 1988). While traditional counseling appears to be more situational and addresses the individual and those who surround them, western counseling tends to focus more on the individual and his/her problems. One good aspect of western counseling is that if a counselor realizes his/her limitations or feels for some reason - not able to help the client, they can refer to those they think have appropriate skills such as highly experienced counselors or psychologists. In the traditional set up the counselor gives advice and expects the counselee to take it as words of wisdom. The counselor is always expected to be older than the counselee whereas in the western culture a counselor is determined by qualification and experience.

Counseling in Learning Institutions

For counseling to be effective in school and other Institutions of Learning, the two approaches of counseling should be used wherever appropriate with culturally suitable students. Both approaches aim to help the client resolve his/her problems. Confidentiality and trust are observed in both cases.

The departing point of the two approaches is marked in culture, beliefs, resources and demographics. This is where school counselors need to exercise their knowledge and experiences of dealing with students from different cultural backgrounds. While the desires and goals to offer counseling to all Zimbabweans may be similar, the practices differ vastly due to different religions, beliefs and cultural ties.

Indigenous Zimbabweans who experience problems usually consult with family and or friends before approaching any other counselors. And yet their counterparts whose origin is not Africa find it easy to approach and open up to modern counselors. Counseling in schools is dealt with in detail in the next chapter.

CONCLUSION

The diversity and complexity of counseling in the African context is embedded in the cultural interpersonal rituals and the management of spiritual family cleansing and physical activities. African indigenous counseling is deeply rooted in the emotional, physical, spiritual, beliefs, cultural and family ties. While the nuclear family is battling to break away from the traditional counseling, family ties remain too strong for a family to be autonomous. The way forward for counseling in Zimbabwe and other African countries would be to use a multi-cultural approach. Depending on the background of the client being counseled, marrying the two approaches where appropriate is likely to yield better results. Counseling practiced in the western world should not be transported to Zimbabwe wholesale for use. There is need to make suitable adjustments in order to cater for clients of different backgrounds. As it stands, the conclusion that there is no set pattern of counseling in Zimbabwe that caters for different ethnic groups would be undisputed.

This chapter discussed the origin of counseling and theories of counseling. It further dealt with counseling in the African perspective and Zimbabwe in particular. In the process the author discussed the complexities and challenges that face counselors today. The chapter further compares and contrasts the traditional and western methods of counseling.

Reflection Questions

1. What do you understand to be counseling?
2. Describe and evaluate theories of counseling.
3. Identify the most appropriate counseling theories to apply in a school set-up?
4. Critically evaluate both traditional and western counseling systems.
5. Suggest ways of improving counseling in Zimbabwe.
6. Why is multicultural counseling necessary in learning institutions?

Chapter 8

TEACHER PREPARATION IN ZIMBABWE

Moses Rumano

Chapter Overview

This chapter traces the historical development of teacher preparation programs in Zimbabwe. Primary and secondary teacher programs will be examined in light of the fast social, economic and technological changes taking place at the global level. The sustenance of a democratic 21st century society revolves around quality education whose impetus comes through vibrant teacher education programs. The role of technology in teacher education will be highlighted. The history of teacher preparation programs in the country, including successes and challenges, will be discussed while the government's initiatives in combating HIV/AIDS through education sector and social responses to HIV/AIDS epidemic will be explored. The chapter concludes with a set of recommendations on the way forward insofar as teacher preparation is concerned.

Key Topics
Primary teacher education before independence
Teacher preparation and certification
Role of the University of Zimbabwe
Zimbabwe Integrated Teacher Education Course (ZINTEC)
Africa University's teacher preparation program
Bindura University of Science and Technology
Role of technology in teacher preparation programs
Teacher preparation in the advent of HIV/AIDS

Learner Outcomes
Upon completion of this chapter, readers will be able to:

1) Identify the reforms that took place in teacher education programs before and after independence.
2) Describe the fundamental roles that were/are played by church-related teachers' colleges.

3) Evaluate the strengths and weaknesses of Zimbabwe's teacher education programs in general.

INTRODUCTION

Teacher education can be defined as a systematic process of equipping both in-service and pre-service teachers with the essential skills and knowledge necessary to teach effectively. Teacher preparation in Zimbabwe starts with initial training either at a primary or secondary teachers' training college or university. Once a student teacher has completed the prescribed program, he or she receives a diploma in education, or a degree if enrolled at a university.

Zimbabwe has had teachers of varying academic and professional qualifications since 1939. Teacher qualifications range from a Primary Teachers' Lower Certificate (PTL), which was a two-year post Standard six course to degreed teachers (Chiromo, 2007). From 1939 significant changes in formal teacher training were experienced. According to Musarurwa (2011), many of Zimbabwean teachers are trained at one of the country's 15 teacher training colleges, 12 are state-owned and three church-related private institutions. Twelve of the 15 colleges are primary teacher training institutions and the remaining three are secondary teachers' training colleges. Teachers' colleges have made a tremendous effort to provide highly qualified teachers. By 2007, over 18,000 teachers were trained from these colleges since the attainment of political independence in 1980. Many of the teachers were trained to teach at the primary school level (National Status of Education in Zimbabwe Report, 2008). A sizeable number of teachers graduated from universities that offer education degree programs. According to Musarurwa (2011) the University of Zimbabwe's Department of Teacher Education is responsible for running a scheme of association with all 15 teacher training colleges in the country. Through this scheme of association, the University of Zimbabwe has the certification authority, which empowers it to monitor and control academic standards. However, each of the colleges has the autonomy to design their own syllabi, which should be approved by the University of Zimbabwe's Department of Teacher Education (DTE).

PRIMARY TEACHER EDUCATION BEFORE INDEPENDENCE

According to Chiromo (2007) Zimbabwe started training teachers at Morgenster Mission, a Dutch Reformed Church institution, as early as 1902. Most of the trained teachers then were called Jeannes teachers and had varying academic qualifications – at most Standard 4. The Jeannes teacher program was a teacher training program started in honor of a Philadelphia philanthropist, Anna T. Jeannes, who had given support for such training in the education of blacks in the United States. The program was widely used in British colonial Africa, including Southern Rhodesia (Zimbabwe), beginning in 1924. Chiromo further states that:

> In 1934 George Stark who had replaced Harold Jowitt as Director of Native Education, quickly recognized the need for better trained teachers and so in 1939, the entrance qualification for teacher training with the concurrence of the missionaries was

raised to Standard 6 and this marked the beginning of a somewhat formal training program in Zimbabwe. (p. 14)

Primary Teachers' Lower Certificate (PTL)

The Primary Teachers' Lower Certificate (PTL) was introduced in 1939. This was a two-year post Standard six course (Chiromo, 2007). It must be noted that the entry qualifications for the PTL could not have been higher than Standard six because by then there were no schools that offered secondary education to Africans. Some of the first secondary schools for Africans were St. Augustine's Penhalonga, Kutama, Gokomere, Inyati, Hatzel, Goromonzi and Fletcher, among others, which started enrolling students for secondary education from the late 1930s (Chiromo, 2007).

Before 1956, PTL courses were only offered by church-run institutions scattered all over the country. There were no government teacher training schools until 1956 when Umtali (now Mutare) Teacher Training School was opened. The opening of Umtali Teacher Training School was a result of the recommendations of the Kerr Commission of 1952. The Commission had recommended the establishment of a government teacher training school to augment the efforts of missionaries (Chiromo, 2007).

Primary Teachers' Higher Certificate (PTH)

The Primary Teachers' Certificate was introduced in 1949. The first teacher training school to enroll students for this course was Kutama (Chiromo, 2007). PTH was a two-year post-junior certificate. PTH holders taught the upper grades of primary school, i.e., Standards four to six or Grades six to seven. Some of the church-run teacher training schools that offered PTH courses were the same institutions that offered PTH courses. The structure and curriculum of the PTH program was similar to that of the PTL program. The only difference was its emphasis on the content and methodologies of the upper grades of the primary school system. The major reason why the PTH program was discontinued, according to the secretary for African Education, was that the course had tended to produce instructors who had been drilled in certain skills but had little idea of how to analyze their own work or diagnose the difficulties experienced by children in their classrooms. Therefore, there was need to come up with teacher education programs that were in line with progressive modern methods such as child-centered approach. According to Shaw (1992), "while the PTH and PTL courses were meant to produce a teacher who could teach good lessons, the new course (T3) emphasized the production of a teacher who could teach children and develop their personalities" (p. 137).

Teachers' Certificate Grade 4 (T4)

Teachers' Certificate Grade four (T4) was pioneered at Hope Fountain Mission replacing PTL courses in 1967 (Shaw, 1992). The last intake of PTL teachers was in 1968. The T4 course was a two-year post-Standard six program meant to train specialist teachers for the infant classes, i.e., grades one to two. The T4 graduates were grounded in infant methods. The difference between PTL and T4 program was that PTL teachers were trained to teach up to Grade five and therefore, were not specialist teachers in infant methods. The course was biased towards women since only women were allowed to enroll for the T4 course.

Teachers' Certificate Grade 3 (T3)

Chiromo (2007) pointed out that the year 1968 was a turning point in teacher education with a number of changes being effected. Some of the changes were a direct response to the provisions of the 1966 Education Act. The idea that the T3 course was introduced in 1968 to replace PTH was met with mixed feelings. Initially, the minimum entry qualifications for the T3 course were raised to a Junior Certificate until 1976 when the minimum entry qualifications were raised to a Cambridge School Certificate. The major difference between the T3 program and the PTH program was the duration of the course. An increase in the duration of the course was meant to produce a better-trained teacher than the PTH teacher. In addition, Shaw (1992) observed that in the "new" T3 course, greater emphasis was placed on the theory of education and background knowledge in the curriculum subjects of primary school, but of course with due care taken to see that practice of education and methodology received their share of attention. A number of institutions were offering T3 education by the year 1971. These were, Mt. Silinda, Mtshabezi, Darambombe, Morgenster, Nyadiri, Kutama, St. Paul's (Musami), Bondolfi, Howard, Lower Gwelo, Waddilove and United College of Education (Shaw, 1992).

PRIMARY TEACHER EDUCATION AFTER INDEPENDENCE

By 1980, a number of church-run primary teacher training colleges had folded up due to a variety of reasons. One of the major reasons was the recommendation made by the Judges Commission (1962), which recommended the grouping of small teacher training schools to allow the colleges to benefit from adequate staff and resources. This recommendation resulted in a number of church denominations pooling their resources and opening the United College of Education in Bulawayo in 1968 (Chiromo, 2007). The intensification of the liberation war in the late 1970s also saw a number of small teacher training schools closing down since most of the rural areas where all these teacher training schools were located had become no-go areas. Shaw (1992) noted that the only church-run teacher education colleges that survived and are still operational are Nyadire in Mutoko, Morgenster and Bondolfi, both in Masvingo. The efforts of these three church-run institutions are complemented by Mkoba, Seke, Masvingo, Morgan, Marymount, Gwanda, and United College of Education (Chiromo, 2007).

By the end of 1985, most of the teachers' colleges had attained associate status with the Associate College Center (now Department of Teacher Education) of the University of Zimbabwe. Figure 8.1 indicates the colleges and the year they attained associate status.

Name of College	Year Attained Associate Status
United College of Education	1978
Mkoba	1978
Mutare	1979
Seke	1981
Nyadire	1981
Bondolfi	1982
Gwanda	1983
Marymount	1983
Masvingo	1983
Morgan	1983
Morgenster	1985

Source: A Handbook for the Department of Teacher Education, University of Zimbabwe 1993.

Figure 8.1. Colleges and the Year they Attained Associate Status.

Affiliation with the University of Zimbabwe

The associate status with the colleges meant that the University of Zimbabwe, through the Department of Teacher Education, was responsible for the certification of successful students (Musarurwa, 2011). This association made the teachers' certificates a standard qualification that could be recognized internationally. The scheme of association applies to those institutions that do not seek to participate in the work of the university but that seek to obtain the university's participation in their work. National teacher education standardization became universal to all teacher-training colleges in Zimbabwe. This meant that all associate colleges had their syllabi designed according to the broad principles suggested by the University of Zimbabwe and subject to the approval of Senate.

Zimbabwe Integrated Teacher Education Course (ZINTEC)

The Zimbabwe Integrated Teacher Education Course (ZINTEC) program was a four-year (now three-year) teacher education course initiated in 1981 soon after Zimbabwe attained political independence as a way to meet the high demand for new teachers. It became one of the success stories in teacher preparation programs initiated by the government in post-independent Zimbabwe. The main purpose of the program was to effectively improve teaching practice by deploying the student teachers to teach in schools during their training. While on teaching practice, student teachers received some teaching materials that helped them to gain more theoretical foundations. They were routinely supervised by both college lecturers and school heads. The need for trained teachers was underscored by the governmental policy that viewed human development as a catalyst for the empowerment of the citizens especially in rural areas. Trained teachers were expected to lead in the war against ignorance, illiteracy and underdevelopment (Dzvimbo, 1989). An effective teacher education in particular and education in general were viewed as the ingredients of bringing about desired socio-economic and cultural changes in Zimbabwe. According to Chung (1996) "the

ZINTEC concept had its foundations in the Zimbabwean liberation struggle, when in the late 1970s, refugees in Mozambique who numbered about 30,000 were taught by only three qualified teachers" (p. 1). ZINTEC marked a point of departure from the previous conventional method of teacher preparation. All student teachers enrolled through ZINTEC had successfully completed four years of secondary education and a few had served as primary and secondary school temporary teachers.

According to Dzvimbo (1989) the teacher trainees spent 16 weeks of initial training at the colleges. After 16 weeks of intensive course-work, students were posted to all regions across the country. For the rest of their four-year education course, student teachers were given the privileges and conditions of service just like full-time teachers and received a graduated salary. However, their counterparts in conventional teachers' colleges did not receive a full salary. Rural areas were the targets where student teachers were actively involved in community projects such as adult literacy projects and night schools. The program was designed to empower students who did not have any access to quality education to be active and engaging in the remote and rural areas. The colonial government did not have a plan to develop the rural areas where the majority of black people resided.

To effectively equip the student teachers with theoretical foundations of education while on teaching practice, educational broadcasts were used to supplement the materials from their colleges. These modules were carefully prepared by trained staff at the national center and broadcast from the regional centers in the six provinces. Student teachers returned to college at the end of four years to take final examinations. After successful completion of the program the students received a certificate in education (now diploma in education), which was (and still is) issued by the University of Zimbabwe in conjunction with the Department of Education. Insights from the ZINTEC program influenced the government to move teacher preparation toward this model in 1983. Teacher preparation at both the primary and secondary levels in the country was eventually modeled along the ZINTEC. The only technical difference is that instead of spending 16-week residency program student teachers spend their first year at college. The second year was assigned for teaching practice whereby student teachers spent the entire year in schools as full time teachers. The third and final year was college based, where students had to complete their major projects and had to take their final examinations.

The Aims and Goals of the ZINTEC Program

At independence in 1980, primary and secondary education was made more accessible to a majority of the people; therefore, the need for trained teachers correspondingly rose. The aims and objectives of the ZINTEC program were as follows:

- to train as many primary teachers as possible to reduce the perennial teacher shortage through an in-service type of teacher education
- to start a teacher education program relevant to alleviate poverty levels in rural areas
- to initiate an effective teacher education program based on scientific socialism
- to effect significant infrastructural and developmental changes through teacher education by infusing theory into practice

- to develop an effective and reflective teacher with essential professional skills needed for the provision of effective learning experiences

Successes and Challenges of the ZINTEC Program

The ZINTEC program was introduced at a time when the country desperately needed qualified primary school teachers. The need for such a program was apparent in order to complement the efforts of the few conventional teachers' colleges which were producing insufficient teachers at that time. As such Chivore (1993) reported that, "by 1988, the four ZINTEC colleges had produced 5,887 teachers compared to 5,416 produced by seven conventional colleges during the same period" (p. 44). In addition, Chiromo (2007) argued that the "success" story of the ZINTEC program led to the "Zintecnization" of the conventional teacher education program with effect from 1982. Instead of the three years of conventional training, a four-year program was introduced. The introduction of ZINTEC was a cost effective way of producing teachers in terms of both money and time. As such, "an evaluation carried out in 1986 claimed that the cost of preparing primary school teachers under the ZINTEC program was relatively cheaper than the three-year conventional pattern" (Chivore, 1993, p. 45). The idea of producing a teacher with a socialist orientation was considered appropriate by the government of the day.

The ZINTEC program was not a story of successes only; it had a fair share of challenges, too. Some aspects of the ZINTEC program, though relevant on paper, proved to be problematic in the real training of the teacher. An evaluation by Chivore (1993) showed that ZINTEC teachers were found to be ineffective in "education with production." This was problematic because most educationists did not understand the concept of "education with production" which refers to students learning practical skills alongside academic skills. There was a strong perception among prospective students that conventional colleges did a better job in preparing teachers than the ZINTEC program. Many of them believed that teacher preparation through distance education was inferior to what was still being taught in the classrooms.

Chiromo (2007) argued that the increase in the duration of the initial residential part of the ZINTEC program from 16 weeks to 24 weeks could have been because of the realization that there was need for student teachers to have more time to master the "survival skills" before they went on teaching practice. Some of the problems associated with the ZINTEC program emanated from lack of relevant and adequate resources and the inaccessibility of libraries to the majority of the students.

SECONDARY TEACHER EDUCATION

Prior to the 1960s, there was no institution that trained non-graduate black secondary teachers. The only teachers' college that trained non-graduate secondary school teachers was the Teachers' College (now Hillside Teachers' College) but it was strictly for Whites, Coloreds and Asians. In the early 1960s, Gwelo (Gweru) Teachers College (now Midlands State University), started training black secondary school teachers (Annual Report of the

Secretary for African Education, 1972). Gwelo Teachers College was to remain the only institution for training non-graduate secondary teachers until the advent of independence in 1980 when more secondary teachers' colleges were opened.

The entry requirements for the Teachers' Certificate Grade 1 (T1) course were a first-class Cambridge School Certificate (Shaw, 1992). The duration of the course was three years. The T1 trainees were supposed to teach up to form two (Annual Report of the Secretary for African Education, 1972). Ordinary level pupils were supposed to be taught mainly by graduates from the University of Rhodesia and other universities outside the country. Gwelo Teachers' College started with an enrollment of 40 male students. Female students were not enrolled during the inaugural year because of insufficient accommodation (Chiromo, 2007). In 1972, the T1 course was found to be producing more teachers than could be absorbed into the secondary school system. This was mainly due to the strict bottle-necking at form one. The year 1979 saw the discontinuation of the T1 and T2 courses. A new certificate known as the Secondary Teachers' Certificate in Education was introduced in 1979. The course did not make a distinction between teachers of academic subjects and practical subjects. The bottleneck system was removed at independence resulting in high demand of secondary school teachers; this led the government to open Belvedere Teachers College in Harare in 1982 (Chivore, 1990).

In an effort to produce more teachers of practical subjects, Chinhoyi Technical Teacher Training College was opened in May 1991. The curriculum at Chinhoyi was/is structured in such a way that student teachers would do a three-year skills training course resulting a National Certificate. After successfully completing three years of skills training in the various practical skills, interested students would do the pedagogy course in their fourth year. Because of the apparent effectiveness of the Chinhoyi Teacher Training College curriculum, Belvedere changed its curriculum to be in line with that of Chinhoyi (Chiromo, 2007).

In line with the significant developments that were taking place in secondary teacher training, Gweru Teachers College and Hillside Teachers College revamped their curricula to offer training to advanced level graduates except for Physical Education, French, Music, Arts and Crafts, and Home Economics. Today the only operational secondary school teachers training colleges are Mutare Teachers College, Hillside Teachers College, and Belvedere Technical Teachers College.

UNIVERSITIES INVOLVED IN TEACHER PREPARATION PROGRAMS

A number of universities are actively involved in teacher preparation programs in Zimbabwe. To illustrate some of the specific teacher preparation programs we will only focus on one private university and one state university in this chapter to highlight how teacher preparation has progressively advanced in Zimbabwe.

Africa University

The Africa University Handbook (2010) states that the development of Africa University came as a result of the growth of United Methodism in Africa. The emerging socio-economic and political needs in the continent convinced the African bishops of the United Methodist Church (UMC) to call on their church to establish an institution of higher learning. In the 1980s, Bishop Arthur Kulah of Liberia and Bishop Emilio J. M. de Carvalho of Angola spearheaded the idea of setting up a United Methodist related university for all of Africa. Their efforts resonated quite well within the United Methodist Church worldwide. In 1985 the "Africa Initiative" was born due to the concerted effort by the inspirational and hardworking bishops.

According to the Africa University Curriculum Guide (2011), the mission statement of the faculty of education at Africa University is to prepare competent and effective educational leaders who can contribute toward sustainable development of their communities and countries.

The Aims of Teacher Preparation Program at Africa University
Africa University seeks to prepare teachers who are able to:

- have a strong theoretical foundation and principles of education;
- understand the stages of human development in their instructional methodologies;
- develop and implement age appropriate learning objectives;
- appropriately evaluate student learning in different settings;
- communicate effectively to all students;
- engage in constructive dialogue and conversation with their students;
- build good rapport with all students irrespective of their cultural background;
- develop effective classroom management techniques;
- demonstrate competence and proficiency in their subject areas;
- value basic human rights and celebrate diversity of opinions;
- advocate for students, parents, and the community at large;

Four-Year Bachelor of Arts with Education (B.A. Ed.) Program
The four-year Bachelor of Arts (Education) study program is designed for students who are interested in becoming teachers. Students admitted into this program should have successfully completed their Advanced level education. The content majors offered on the program are as follows: English, Geography, French, Music, History, Religious Studies and Portuguese. In order to complete the program, students need to have their coursework covered in seven semesters and go for student teaching in their final semester. While on teaching practice, cooperating teachers, school leaders and university lecturers supervise them. Student teachers are placed in various school districts that help them to become professional teachers and appreciate student diversity (Africa University Curriculum Guide, 2011).

Four-Year Bachelor of Science with Education (B.Sc. Ed.) in Business/Commerce Program
Students enrolled into this program are required to take all specified Business courses in the program. The main focus of this program is to adequately prepare students to teach Business or Commerce courses at the secondary school level. After successfully completing their coursework students go for their student teaching (Africa University Curriculum Guide, 2011).

Four-Year Bachelor of Science in Agriculture with Education (B.Sc. Agric. Ed.) Program

The program prepares students to teach Agriculture at the secondary school level. Students are expected to take all specified courses in Agriculture and Natural Resources. Like the study programs discussed above, this program involves seven semesters of coursework plus an additional semester of teaching practice. All student teachers are placed in school districts that help them to mature in the profession (Africa University Curriculum Guide, 2011).

Two-Year Bachelor of Education (B.Ed.) Program

The two-year Bachelor of Education program is intended for applicants who are either holders of a certificate in education or a diploma. The main purpose of this program of study is to help qualified teachers to further their academic and professional knowledge. Unlike in the four year program, students enrolled in this program are expected to complete coursework in one or two content subjects. The following major subject areas are on offer: English, French, History, Agriculture, Business, Geography, Music, Portuguese and Religious Studies. Since the duration of study for this program is two years, not all courses may be available in any one year. Many of the students enrolled in this program already have teaching positions either as primary or secondary teachers (Africa University Curriculum Guide, 2011).

Bindura University of Science Education

A state university chosen in this chapter to highlight the advancement of teacher preparation in Zimbabwe is the Bindura University of Science Education. Historically, the establishment of the Bindura University of Science Education can be traced to the government initiated Zimbabwe-Cuba Teacher Training Program that was started in the mid-1980s. The need for qualified science teachers after independence motivated the government to send Zimbabwean student teachers to Cuba for training in Science Education. The Ministry of Higher and Tertiary Education Report (1997) pointed out it was economically prudent to relocate the teacher training program to Zimbabwe in 1995. After consultations and deliberations, a college in Bindura was established under the auspices of the University of Zimbabwe. After a couple of years, the program was turned into a full-fledged university. In 1996 Bindura College roared into life by admitting its first group of 125 students in March.

The Bindura University of Science Education became a fully-fledged state institution of higher learning through an act of parliament that was passed in February 2000. More science teachers were locally trained that significantly alleviated the shortage of qualified science teachers in the country. The first graduation ceremony was held in 2003 where 140 graduates were capped (Ministry of Higher Education and Tertiary Report, 1997). This university has four faculties: Agriculture and Environmental Science, Science, Science Education and Commerce. A total of 58 programs are offered by the university's 19 departments.

Faculty of Science Education

The department of education seeks to prepare science educators with essential pedagogical skills in Science and Mathematics. To accomplish its objectives, the following programs of study are offered.

Undergraduate Programs
- Diploma in Science Education;
- Bachelor of Science (BSc.Ed.), which is a three-year study program. Students have the option to major in Biological Sciences, Chemistry, and Geography;
- Bachelor of Science Education Honors Degree (HBSc.Ed.), a three-year study program; the following majors are offered: Biological Sciences, Chemistry, and Computer Science,
- Bachelor of Science Education Honors (BSc.Ed.), which is a four-year program. The following majors are available to students: Biological Sciences, Chemistry, Physics, Mathematics, and Computer Science (Bindura University of Science Education Curriculum Guide, 2014)

Postgraduate Programs
- Master of Science Education (MSc.Ed.), with major options in Biology, Chemistry, Physics, Mathematics, Geography, and Computer Science, and
- Master of Science Education in Curriculum Studies (MSc.Ed.) (Bindura University of Science Education Curriculum Guide, 2014).

Incorporating Technology in Teacher Preparation Programs

The need to embrace technology in teacher preparation programs in the twenty-first century cannot be overemphasized. All student teachers should have extensive knowledge on how to effectively use technology into the classroom before they graduate from colleges. Few teachers today are prepared to incorporate technology into their instructional methodologies after graduating from teachers' colleges due to the lack of technological infrastructure and training in that area. Many high school students are graduating into a world that is more technologically networked than ever before. In Zimbabwe, more citizens now have access to the internet than a decade ago. If teachers are to be considered active nation builders and agents of change, they have to teach their students to embrace technology. The Zimbabwean government and the private church-related institutions have made significant strides in opening up teacher preparation programs. These opportunities should transform the lives of many citizens by using technological advancement to alleviate poverty, suffering, and economic stagnation.

Research has shown that the role of a teacher has been transformed tremendously as technological advances have made the learning process increasingly information-rich. Black (1999) argued that student teachers should be fully prepared and equipped to move from the traditional role of instructor to the role of a well prepared facilitator. In addition, teachers must be technologically prepared to deal with the challenges of moving from a system that is teacher-oriented to student-oriented. In agreement, CEO Forum on Education and Technology (1999) states that we should train teachers in technology by raising the mandatory requirements for technological literacy a teacher needs to possess, and provide teachers with more intensive training in using computers and digital technology. Teacher preparation programs should also focus on how to equip their students with practical training in the handling of instrumentation and equipment.

Dugger (2001) observed that one area of inherent weakness often noted in teacher preparation programs is the lack of integration of technology. With frequent power outages and lack of computers in Zimbabwe, technological integration remains an elusive dream to many student teachers. Very few schools in the rural and farming communities have electricity, manpower and computers. In spite of all the challenges, teacher preparation programs should require pre-service teachers to take technology courses before they graduate. Merkley, Schmidt, and Allen (2001) state that "required technology courses in a teacher preparation program must be complemented by faculty who model effective use of technology for instructional and administrative tasks throughout the teacher preparation coursework" (p. 221). Research indicates that lecturers who use technology well in their teaching motivate their students to embrace it well. For lecturers who lack technological expertise, staff development can be used as a most effective enrichment course (Lacey, 2001). The significance of intensive and extensive, and continual, teacher training in appropriate technology use and curricular application is fundamental (Cooley, Cradler, & Engel, 1997).

In addition, Darling-Hammond (1996) articulates the notion that teachers' preparation programs need to encourage the teaching of skills in using an array of teaching strategies like cooperative learning, classroom management, and technologies, as this will increase effectiveness in working with students from diverse backgrounds. Twenty-first century teachers need to be familiar with the new technology and incorporate it in classroom teaching. This use of technology in learning helps the students to interact with the content, programmed interface, the instructor, and other learners, both individually and in groups (Geer, 2000).

The appropriate use of technology in teaching requires student teachers to have used the facilities before and be well acquainted with the use of instructional technology in their classes. Indeed, the teachers need to have skills on how to operate particular technologies, such as use of standard sets of software tools, word processors, and spreadsheets, among others. Furthermore, teachers need to understand the subject matter and the manner in which it can be changed through application of technology. It is of great importance also for both student teachers and practicing teachers to understand curriculum materials and technologies in order to mutually connect with their students. For example, learners can play with the computers and construct shapes and forms which change the nature of learning geometry (Darling-Hammond, 2005). In order for this to happen, teachers need to be trained to use technology.

TEACHER PREPARATION IN THE ADVENT OF HIV/AIDS EPIDEMIC

UNAIDS (2011) indicated that the HIV/AIDS National policy encourages voluntary counseling and testing to all interested people in Zimbabwe. There are over 400 sites in the country where voluntary counseling and testing is provided by the government. International donors have poured in substantial amount of money in order to stop mother to child transmission. Educational programs offered in villages, wards, districts, and provinces have helped many people to deal with HIV/AIDS epidemic from an informed position. The effectiveness of education in the fight against HIV/AIDS epidemic is underscored by the fact that children in Zimbabwe are taught about HIV/AIDS from the age of eight. Both government and non-governmental organizations efforts are gearing towards making the subject examinable.

The need for a comprehensive and well established HIV/AIDS education curriculum in all teachers' training colleges and universities cannot be overemphasized in Zimbabwe. Given how devastating this epidemic has been to the country's economy, social, and cultural facets of the society, teacher preparation programs are strategically positioned and academically empowered to play an effective role in combating the disease through accurate dissemination of vital information. The proponents for HIV/AIDS education call for all pre-service and in-service teachers to be adequately trained on how to pass information to combat this deadly HIV and AIDS epidemic especially among youths. The UNDP (2013) reported that around 15% of the total population is living with HIV in Zimbabwe. Conservative figures projected by some organizations working with HIV and AIDS-orphaned children suggest that over one million of them are living with the deadly virus that causes AIDS. The average life expectancy is around 53 due to this scourge.

Efforts to prevent and combat HIV/AIDS were stepped up when the Ministry of Higher Education and Tertiary Education (2005) developed a policy on HIV/AIDS for teachers' colleges. The main purpose of this policy framework is to guide colleges and institutions of higher learning on how to implement effective measures to combat HIV/AIDS epidemic. This policy was established to strengthen and embolden the effectiveness of the National Policy by developing pragmatic and appropriate solutions to fight the HIV and AIDS pandemic. The devastating effects of the HIV and AIDS on all entities of the country compelled the Ministry of Higher and Tertiary Education to collaborate with other organizations working with the HIV/AIDS affected and infected people in Zimbabwe. There was agreement between the Ministry of Higher and Tertiary Education and many non-governmental organizations that the need for HIV/AIDS education was of paramount importance. This combined group mutually concurred that that teachers in society are potentially powerful and effective emissaries in the dissemination of HIV and AIDS information to many young people.

Children in Zimbabwe have a mandatory HIV/AIDS curriculum that is taught by qualified teachers. The Ministry of Education, Sport and Culture in conjunction with UNICEF initiated an in-service training scheme of primary and secondary school teachers in 2006 on HIV/AIDS and life-skills; all teachers are trained to deliver age appropriate information on combating HIV/AIDS epidemic. In Zimbabwe many communities look up to teachers for informed advice and leadership; therefore, their close connection with the students and parents place them at an elevated position to reach out. Teachers' training colleges and all the institutions of higher learning need to adequately empower and equip all the student teachers and university graduates with the necessary training and tools so that they can effectively educate the nation on the dangers of HIV and the AIDS epidemic.

Challenges in the Implementation of the National HIV and AIDS Policy

The combined effort by the Ministry of Higher and Tertiary Education and non-governmental organizations to have teachers' colleges and all institutions of higher learning run effective HIV and AIDS programs have been stifled by a number of reasons such as: negative attitudes by both lecturers and students who feel that HIV and AIDS is not their problem, lack of learning and teaching materials, and enthusiasm in the subject. In spite of these obstacles in the full implementation of HIV/AIDS policy, however, it is still agreed in principle that the first step towards strengthening and empowering college-based HIV and AIDS programs is a policy customized to meet the challenges of passing accurate information to all the vulnerable groups. Another challenge to grapple with is the lack of qualified and enthusiastic personnel for HIV and AIDS education that has resulted in most teachers' training colleges failing to put in place effective and meaningful programs. It is regrettable and unfortunate that many teachers are deployed to teach at schools without the necessary skills to handle HIV and AIDS education. In a country where there is stigma, ignorance, and denial by those infected and affected with HIV/AIDS, the only hope and optimism squarely remains in empowering educators.

Conclusion

The historical development of teacher preparation programs went through several reforms. Political events, economic cycles, and social challenges were instrumental in the reshaping of teacher education programs. Academic entry qualifications were reviewed many times with the hope of improving the quality of teachers since the colonial times. Teacher preparation programs in post-independent Zimbabwe ushered in radical changes that sought to empower the Black Zimbabweans that were racially excluded from an active participation in the teacher preparation programs. Initiated in 1981, the ZINTEC program was the most acclaimed post-independence teacher education program in Zimbabwe. Currently most of Zimbabwe's teachers are trained through the 15 teacher training colleges, 12 of which are state owned and three are church related institutions. A number of universities are preparing teachers in specific disciplines too across the country.

Another important area that teachers' colleges and universities need to embrace is the use of technology in their instructional approaches. The demands of the twenty-first century require all teacher preparation programs to be proactive in order to empower all citizens. Technological advancement has literally turned the world into a borderless global village through unlimited access to information. In the advent of the devastating HIV/AIDS epidemic, all teacher preparations programs are called upon to be champions in combating the further spread of this hitherto incurable epidemic. Teachers' colleges and other institutions of higher learning are well positioned to disseminate accurate information about HIV/AIDS to both in-service and pre-service teachers. Teacher preparation programs in the country need to empower student teachers with accurate information to combat the HIV/AIDS epidemic.

Reflection Questions

1) Discuss the influential reforms that were taken before and after independence in teacher education programs?
2) What fundamental roles were/are played by church-related teachers' colleges and universities in Zimbabwe?
3) What are the successes and challenges encountered by teacher preparation programs in fostering the government's effort to combat the HIV/AIDS epidemic?
4) How can teacher preparation programs prepare students for the new challenges of the global demands such as technologically literate citizens?

Chapter 9

THE ROLE OF COUNSELOR EDUCATION TODAY

John Charema

Chapter Overview
In this chapter we explore the role of counselor education in learning institutions and how counseling enhances the education of students in primary secondary and tertiary education in Zimbabwe.

The various challenges that students face thereby exposing them to social, psychological and emotional problems are discussed. We also look at environmental, socio-economic, personal and family factors that impact students' welfare and behavior as well as the role that counselor education plays in alleviating student experiences. The place of evaluation and cultural counseling is also addressed.

Key Topics
- Policy and legislation
- Counselor training
- Counseling practice
- Counseling in schools
- Diversity and multi-cultural counseling

Learner Outcomes
By the time readers complete this chapter they should be able to:

- Describe counseling
- Identify counselor training organizations in Zimbabwe
- Explain why students need counseling
- Identify the challenges of counseling in schools
- Explain how counseling can be improved

INTRODUCTION

Due to a number of challenges that students experience in Learning Institutions, the role of counselor education has become paramount in the life of a student. For students to succeed in their learning they need among other things, emotional, social and educational support, from the community, parents, teachers and school counselors. Education is a vital transformational tool and an efficient instrument for socio-economic empowerment. Therefore to achieve economic freedom, the goals of wealth creation, employment generation, self-sustainability, poverty reduction and orientation can be effectively pursued, attained, and sustained mainly through an efficient, appropriate and functional education system (NEEDS, 2004 as cited in Alao, 2009). Educating people is one important way of effecting change in human thinking, attitudes, values, morals, beliefs, orientation and perceptions. However, students in learning institutions experience social, psychological, personal and academic problems at school and at home (Chireshe, 2008). Some of these problems are caused by family discord, divorce or separation, poverty, poor living conditions, and long and short-term illnesses in the family. While most of the problems cited from home-related challenges, some of them are socially and psychologically behavior-related. Quite a number of studies have documented the existence of behavior problems in schools (Alao, 2009; Gesinde, 2009; Shayo, 2011). While not all, some of the behavior-related problems are caused by some form of disorders and or disabilities and yet most of them are created by students themselves. Such problems include among others: drug and alcohol abuse, truancy, lying, cheating, emotional disorder, teenage pregnancies, hyperactivity, abortion, aggression, fighting, disobedience, sex indulgence, rudeness, lateness, smoking, uncompleted work, bullying and dirtiness. Whether the problems come from home or school or are self-imposed, they expose students to stress triggers and emotional depression that impact negatively on their learning.

Basically, most of the undesirable disruptive behaviors cannot be easily addressed or dealt with by regular class teachers without special training in guidance and counseling. The need for counseling has become paramount in order to promote the well-being of the child. Unprecedented world recession, socio-economic and social interaction changes have, over the years, changed the ways in which we manage our lives (Shayo, 2011). Consequently, not all the lessons of the past can help us effectively deal with the challenges of modern times. Effective counseling, especially in institutions of learning has now become important and should be embedded in the education system. It therefore stands to reason that the importance of guidance counselors in schools cannot be underestimated. Students in institutions of learning from primary school through college all need to be guided in the relationships between health and the environment, developing skills, knowledge, and attitudes that lead to success in life (Shayo, 2011). Considering the host of problems encountered by students in the present age, it is undisputed that the need for counseling has never existed before than now. Counseling helps to develop a holistic child who is well groomed spiritually, morally and socially. Effective guidance and counseling could help to improve the self-image of young people and facilitate achievement in life tasks. Counseling should empower students to participate fully in, and benefit from, the economic and social development of the nation.

POLICY AND LEGISLATION

According to the Ministry of Education circular number 3 of 2005, the main goal of the education system of Zimbabwe is to promote national development through the production of disciplined, socially well-adjusted and productive individuals with sound physical and mental health practices. The policy further indicates that learner welfare is the priority focus of the Ministry's Client Charter in pursuance of quality education.

This is the basis on which the government of Zimbabwe in conjunction with the Ministry of Education Sports and Culture recognizes guidance and counseling as an essential service that must be provided to every individual learner who needs it in all schools, colleges, in the work place and the community at large. It is government policy to ensure that operational and sustainable Guidance and Counseling programs established in all learning institutions are functional. The policy emphasizes that academic education by itself cannot produce an all-round person. Counseling can positively develop students emotionally, socially, psychologically and intellectually. The ability for students to produce the best and derive maximum satisfaction from the adult life will depend largely on the education, self-discipline, good moral behavior and social skills acquired for future development.

COUNSELOR TRAINING

Zimbabwe has a few training institutions for counselors. The University of Zimbabwe trains graduate psychologists who practice counseling in different organizations upon demand or as part of their employment duties. CONNECT, a trainer counseling organization, trains child, general and family counselors. Most school counselors are trained at CONNECT, which offers child counseling. The Ministry of Health and Child Welfare also trains counselors who offer counseling services to patients who experience complications at birth or give birth to children with disabilities, terminal patients who suffer from different ailments including cancer and HIV/AIDS. They also offer bereavement counseling to people who lose their loved ones. The main challenge with most trained counselors in Zimbabwe is that they are not licensed. One other challenge is that most people who enroll to train as counselors do so holding different professional and academic qualifications at different levels. It is necessary to establish entry qualifications for different levels of training and further have all qualified counselors licensed such that the practice is standardized, governed and regulated.

CHALLENGES STUDENTS FACE IN EDUCATIONAL INSTITUTIONS

Counseling has an important role to play in the life of students at all levels from primary school, high school, and college or university education. In most developing countries counseling has increasingly become of high demand than ever before, due to the shrinking economy, shortage of food due to drought, poor farming methods, civil wars, limited job opportunities, the increasing gap of poverty, serious levels of social and emotional distress, corruption, the HIV/AIDS pandemic, increase in crime and suicidal deaths (Charema, 2009; Webb, 2000). It would appear as though young people are on the receiving end of these harsh and rough conditions. Young people who experience challenges either from home, school, social relations friendship circles and peer pressure are all candidates for counseling. Some of the common problems that manifest in young people of today include but are not limited to; drug and alcohol abuse, eating disorders, absenteeism, petty pilfering, depression and stress, low self-esteem, teenage pregnancy, physical and sexual abuse, bullying, gangsters, divorced and loss of parents (Charema, 2009). Many students lack life and survival skills and so are prone and easy prey to most of the above mentioned. There is need to have counseling and behavior modification programs that complement academic work to better equip students to cope in the prevailing harsh, social and economically depressed environment.

GOALS OF COUNSELING IN EDUCATIONAL INSTITUTIONS

Institutions of learning can only be conducive and productive when there is order, emotional stability within students, peace and harmony in the family, healthy relations among students, focus on tasks and positive peer interaction. All these in the absence of or in addition to family support unit, need to be enhanced by a vibrant effective counseling school program. The goals of a counseling program are to support all students who experience family, educational, relational, emotional and psychological problems I one way or another. Initially school guidance was perceived as vocational in nature mainly to provide high school, college and university students with career guidance. However, this trend has changed, to date counselors deal with diverse problems with respect to concerns and needs of students. Counseling helps to equip students with life skills rooted in their belief systems thereby further enhancing their decision making in career choices and personal social life in a complex ever-changing world.

COUNSELING PRACTICE

According to Charema (2004) counseling is a dynamic process that involves professionally trained counselors assisting clients with particular concerns to make decisions and change behavior. It is an interactive learning process between a counselor and a client, (in this case a student) whether individual or group, using appropriate approaches, with the aim of developing a holistic student, dealing with personal, educational and vocational issues. Nystul (1999) states that the counselor uses a variety of strategies such as individual, group, or family counseling to assist the client come to terms with and resolve conflicting issues. The counselor can create a conducive environment for the client to embrace change, enhance coping skills and promote decision-making.

Basically, the availability of a counseling service is there to support individual students inside and outside the classroom context. As mentioned before, undesirable behaviors such as unhealthy competition, social exclusion, scholastic under-achievement, sexual and substance abuse, homophobia, peer pressure, and racism are some of the problems which can be resolved through counseling. Students are also helped to cope with family crises and other personal problems. Counseling helps to enhance discipline in a school.

Individual Counseling is an interactive process, which facilitates meaningful understanding of the self, environment, positive attitudes, spiritual and mental healing, and clarification of goals and values for the future. Group Counseling involves counseling people in a group engaging them to take an active part. Members of the group are encouraged to listen attentively, support and encourage or challenge each other's ideas without necessarily creating conflict, thereby learning to be open, constructive, assertive, and to learn others' views. The emphasis is on dealing with behavior or views not the person. Once students have mastered the concept of separating the behavior or any other problem from the person then they graduate to peer-counseling on issues at their level of skill. Peer-Counseling occurs on limited and well prepared occasions where pupils help and support each other on topics that deal with general behavior, educational and vocational aspects, but not necessarily on personal issues.

Essentially, counseling services within the school are expected to operate in collaboration with the school administrative structures which include the disciplinary team thereby promoting harmony in the school operating system. Working within the guidelines of the counseling code of conduct, respecting ethical considerations and client confidentiality, ensures that the service is properly supervised and monitored so that the student's needs are prioritized and their rights respected and protected. The service should operate above board fulfilling the mandate of the protection, guidance and welfare of children.

COUNSELING IN SCHOOLS

Most high schools in Zimbabwe already have established guidance and counseling services administered by professionally trained School Guidance Counselors (SGC). The SGC, as part of a school team, focuses primarily on the development of the whole child. This involves the personal, academic, social, educational and vocational development of the student. The aim of the service is to equip every student to function effectively in a stable and sound mind. Typically, the objective is to meet the guidance and counseling needs of every student and to further enhance their learning process in the context of the overall school mission. School counselors help to make learning a positive experience for every student observing individual differences. They know that a classroom environment that is good for one child is not necessarily good for another, therefore, they are sensitive to the needs of individual children. Counselors facilitate communication among teachers, parents, administrators, and students to adapt the school environment in the best interests of each individual student. They help individual students make the most of their school experiences and prepare them to face the future with confidence and to make use of skills whenever they meet challenges.

It is important to note that while Zimbabwe has implemented SGC programs in primary and secondary schools, the roles of a school counselor are somewhat different at various grade levels. At primary school level, particularly for ages five to eight years, counselors are expected to spend most of their time with individual children, small groups, classes, in an effort to connect with every child in the school. The counselor should make an effort to create a working relationship with children's parents, and other stakeholders. Their contribution plays a very important role towards the positive and appropriate development of the child.

Although the roles of counselors vary from one school to another due to settings, cultural values and beliefs, common roles include, among others, individual counseling, small-group counseling, class lessons on various topics, school-wide promotion of positive behavior, stamping out negative behavior. The counselor also engages and consults other teachers, parents, and the community on a variety of issues. It is important for the counselor to evaluate the program through his/her activities regularly in order to check their effectiveness. Effective counseling will lead to more positive behavior outcomes both in the classroom and the school environment in general. This further helps to steer the school in the right direction.

The roles of the counselor vary depending on the level of students he or she will be dealing with as well as the expectations of the administrators. At the secondary and high school levels, for example, counselors deal with a vast array of student problems from personal, academic, social, and career issues (Gale Encyclopedia of Education). Typically, most problems that students exhibit are interwoven that one cannot compartmentalize them on the basis of what is presented to the counselor. A counselor's role covers all areas of the student's life whilst at school. Counselors develop experiences to deal with all types of problems with the help of other teachers, parents, the community and the administration. Where there are major challenges, the school counselor assesses the severity of the problem in order to provide appropriate support or refer to psychologists. Sometimes school counselors are assigned by the administration responsibilities to schedule classes, work on discipline, and carry out administration work. These tasks can be integrated with the goals of school counseling but must not impact negatively on the time allocated for other subject areas.

DIVERSITY AND MULTI-CULTURAL COUNSELING

There is a growing trend in the field of counseling that counselors must not wait for crises to happen but to work on prevention measures instead of remediation. Over the years, the belief was that counselors would have interactions with students only after some crisis or incident had occurred. There is now a shift for school counselors to intervene prior to any incidents and to become more proactive in developing and enacting school-wide prevention plans. We live in a global village where geographical boundaries mean less and less, therefore, counselors should be sensitive to cultural differences and value systems, by employing multi-cultural counseling methods (Charema, 2009a). Tolerance of diversity is an important goal to work towards in a multicultural society.

School counselors help all students to accept others regardless of sex, age, race, sexual orientation, culture, disability, or religious beliefs. Bearing in mind that students come from different backgrounds with cultural differences, school counselors should be sensitive to individual differences and embrace diversity as an opportunity to expand educational horizons. Studies carried out by Levers & Maki (1995) and Mpofu (2006) involving Botswana, South Africa, Tanzania, Zambia and Zimbabwe on rehabilitation counseling indicate that the majority the indigenous Africans use both traditional and modern counseling services. Basically this is a clear indication that counseling must be multi-cultural in order to cater for individual students from different backgrounds. This might be achieved through community involvement. Therefore schools, community, and families need to join hands in guiding and keeping students out of inappropriate activities that involve participating in gangs, dropping out of school, becoming a teenage parent and participating in or becoming victims of acts of violence. It must be noted that high school years are crucial in the adjustments of students as they represent the transition from the relatively sheltered life of the primary school to the adult life where they are expected to be responsible either at tertiary education or in a work-related environment (Charema, 2009b). This transition from high school to tertiary education or work environment presents students with problems of an educational, vocational, social and personal nature. The breakdown of the extended family makes it worse for our students whose culture is strongly dependent on the family support system. Counseling programs in Zimbabwean schools are left with the responsibility to shape students behaviors and create more positive school environments.

All students have a right to confidentiality in their dealings with the SGC. However, the right is not universal due to some cases in which, in the student's best interest, confidentiality cannot be guaranteed. Such cases include abuse, suicide, bullying, and risk to another student's life. In such cases the counselor should make the student aware that confidentiality could not be guaranteed in any of the above cases and that information of this nature would have to be acted on. At the beginning of all counseling sessions rules must be spelt out clearly with one of them being that all things discussed are confidential between the student and the SGC except when the student himself or another person is at risk. In the absence of legislation to register certified counselors for legal practice, the SGC's primary focus is the welfare of the student and therefore is ethically bound to act in the best interest of the student.

To further strengthen SGC, there is need to allocate adequate time for the service in the curriculum. Short courses with teacher trainers, administrators and other teachers can help accelerate the improvement of guidance and counseling. A major trend in education is the demand for accountability and evaluation. School counselors are expected to account for their work and progress. Similar to the academic standards used nationally by the department of education, the counseling standards should be provided with a blueprint of the tasks of and goals for school counselors. If these standards were implemented, counseling in schools would improve. A study carried out by Chireshe in 2008 in Zimbabwean high schools indicated that programs were not evaluated and did not seem to be effective. Therefore, if counseling is to be effective, counselors and other staff members should be able to evaluate the programs and establish that students have made academic progress, have positive attitude towards school work, and exhibit appropriate behaviors (Chireshe, 2008).

We suggest the following in order to have more effective counseling in Zimbabwean schools:

- Counseling programs must be run by qualified counselors who have the necessary skills to deal with social, socio-economic, psychological and personal teenage problems.
- Workshops and short courses should be conducted to re-train, in-service counselors and the general teaching staff in order for them to appreciate and support the counseling program.
- Students should be fully involved in the evaluation process and contribute towards changes to the program.
- Schools should have adequate resources and support systems to facilitate effective counseling.

- The school guidance counselor should plan purposeful activities that can be used by teachers and parents to keep students away from undesired behavior.
- Provision for regulatory bodies like the counselor ethics and disciplinary body and the counselor licensing body is necessary.

All these factors help to monitor, regulate and standardize guidance and counseling services.

CONCLUSION

Guidance and counseling is a valuable component of the school curriculum, which benefits students, academically, socially, psychologically and socio-economically. The involvement of all stakeholders such as teachers, parents, administration, the community and students themselves cannot be overemphasized. Carefully prepared programs, adequate time allocation, short training workshops and the use of multicultural-counseling can bring about the desired results. Accountability and evaluation of programs by counselors can enhance effective counseling education in Zimbabwean schools. In this chapter we have explored the benefits of counseling, the challenges students face in leaning institutions, counseling programs and practice. We believe that if counselors in schools implement practical ideas from this chapter students will benefit academically, socially and in career choice -making.

Reflection Questions

1) What challenges do youths face in today's life and how can counseling help to resolve these challenges?
2) In what ways does the role of a SGC pose challenges?
3) Why is school counseling important?

Chapter 10

ASSESSMENT IN EDUCATION

George Chitiyo

Overview
This chapter introduces the reader to key concepts of measurement and assessment in education, including tools that the teacher needs in order to more effectively assess student performance. We will give the reader the take-home message, without complicating the subject.

Key Topics
Key topics covered in the chapter include:

- Why assessment?
- Types of assessment
- Assessment tools

Learner Outcomes
The goal of this chapter is to introduce the readers to the broad topic of assessment, and hence enable them to be effective practitioners who make decisions everyday based on the feedback they constantly get from the students. After studying this chapter, it is our hope that the classroom practitioner will be able to:

1. State the goals of assessment
2. Link each assessment used with specific instructional objectives
3. Reflect on and revise their current assessments to ensure that they are valid and reliable
4. Design meaningful and effective assessment tools
5. Interpret accurately results from student assessments.

INTRODUCTION

One of the key issues in education is assessment. The term assessment broadly refers to the process of systematically monitoring performance of students, institutions, or programs through the careful collection and analysis of data using both formal and informal observation methods. Classroom teachers have the ongoing obligation to constantly determine if what they are doing is really having the intended impact, and the goal, of course, is to facilitate student learning and improve their performance academically and otherwise. Without a consistent mechanism in place for assessing student performance, instructional programs, and intervention activities, it would be difficult for educators to determine whether progress towards intended objectives is being made.

All procedures that are used to evaluate educational outcomes and interventions fall under assessment (Chase, 1999). Having said this, we wish to emphatically say that assessment should not be used as a means to simply classify students into groups based on their performance but rather to help the teacher and student make decisions about their teaching and learning respectively. Classifying students into groups can be viewed as labeling, and it can have negative connotations particularly for the students some of whom may feel stigmatized.

WHY ASSESSMENT?

Research has shown that assessment can help both the teacher and student (Black & Wiliam, 1998; Popham, 2014). For the teacher, it points to areas that need further instruction for individual students or for the whole class. It can be a diagnostic tool to identify particular students who are at risk of failure and who thus require remedial instruction or behavioral interventions. For the students, assessment helps them see the areas in which they are doing well, and those that they need to improve or seek help in. Chase (1999) summed this discussion in the following words: "Assessment can show teachers where instruction has been effective and where it has not. Teaching without competent assessment will surely be less effective for both students and teachers" (p. 3). Sound decisions should always be guided by evidence.

MEASUREMENT

The term measurement is defined broadly as the process of assigning numbers to attributes using some predefined rules. Examples of attributes abound – test scores, age, intelligence, income, length, height, and weight, just to name a few. Part of one's job as a teacher is to "measure" whether students have mastered the content in a discipline such as Geography, Mathematics, Science, and so forth. Teachers often use tests and quizzes to measure such performance. In order to ensure that one is *reliably* and *validly* measuring student performance, they need to have the right assessment tools. In other words, the tests that teachers use must be well developed in order to accurately and consistently capture the intended concepts that are desired to be assessed.

Validity refers to the degree that a test or an instrument measures what it is designed to measure. A test on geometry needs to have geometry content, and all the items on the test need to be constantly assessing geometry concepts. Reliability, on the other hand, is the degree to which a test consistently measures what it is measuring. According to Gay (1996), "an unreliable test is essentially useless; if a test is unreliable, then scores for a given sample would be expected to be different every time the test was administered" (Gay, 1996, p. 145). Reliability sets an upper limit for validity. We will expound on these two concepts and illustrate them in the next section.

RELIABILITY AND VALIDITY IN ASSESSMENT

We want to make sure that the reader has an appreciation of these important terms. Here is a scenario. Mr. Rugare has been teaching Social Studies to 7th grade students for 12 years. He developed end of term tests during his first two years of teaching which he has been using with every new group of students ever since. Five years ago, the Ministry of Education revised the curriculum substantially such that the syllabus that Mr. Rugare was using 12 years ago became very much out of date. About half of the old content in Mr. Rugare's syllabus was replaced with newer content. In response to these changes, Mr. Rugare developed new lesson plans to reflect the new curriculum. He just "recycles" these lesson plans every school year that is, he changes the dates on them and uses them over and over again. However, Mr. Rugare's end of term tests have remained the same, consisting of questions which are not relevant anymore. While browsing over the results of his students on the national standardized exam, he somehow noticed about three years ago that his students were not doing very well on certain sections of the exam, but he quickly brushed that aside, instead opting to believe that students these days are less interested in school than when he first started teaching. Unsurprisingly, Mr. Rugare's students have not been doing as well as Mrs. Muzenda's, his colleague, on the national exam over the last three to five years.

Let's Analyze this Scenario

When he first developed the tests, it is reasonable to believe that they reflected the content that was supposed to be covered. This is a type of content validity called curricular validity. The test content at every grade level needs to reflect the content that the curriculum for that grade level contains. In other words, the test items all need to be a representative sample of the universe of content in the curriculum.

Secondly, we do not have any information about how Mr. Rugare actually taught his lessons. Do his tests contain the actual content that he taught? If the tests do so, then they have instructional validity, another type of content validity. Remember that Mr. Rugare somehow noticed how students have not been doing so well over the last five years on both his tests and the national examinations. This is most likely because his tests contain information not covered in the class. They do not have content validity anymore, at least not when the curriculum was changed. There are other types of validity such as face validity, criterion related validity and construct validity. We will address these momentarily.

One other problem that we see with Mr. Rugare's approach is that he never systematically looked at the students' performance data to determine whether his students were actually learning what they were supposed to learn. It is the characteristic mark of an effective teacher, or one who aims to be effective, to constantly and systematically look at students' performance data to see how well they are performing so that he can improve his instruction if necessary. Mr. Rugare did not even care enough to revise his tests after the curriculum changed. Secondly, he needed to look at the students' test performance after every administration of the test to see which sections the students did well on, and which ones they did not perform so well on. For instance, why might 75% of the students have struggled with one particular section of the test (of course we just made that percentage up)? Could it be because the items are not worded clearly? Could it be because he did not cover them well in class? We are not expecting Mr. Rugare to be an expert in test item analysis, but that he needs to care enough to notice that some items on the test just are not working. That will be a good starting point.

We have mentioned systematic assessments. This simply means that one needs to collect data regarding students' performance at certain points in time, say after completion of every unit. Examining how well the students would have performed on each unit will show areas that need to be revisited. Many teachers already do this, and this is commendable. Those who somehow get tired of continuously testing their students' performance perhaps need to be reminded that the education enterprise thrives on the success of the students, and our purpose as teachers is to ensure student success. Needless to say, if our students are doing well, we are assured that we keep our jobs as well.

We also we need to make it abundantly clear that tests are only one component of assessment, there are many other ways that teachers can use to gauge student performance. These include term papers, in-class observations, students' homework, class projects, benchmark tests, and many others. All of these supply the teacher with lots of data which, if correctly recorded and analyzed, will provide rich information about the effectiveness of teaching on the part of the teacher, and learning on the part of the student. Mr. Rugare does not seem to be using any of these other forms of assessment – or at least we are not told that he does.

Types of Validity

There are several types of validity which all assessments should exhibit, at least to some degree. We will define them here.

1. Content validity: We already addressed this earlier. There are two types of content validity, which are, (i) curricular validity and (ii) instructional validity. A teacher's tests must reflect both types of validity for them to have content validity. What type of teacher will test his or her students on what he or she did not teach them? What type of teacher will simply dream of items to include on a test which are not included in the curriculum that is supposed to be taught? It must be the uncaring kind!
2. Criterion related evidence of validity: With this type of validity, performance on the test is judged against a specified criterion. There are two types of this form of validity, (i) predictive validity and (ii) concurrent validity. Let us address each in

turn: (i). Predictive validity: The end of term tests that Mr. Rugare developed were meant to be a reflection of how well students ought to do on the standardized test at the end of the year. To the extent that the tests predict how well a student will do on the national standardized exam, then his tests would be said to have predictive validity. Basically, this means that the tests are able to predict what will happen in the future – kind of what seers or foretellers do, only that in this case the predictions are done using a mathematical application called regression analysis. Let us not be overly concerned about how regression works for now. It should suffice to simply say that if one designs a test that is meant to be a mock-exam, then if students do as well on the final exam as on the mock exam, the test is doing its job well. In this case it is said to have predictive validity. (ii). Concurrent validity: A test is said to have concurrent validity if it correlates highly with another already established test. The established test will be regarded as "the criterion" in this case. Hang on for a brief moment, we will tell you more about correlation at the end of this section.
3. Construct Validity: Construct validity is the extent to which a test measures a hypothetical construct or nonobservable trait that it is intended to measure. An example of such a hypothetical construct is intellectual ability or intelligence. There are several aptitude tests that are often administered to assess intellectual ability. To the extent that performance on any such intellectual ability test correlates with the student's measurable achievement (e.g., scores on a science test), then the said test has construct validity.
4. Face Validity: When a person looks at a test (not just the common man on the street but somebody who has some familiarity with the content), will they have the impression that the test is assessing the intended content? If so, the test has face validity. To ascertain face validity, it is not necessary to employ a rocket scientist to do so; a fellow teacher from across the building can do the job just fine.

Types of Reliability

In this section, we will define different types of reliability without going into much detail about them. Our purpose is simply to introduce the concepts so that the reader has some familiarity with them. One can always look them up in more detailed texts.

1. Stability reliability: Also referred to as test-retest reliability, this refers to consistency of test results upon retesting at different times. Let us suppose that Mr. Rugare gives one of his tests to his students at two different times without any further instruction. Each student performs quite differently than they did the first time. Performance at different occasions of testing is *unstable*. This signals that the test does not assess the content in a consistent manner. It is not a reliable test. Might this be the reason why the test is not valid? Most likely so. A test can only be valid to the extent that it is reliable. If experts were to look at Mr. Rugare's assessments, will they see any reflection of the content that students are supposed to learn? Test-retest reliability can be expressed numerically using a reliability coefficient. This is simply a correlation coefficient between the scores from the two administrations of the test. The higher the coefficient, the more reliable (or stable) the test is.

2. Alternate form reliability: When there are at least two different forms of the same test, and the results from either form are similar to the other, the test is said to have alternate form reliability. A teacher can alternate the tests they give, rather than administer the same one all the time. After all, the different forms are equivalent. Suppose a student misses a test on a particular day because they missed the test (actually, it could be for any number of reasons), the teacher could simply give the student a different form of the test.
3. Internal consistency: This form of reliability refers to the consistency with which the items on a particular test measure what the test is supposed to measure. In other words, one might ask, do the items on the test measure the same general construct or theme? A good test will have all of its items consistently addressing the content that the test is aimed at measuring. Unlike test retest and alternate forms reliability, checking for internal consistency requires administering a test only one time. There are basically two ways to calculate internal consistency reliability. The first one is to compute the Split-half correlation. With this method, the test is divided into two sections e.g., odd numbered items vs. even numbered items. Each student's score on both halves of the test is computed, and these totals are then correlated. Longer tests will have more reliability as correlation is reduced in small samples. The Spearman-Brown's Prophecy formula can be used to adjust for the reduced sample size. The latter formula basically computes an average of all possible split halves. The second way to ascertain internal consistency reliability is to use one of several formulas such as the Cronbach's alpha or the Kuder-Richardson (KR-20) coefficients. Whereas the Kuder-Richardson can be used with test items that are scored dichotomously, the Cronbach's alpha can be used with tests that have items of any form (Blerkom, 2009). We will spare you the technical details about these formulas.

Having highlighted the above types of reliability, it is important to state that they all are not equivalent to each other. If a test displays one form of reliability, it does not translate that the others are present also.

4. Interrater reliability: Sometimes teachers may be interested in observing actual performance by students as they perform a task. In some situations, it will be necessary for at least two people to observe the same behavior to ensure that they both agree that the behavior has occurred. The extent to which the different raters or scorers agree can be expressed numerically e.g., as a percent of agreement, and this is called interrater reliability. This type of reliability is commonly used in applied behavior analysis and in special education when interest lies in scoring the occurrence of a certain behavior being studied.

Expressing Validity and Reliability Using Correlations

Validity and reliability can be expressed as a correlation coefficient, which is a number between zero and one. The closer the number is to zero, the weaker the reliability/validity, and conversely, the closer the number is to one, the stronger is the evidence of reliability/validity. Correlation is a tool that is used to analyze the relationship between two variables. A variable is any attribute that can assume different values, for example test scores, grade point average, length, age, etc. There are different kinds of correlation coefficients (Pearson's r coefficient, Spearman's rank-order coefficient, Cramer's phi coefficient for nominal variables, to name a few). The nature of the variables being correlated and their level of measurement (nominal, ordinal, and interval/ratio) determine which type of coefficient to compute. Regardless of which type of coefficient is computed, the interpretation is always the same. Blerkom (2009) suggests that coefficients of at least .70 indicate that validity/reliability is present. However, we need to state that validity coefficients are often less than .70. A rule of thumb regarding cutoff values for such coefficients may be hard to establish.

To illustrate test-retest reliability, we would take students' scores on both instances that they took the test. Basically we want to determine whether high scorers upon the first administration of the test will still score high on the second administration. Similarly we want to see if low scorers will also score low the second time. If this pattern occurs, the reliability coefficient will be very close to one, and the test is said to be reliable, or rather, that it exhibits stability reliability.

How much should the teacher be concerned about validity and reliability? We think every teacher needs to have an appreciation of these concepts so that they are able to easily look for and find solutions to fix any of their assessment tools that may not be working well. People should not be making important decisions based on one test that has questionable reliability and validity (Blerkom, 2009). It would be necessary to use information from multiple assessments, even if each of them has moderate reliability. We will conclude this section using Popham's (2014) words:

> The classroom teacher needs to understand what the essential nature of the [different] types of validity [and reliability] is, but I don't think classroom teachers need to go into a frenzy of evidence-gathering regarding validity. Clearly if you're a teacher or a teacher in preparation, you'll be far too busy in your classroom trying to keep ahead of the students to spend much time in assembling validity [and reliability] evidence. I do recommend, however, that for your most important tests, you devote at least some *attention* to content-related evidence of validity. (p. 119)

EVALUATION

One frequently encountered term in assessment is evaluation. This refers to the process of judging the worth of an instructional strategy, an intervention, or a program by comparing its merits against the stated objectives. Almost every teacher knows what they want their students to know at the end of the school term or school year. In order to be able to determine whether effective learning has taken place, one must have clear goals and objectives. Goals are broad general intentions which a teacher will have for her students. They are usually not measureable and thus generally difficult to assess. Objectives, on the other hand, are specific and measurable targets which emanate from the goals. Thus for each goal, there can be any number of objectives. A few goals and corresponding objectives are illustrated in Figure 10.1.

The purpose of having goals and objectives is so that one will be able to evaluate the data and determine whether the objectives have been met. The extent to which the objectives have been met determines whether the goal has also been satisfied. This is what evaluation is all about. We hope that you can now make a connection between assessment and evaluation. Assessment is quite broad and involves a systematic process of gathering, analyzing, and making sense of data. Evaluation ties the data to specific and measurable objectives.

Subject	Goal	Objective
Elementary Mathematics	Students will learn basic mathematics concepts	Students will demonstrate an understanding of the concepts of addition and subtraction using two digit numbers with 80% accuracy on a test
Elementary English	Students will be proficient in English	Students will write a two page English essay on a given topic by the end of the school term
Secondary History	Students will gain knowledge of how colonization in sub-Saharan Africa enhanced or hampered the development of the region	Students will identify and describe the key events that happened during the scramble for Africa between 1870 and 1914 eight out of ten times
Special Education	Shamiso will improve interest in mathematics	By the end of the month, Shamiso will be able to increase her on-task behavior from 1 minute to 10 minutes during the mathematics lesson period.

Figure 10.1. Examples of Goals and Objectives.

TYPES OF ASSESSMENT

Let us turn our attention to the two main types of assessment that are used for decision making. When people collect data on certain measures and use these data in order to make changes to the way that they are implementing an intervention or a teaching strategy, such assessments are called formative assessments. In other words, the practitioner or implementer is using the data to help make decisions about how to continue implementing the intervention. This is important in that it makes all the decisions that are made towards the program to be data-based, or data-driven.

Formative Assessment

Formative assessments are usually used to inform decision-making. Data are collected and evaluated while a program is being implemented in order to help make decisions about the subsequent phases of the program. Popham (2014) defines formative assessment as:

> …a planned process in which assessment-elicited evidence of students' status is used by teachers to adjust their ongoing instructional procedures or by students to adjust their current learning tactics. (p. 290)

Popham (2014) highlights that this is a planned process which involves several steps rather than it being a single test as most people would think it to be. There has to be a deliberate effort on the part of the teacher to monitor how an instructional strategy is going and, most importantly, whether, and how much students are making adequate progress. Data will have to be collected and analyzed. The results of this data analysis process will then help the teacher make a decision about what areas to improve in the current implementation of the instructional strategy. Of course formative assessment can be applied to many other areas apart from instructional strategies.

The special education teacher can also formatively assess the progress of her intervention on children with varying needs. The interventions can be of varying nature, including those for a wide-ranging spectrum of autism disorders and learning disabilities. The main point to be made here is that every practitioner who is genuinely interested in improving students' outcomes will look at their students' data and make decisions on how to improve the delivery of the instruction or the implementation of an intervention program.

Summative Assessment

Summative assessment is used when interest lies in judging the overall success of an instruction or educational or behavioral intervention. In this case, one looks at the goals of the instruction and then examines the evidence collected from the assessments to determine the extent to which the goals have been met. One can view summative assessment as "the sum of it all," or the assessment which occurs at the conclusion of the program, intervention or instructional strategy. Questions that this type of assessment will answer include; was the program helpful? Did effective learning take place? Was the intervention effective? Did the remedial lessons result in the desired goals of increasing student performance to a certain level of proficiency?

Tests are regularly used by teachers as assessment tools. In and of themselves, tests are neither formative nor summative (Popham, 2014). The purpose why they are used determines whether they are either formative or summative. In Popham's words, "although a given test may be employed in connection with a summative assessment function, it is possible (if the test is carefully crafted) for this very same test to be used also as part of the formative assessment process" (p. 291).

Questions are usually asked about how much assessment should one implement – for example, how many tests to administer, how much data to collect etc. While there cannot be a definitive answer to this, we suggest that one should be able to judge the amount of formative assessment that each context and situation calls for. It may help to decide together as a team (that is, with your colleagues) what activities will be done, what data will be collected, how the data will be analyzed, etc.

Once all the data have been collected, it would be helpful to look at it as a team, and them make recommendations for areas of improvement collectively. In a multitude of counselors, there is safety.

-
-
-
-
-
-
-

ASSESSMENT TOOLS

In Figure 10.2, we provide a few examples of assessments, the list can be longer, depending on the subject involved. Our hope is that these examples will serve as a guide for the teacher who would wish to design or revise their already existing key assessments.

Type of Assessment	Formative or Summative	Tips
Quizzes and end-of unit/module tests	Formative or summative depending on the intended use of the results.	Make them specific to a particular module or to address a specific learning objective
End of term tests	Usually summative, but can be formative as well e.g., if the results will be used to inform next year's instruction.	For end of course tests, the items need to be a representative sample of the whole content covered in the syllabus, that way all instructional objectives are addressed We suggest longer rather than shorter tests as longer tests will have more reliability
		Depending on the subject area, many short answer questions will ensure more representation of content than one or two essay questions.
Informal and informal observations	Formative or summative depending on the intended use of the results	Operationally define the behavior being observed Document the behavior using a recording chart or computer spreadsheet
Student projects	Formative or summative	Use a clear rubric for scoring student projects Specify *a priori* how the project will be graded so the students know beforehand
Mock-exams	Usually formative – to help the	Make them as identical to the final

	teacher prepare the students for standardized exams	exam as possible Sample the whole content taught We suggest longer rather than shorter tests as longer tests will have more reliability Depending on the subject area, many short answer questions will ensure more representation of content than one or two essay questions.

Figure 10.2. Suggestions on Designing Assessments.

STUDENT INVOLVEMENT IN ASSESSMENT

According to Stiggins (2008), an important component of the assessment process is student involvement. The students need to be involved in repeatedly monitoring their own achievement and hence tracking their own progress over the course of time. The teacher thus needs to put in place or adopt a mechanism which enables such student self-assessment. Stiggins provides the following list of activities that the teacher can let students do as he or she begins involving them in the assessment process.

- Take the test and receive the grade
- Be invited to offer the teacher comments on how to improve the test
- Suggest possible assessment exercises
- Actually develop assessment exercises
- Assist the teacher in devising scoring criteria
- Create the scoring criteria on their own
- Apply scoring criteria to the evaluation of their own performance
- Come to understand how assessment and evaluation affect their own academic success come to see how their own self-assessment relates to the teacher's assessment and to their own academic success. (Stiggins, 2008, p.23)

Involving students in assessment will increase their self-confidence and it will make them to take ownership of their own learning. By identifying areas that need improvement on their own, they are more likely to devise strategies on how those areas can be improved rather than wait for the teacher to dictate to them how to improve. Unless the student sees the need to improve, hearing it from the teacher will likely have minimal impact.

USING MEASUREMENT TO IMPROVE THE QUALITY OF EDUCATION

One of the goals of measurement in education is to improve the system so that students will get the best possible outcomes. The Learning Metrics Task Force, a task force set up by the UNESCO Institute for Statistics and the Center for Universal Education at Brookings in 2013, generated a list of seven domains and their subdomains that all children and youths from early childhood to post-primary education should have learned. Developing competencies across these seven domains of physical well-being, social and emotional, culture and the arts, literacy and communication, learning approaches and cognition, numeracy and mathematics, and science and technology, is essential to prepare children for their future lives and livelihoods (Learning Metrics Task Force, 2013). Data from assessments would thus be used to inform both practices at the local level, such as the development of interventions for different students, and policies at the macro level.

According to the Learning Metrics Task Force, there is dearth of data globally that can be used to improve the education systems of many countries, and this is compromising the quality of the education that students receive. According to the Learning Metrics Task Force:

> Poor quality education is jeopardizing the future of millions of children and youth across high-, medium-, and low-income countries alike. Yet we do not know the full scale of the crisis because measurement of learning achievement is limited in many countries, and hence difficult to assess at the international level. A global data gap on learning outcomes is holding back progress on education quality. Because many countries lack sufficient data and capacity to systematically measure and track learning outcomes over time, evidence-based decision-making and accountability become impossible. There is a critical need for robust data to understand the full scale of the learning crisis. Only then can we target policy to address areas of need, track progress and hold ourselves to account. (Learning Metrics Task Force, 2013, p. 10)

In line with some of the recommendations of the Learning Metrics Task Force (2013), in order to reduce this data gap, the education system needs to track indicators of child development and learning at different levels. Analysis of such data, will inform practices at the classroom and school levels (such as developing appropriate interventions for certain students), and policy at the macro levels. The measurement of educational performance indicators can be one of the best tools that school systems can use to improve practice.

Assessment data across the aforementioned domains can be used to make international comparisons in order to see how the country's education system is faring relative to similar countries. In order for Zimbabwe to position itself to compete in the global world, it must ensure that its citizens are well-educated and competent in these key areas identified as important by world education experts. This makes the process of determining what changes need to be made to the process of educational delivery in order to ensure global competitiveness of the Zimbabwean students easy.

CONCLUSION

In this chapter, we introduced some of the most important terms in assessment. The chapter is meant to serve as a starting point as one begins the quest for knowledge on the subject. There are books that have been written on this, and we would encourage those who wish to learn more about this subject to refer to these more in-depth sources. We have a very ambitious goal to have a society whose teachers care about their students so much that they are willing to invest in knowledge to be better and more effective educators. The chapter concludes with a presentation of areas identified by researchers as key learning areas for students that the Zimbabwean education sector can focus on in order to be competitive globally.

Reflection Questions

1) Select a broad area that you might be interested in researching. What possible research question(s) can you ask about this topic? What does the existing literature contain about this topic? (Hint: a good place to start looking for research articles will be to use Google Scholar.)
2) What are some ideas of activities (about two or three) that you might implement in your classroom in order to improve outcomes for specific students, e.g., implementing an intervention for students who struggle with a particular subject?
3) Select one of the ideas you identified for question 2 and design a rough plan of a research study which you may possibly conduct in order to test to see if the activity will benefit the students over a period of time. How might you possibly measure the student outcomes e.g., through a test? Share your plan with a colleague so that they can help refine your idea.

Chapter 11

RESEARCH IN EDUCATION

George Chitiyo

Overview
This chapter provides the classroom teacher who is eager to improve his or her practice with a rationale for implementing research. The chapter also highlights the different types of research designs that a teacher can choose from, depending on his or her particular area of research. Classroom research is a deliberate act that teachers engage in with the intention to get better at what they do, and in the process, improve student outcomes. By engaging in classroom research, teachers can actually gather evidence that supports the continued use of effective practices, and that justifies discontinuing the use of ineffective ones. Those working with exceptional children will also be in a position to implement interventions and evaluate their efficacy.

Key Topics
Educational research
Action research
Characteristics of scientific research
Basic research designs

Learner Outcomes
Upon completion of this chapter, readers will be able to:

- Appreciate the need to make decisions that are based on research, including their own research within their classrooms and schools in order to solve local problems
- Describe the basic research designs that they can utilize as they conduct classroom research
- Describe the concept of action research and the place of research in the classroom

INTRODUCTION

Some people think of research as simply going on the Internet to find information about a topic. This is a very limited view of what research entails – there is so much more that is involved in the process than simply "googling" a topic of interest. Teachers need to value the importance of research, be informed consumers of research, and be researchers themselves. This chapter addresses the definition of research, characteristics of research, and describes the main types of research designs.

Research in Education

A good place to begin is to define research. In simple terms, research refers to the systematic approach to knowledge discovery and to finding answers to questions by way of collecting and examining empirical data. The key point to note is that it is based on real life observations. People usually have questions about specific areas of interest about which they seek answers. Unless the answers already exist, the best way to solve unanswered problems is to engage in research.

The American Educational Research Association (AERA), one of the largest and most reputable educational research organizations in the world, defines educational research in the following terms:

> Education research is a field of inquiry aimed at advancing knowledge of education and learning processes and development of the tools and methods necessary to support this endeavor. Education researchers aim to describe, understand, and explain how learning takes place throughout the life cycle and how formal and informal processes of education affect learning, attainment, and the capacity to lead productive lives. Scholarship in this arena is undertaken at the individual, situational, institutional, and social structural levels of analysis. The unifying purpose for education research is to build cumulative and sound knowledge about human and social process of fundamental significance to individuals, to groups, and to the larger society. (AERA, 2013)

One of the key elements of the above definition is about the purpose of research. Regardless of the level at which such research is conducted (individual, classroom, or institution) or who conducts it (university professors, teachers etc.), the ultimate purpose is to generate knowledge in order to improve the human condition.

Action Research

The term action research refers to research that is carried out by practitioners with the aim to improve their practice. Such research, as we will demonstrate, needs not be complicated, and yet it can still be credible, provided that it is carried out well following established scientific principles. One important aspect of action research is that it not only leads to generation of new knowledge, but it also leads to the practitioner immediately implementing the lessons learned in order to solve a local practical problem.

Teachers are well placed to directly impact the lives of the students they serve, academically and otherwise, and hence they can use research to increase the impact that they exert. The following are some examples of research problems that can be addressed by teachers working within their classrooms or school settings:

- Will method A of instruction work better than method B in terms of raising student achievement?
- Will treatment X (e.g., the use of visual aids) be effective in redressing the challenging behaviors exhibited by a student who has Attention Deficit Disorder?
- How well do the mock exams that we administer in our school prepare students for the standardized exams at the end of the school year? To what extent do the mock exams predict students' actual performance on standardized exams?
- What are the attitudes of regular education students towards their peers with disabilities? What methods are effective in dealing with negative stereotypes towards students with disabilities?
- Within the context of our school environment, which is a more effective method (from among inclusion, integration, or segregation) of educating children with disabilities?
- What are the advantages of having children attend preschool? Will preschool attendance make children better prepared for school?
- Within our school, are current ways of counseling children suffering from the trauma of caring for parents who are suffering from AIDS or other chronic illnesses effective?
- What factors are associated with orphaned children's self-esteem in school?
- Are buddy-clubs (or peer mentoring) an effective way of fighting the stigma associated with living in a household with an HIV affected parent or guardian?

Characteristics of Scientific Research

Any teacher should be in a position to identify areas that need improvement in their everyday work. That marks the starting point of the journey towards perpetually finding answers to issues surrounding them, and hence the beginning of a lifelong journey as a learner, not an expert. Here we will outline the most important characteristics of scientific research.

Empirical Approach
Scientific research is based on direct observation. By observation, we refer to the process through which accurate measurements of variables are made and recorded. This calls for the use of reliable instruments. If instruments are being developed specifically for the research study, one must make sure that they ascertain the reliability and validity of the instruments. In other words, the instruments must consistently (reliability) and accurately (validity) assess what they are designed to measure. The concepts of reliability and validity are addressed in Chapter 10.

In order to make careful observations, it is necessary to make operational definitions of phenomena. An operational definition (as opposed to a general dictionary definition) tells exactly how a variable is measured or manipulated in that particular study. For example, an operational definition might say that student achievement is measured by test scores on a teacher made test rather than on standardized test scores. In short, an operational definition is very precise and specific to the study in which it is being used.

Research Questions

Any study is guided by sound research questions. The questions must be answerable, that is, one must ask questions that can be answered through available scientific methods and procedures. It would be difficult (if not impossible) for one to answer questions that appeal to faith or religious beliefs. Even if such an answer can be provided, such a study would be impossible to replicate. We posed examples of research questions that can be addressed in educational settings earlier. One may want to use these as rough guides on how they can formulate their own questions. We also need to mention that there is no prescribed number of research questions that must be asked in any given study. It all depends on the topic that one is investigating. After coming up with questions, one can then generate hypotheses for their study. In its simplest form, a hypothesis is a conjectural statement which states the researcher's expected result. Some studies may not require hypotheses a-priori though such as studies that might use qualitative methods or surveys seeking to simply establish descriptive statistics about respondents.

	Relationship Question	Difference Question
Research question	Is there a relationship between student attendance (percentage of schooldays missed during the year) and their performance on end of year exams controlling for the students ability?	Will there be a difference in students' test scores on an end of year exam between students who take Mathematics lessons in the morning versus a similar group of students who take Mathematics classes in the afternoon, controlling for the students ability level?
Independent variable	Attendance	Time of day when students take Mathematics class (morning of afternoon)
Dependent variable	Test scores	Test scores on end of course Mathematics exam
Control variable	Ability level	Ability level
Possible method of data analysis	Partial correlation analysis	Analysis of variance or analysis of covariance

Figure 11.1. Examples of Research Questions and the Independent and Dependent Variables.

In quantitative research, a research question asks how two or more variables are related to each other, or how differences in one variable are associated with differences in the other. Sometimes, but not always, it is necessary to specify independent and dependent variables. An independent variable "is a stimulus variable or input (which) operates either within a person or within his or her environment to affect behavior" (Tuckman & Harper, 2012, p. 67). It is that which has a presumed effect on the outcome of interest. Notice that we deliberately say "presumed." This is because one cannot necessarily infer cause and effect between two variables even if the two variables may be strongly related. Only robust research designs such as randomized controlled trials (RCTs) permit one to make causal inferences.

The dependent variable in a study is the outcome of interest. In Tuckman and Harper's words, "the dependent variable is the factor that is observed and measured to determine the effect of the independent variable; it is the factor that appears, disappears, or varies as the researcher introduces, removes, or varies the independent variable" (Tuckman & Harper, p. 67). Figure 11.1 gives examples of research questions addressing (a) a relationship and (b) differences between groups.

Experiments

When possible, researchers should aim to conduct experimental studies. However, in educational settings, this is not always possible, and so other research designs can be used to answer whatever research questions are posed. When carefully planned and carried out, nonexperimental studies can yield results that are equivalent to those from experimental studies. However, we need to stress that one has limited ability to infer cause and effect, particularly from nonexperimental studies. Generally speaking, experiments in which randomization is utilized are hailed in the research community as the gold standard because of their level of rigor. According to AERA (2008):

> The examination of causal questions requires experimental designs using random assignment or quasi-experimental or other designs that substantially reduce plausible competing explanations for the obtained results. These include, but are not limited to, longitudinal designs, case control methods, statistical matching, or time series analyses. This standard applies especially to studies evaluating the impacts of policies and programs on educational outcomes.

Data Analysis

Data that are obtained through experimental or non-experimental means are analyzed and conclusions are generated. The data analysis methods depend on the design of the study, the nature of the data to be analyzed, and the most importantly, the research questions to be answered. Statistical analyses help researchers to avoid erroneous conclusions from their data.

Replication

Scientific studies must be able to be replicated. Replication is the deliberate duplication of a study in order to confirm the findings from earlier studies. This is usually done to test population or ecological validity of a study's findings. It is thus necessary when one conducts a study to document carefully all their procedures and methods so that others may replicate them.

Basic Types of Research Designs

There are different types of research designs that one can utilize depending on the particular research questions one is trying to address. In this section, we will simply highlight the features of each of the main types of designs, knowing fully that this only whets the appetites of those who are craving the intricate details about each of these designs. We now turn our attention to describing the different types of research designs.

Experimental Research

Experimental research involves the manipulation of at least one independent variable in a study and then observing changes in the dependent variable while controlling for the possible effects of other confounding factors. In other words, the researcher decides which group(s) get(s) certain treatment condition(s), and which one(s) do not. In experimental studies, therefore, at least one independent variable is manipulated. The dependent variable will be the outcome. We will illustrate this with the following example.

Mr. Tambo has been reading about different ways to improve students' performance among students who struggle with reading. He found out about the use of flashcards from the literature and decided to design an experiment with his second grade students to see if this method would work with his students. He implemented this method of flashcards with one of his classes (the treatment group), and used another similar class as the comparison (or control) group. The control group did not use flashcards, they received traditional instruction. He administered a teacher-made test as the pretest to determine the reading proficiency of the students at the start of the experiment and afterwards implemented the treatment for six weeks with the experimental group. At the end of six-weeks, he again administered the same test and compared the performance of the two groups of students to see whether the treatment group had fared better than the control group. This is an example of the pretest-posttest control group design. The point we wish to illustrate though is not about this particular design, but about one feature of all experimental designs, which is manipulation of the treatment variable.

In experimental studies, it is important to ensure that the experimental and control groups are equivalent with respect to almost all attributes such as gender, age, level of academic ability, etc. so that one does not make erroneous conclusions regarding the effects of the treatment. It will be ideal if one could randomly assign students to treatment and control groups; however, we know that this is difficult in educational settings because classes are always intact. Given such conditions, it will be important to simply ensure that the two (or more) classes that one wants to use, are equivalent. Mr. Tambo gave a pretest to both classes and saw that the students performed at about the same level. Another important feature of the study is that he was the teacher for both classes. It would have been a different story if the control group was taught by a different teacher. If that was the case, the treatment and control conditions would be convoluted by the two different teachers.

In order to see if his flashcard method had made a difference, all other things being equal, he needed to administer the same test during both the pretest and posttest, or at least an equivalent form of the test. This enabled him to see the change in performance between the two time periods. There might be other reasons that one group could have performed better than the other, and it is important that one acknowledge all known threats to the validity of their study. We refer the reader to the classical work of Campbell and Stanley (1963) for a rigorous treatment of threats to the internal and external validity of experimental studies as well as to the explanation of all the designs in detail. It is important for us to state that experimental studies fall broadly into two categories, randomized experiments (also called true experiments) and quasi experiments. The latter studies use intact groups, such as was the case with Mr. Tambo.

Single Subject Studies

Single subject studies are a special type of experimental designs which utilize small samples, sometimes consisting of one participant or one entity. Treatments are administered individually to the subject and the subject's performance is monitored consistently over time. Single subject designs are mostly used in behavior modification programs and special education. There are several variations of single case designs, i.e., ABAB, multiple baseline, changing criterion, concurrent designs. We will illustrate this with the following example.

Mr. Kasi, a special educator working with children exhibiting challenging behaviors conducted a study to test whether the use of visual aids and video modeling would decrease the frequency of verbal outbursts in a teenage boy with Down's syndrome. He used a recording chart to document the daily occurrence of the disruptive behavior during 30-minute sessions in the mornings and afternoons for one month. The first week was a baseline phase with no intervention. A baseline phase is the period of time when the researcher collects data to determine the performance of the participant before the introduction of the intervention. The second week was an intervention phase where he administered the use of video modeling and recorded the behavior. During the third week, the treatment was withdrawn, and then reintroduced during the final week of the study. The design used for this study is called a withdrawal design (specifically ABAB). In single subject studies, phases are denoted by letters, for example, A is used to denote baseline, B to denote any kind of treatment. Other letters (such as C, D, etc.) can also be used to denote alternative treatments. The results of the study conducted by Mr. Kasi are shown in Figure 11.2. He was able to conclude that the treatment was an effective way of dealing with Sipho's behavior.

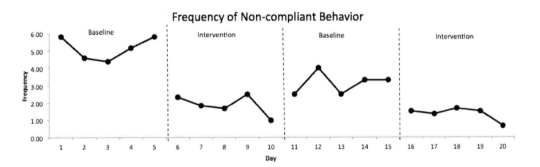

Figure 11.2. Sipho's Average Number of Verbal Outbursts by Phase.

As shown in Figure 11.2, Sipho had an average of 16 verbal outbursts per week. When the treatment was implemented, the average went down to six outbursts per week. Withdrawing the treatment did not change the behavior drastically. Reintroducing the treatment reduced the average to three. This, according to Mr. Kasi was a remarkable change in the student's behavior, considering how severe it was before the treatment was introduced.

Single subject designs are useful in educational and clinical settings when one wants to modify behaviors or outcomes that are specific to certain individuals. Treatments are administered to the individual subject. Before selecting a design, one must consider the design that can best address their end goal, as well as looking at the threats to validity and ethical issues, e.g., the aspect of withdrawing treatment if such an action can have an adverse effect on the participant. For data analysis in single subject studies, the use of visual displays is very common. Sometimes, group comparisons can also be made through the use of some nonparametric tests. An example of simplified visual data analysis from an ABAB design is illustrated in Figure 11.2.

Causal Comparative Studies

It is often the case that researchers want to find out if differences exist between or among preexisting groups of participants. The simplest case is when one begins with two groups which differ on a certain attribute such as gender, type of instruction, school attended, textbook used for a science class, etc. The purpose of conducting causal comparative studies is to look for possible causes of the differences in the performance of the groups. Usually, causal comparative studies are useful in identifying variables for further study, such as, through experimentation. We will illustrate this design with the following example.

Mr. Thomas, a primary school teacher was interested in seeing if a reading program which his school introduced the year before made a difference in students' academic performance. He collected reading achievement data from a group of fourth grade students who had been exposed to the reading program. Similarly, he collected data from a comparable group of fourth graders from the year before who had had the same teachers and took the same tests but had not been exposed to the reading program. In order to ensure that the groups were comparable, he matched the students from both groups using their third grade reading performance. He compared the mean performance of the two groups and found that indeed the group that was exposed to the reading program performed better, and that that difference was statistically significant. This suggested to him that the reading program was probably beneficial to the students. After sharing the results of his study with the school authorities, they decided to continue the program and even expand it to other grades. What started as a curiosity on the part of a passionate teacher ended up benefiting students in the whole school.

Correlational Studies

In correlational studies, the purpose is to establish if two variables are related with each other. One might be interested, for instance, in assessing whether a relationship exists between students' performance on mid-year tests and final exams. If the mid-year test scores are not strongly related with end of year performance, then perhaps the tests are not reliable and should be revised.

Establishing the relationship between two variables is not difficult at all. One can use a spreadsheet program like Excel to generate a scatterplot between the two variables of interest. If the points on the scatterplot form a clear discernible pattern, then that suggests there is a relationship between the two variables. Of course one can always go a step further and compute a correlation coefficient between the two variables to determine how strongly the variables are correlated. Figure 11.3 shows scatterplots that depict different types of relationships between two variables.

Survey Research

Many people are familiar with surveys. We need to mention that a survey is not a research design per se but it is a method of gathering data that can be used either in a causal comparative study or a correlational study. All the same, even without subjecting survey data to some rigorous statistical tests, one can glean a lot of valuable information from the descriptive data that can be generated from a survey.

Let us look at an example. Driven by the need to address the issue of bullying in schools, Ms. Moyo, a guidance and counseling teacher, designs and administers a survey to all seventh grade students at her school. She wants to understand the students' experiences and perceptions regarding the issue of bullying. Ms. Moyo's example is one of the simplest things a teacher who wants to study perceptions, opinions, attitudes, etc., can use. She plans to use descriptive statistics (frequencies, percentages, graphs) to analyze her data.

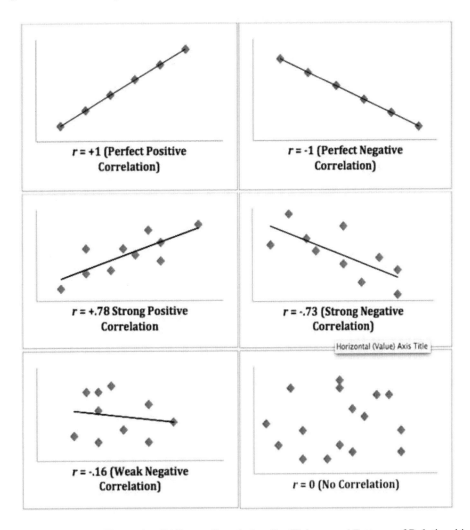

Figure 11.3. Scatterplots Illustrating Different Correlation Coefficients and Patterns of Relationships.

Data from a survey can even be further analyzed using more rigorous tests to uncover possible relationships between variables or differences between groups such as males versus females, experienced versus inexperienced teacher, and so forth. Figure 11.4 is a frequency table with hypothetical data related to Ms. Moyo's survey. It shows that about quarter of the students (26.4%) reported having been bullied and the majority (73.6%) had not been bullied. Figure 11.5 is a crosstabulation that shows the distribution of the same responses by the students' gender. Among those who reported being bullied (23 of them), 52.2% were female and 48.3% were male). Similarly, among those who reported not being bullied (64 of them), 51.6% were female and 48.4% were male. These percentages seem very close to each other to suggest that any one gender is more affected. A test can be done though to determine if these two variables (i.e., whether a student has ever been bullied and ii. gender) are independent of each other.

Have you ever been bullied in the past year?		
	Frequency	Percent
No	64	73.6
Yes	23	26.4
Total	30	100.0

Figure 11.4. Frequency Distribution of Students' Responses on whether they were Bullied.

	Have you ever been bullied in the past year?		Total
	No	Yes	
Female	33 (51.6%)	12 (52.2%)	45 (51.7%)
Male	31 (48.4%)	11 (47.8%)	42 (48.3%)
Total	64 (100%)	23 (100%)	87 (100%)

Figure 11.5. Crosstabulation of Ever been Bullied and Gender.

Ethnographies

Ethnographies are studies where the teacher researcher documents the everyday experiences of their students as they observe them unfold. The teacher will then analyze these notes and reflect upon them. A classic example is given by Goswami and Stillman (1987) when they interviewed a teacher who practiced classroom research, Cindy Myers.

> Every year when I start research by keeping field notes, I keep thinking that this is an exercise and I'm just writing down what's happening and I'm not getting anything out of it. It seems like a bland kind of thing. But when I keep doing that, all of a sudden I'll hear the kids say something that shows they've changed in some way, and I'll put that down too. And then things start to pull together. It's almost like through the field notes that I keep and what I see happening – out of those field notes – the classroom becomes more alive. There are things going on that I didn't realize and we're really getting someplace. Just to stand up there and teach every period and not do the classroom research makes the classroom seem boring. (Goswami & Stillman, 1987, p. 3)

Sometimes, conducting classroom research does not necessarily entail having a hypothesis to test. One can use qualitative methods as well which include simply making observations, documenting them, and sometimes conducting interviews with students, parents, and fellow teachers. Another quotation from Cindy Myers goes like this:

> I guess what I do a lot of times with classroom research is to take special note of things I hear the kids saying. Like at the end of the year when one student turned to another and said, "I've read three more books this year than I've read in my whole life," I wrote that down. My gosh! Now that could have gone right past me, and I could have thought, "Oh, that's nice." But in context with all the other things that happened to that boy during the year, it was such a remarkable change. Sometimes it's just picking up phrases that I hear from the kids and I go ahead and write them down and maybe it doesn't hit me until I've written it down and looked back at it and looked at what's actually there. (Goswami & Stillman, 1987, p. 3)

CONCLUSION

After providing a definition of educational research, this chapter provided reasons why teachers should be actively engaged in research within their classrooms and schools. Teacher research provides evidence that will help in decision-making regarding the implementation of instructional strategies and interventions for certain students. The chapter also summarized important aspects of the research process that every teacher researcher must be conversant with, at least at a superficial level. Finally, the chapter presented the basic forms of research designs that are available for researchers to choose from. A practitioner can choose any one of these designs to use depending on the research problem they wish to solve. More thorough treatments of each of these research designs are presented in research textbooks such as Best and Kahn (2006), Creswell (2008), Fraenkel and Wallen (2013).

Reflection Questions

1) Select a broad area that you might be interested in researching. Search the literature to find out what has been done in this general area. A good place to start looking for research articles will be to use Google Scholar. State the problem in the form of a research question.
2) Write down two or three ideas of activities that you might implement in your classroom in order to improve outcomes for specific students, e.g., students who struggle with a particular subject.
3) Select one of these ideas and design a rough plan of a research study which you may possibly conduct in order to test to see if the activity will benefit the students over a period of time. Think about how you might possibly measure the student outcomes e.g., through a test? Share your plan with a colleague so that they can help refine your idea.

Chapter 12

OVERCOMING CURRENT CHALLENGES AND PREPARING STUDENTS FOR THE 21ST CENTURY

Jonathan Chitiyo

Overview
Education is regarded as the engine driving a country's long-term prospects; hence it is crucial that the sector is not left to collapse. After gaining political independence from Britain, Zimbabwe made huge investments in education thereby creating one of the best education systems in Africa. Not surprisingly, by 2013 Zimbabwe was reported to have the highest literacy rate on the continent. However, the developments made during the formative years appear to have been eroded by social, economic and political instability, among other challenges. This chapter identifies, discusses and recommends possible solutions to problems bedeviling the country's education system. The chapter also discusses how to educate Zimbabwean students in order to meet the unique needs of a 21st Century economy.

Key Topics
Factors negatively affecting the education system:

- The land reform and education
- Political crisis and education
- Economic collapse and education
- Corruption and the education system
- HIV/AIDS and education
- Educating students for unique roles of a 21st century economy

Learner Outcomes
Upon completion of this chapter readers will be able to:

a) Clearly articulate the challenges facing the Zimbabwean education system
b) Explain how these challenges have negatively affected the system
c) Identify strategies which can be implemented to address the current challenges

d) Identify ways to educate Zimbabwean students to meet the needs of a 21st century economy

INTRODUCTION

One of the world's most celebrated heroes, freedom-fighter and the first black South African president Mr. Nelson Mandela, once said that "education is the most powerful weapon which you can use to change the world." Indeed, education can shape the fundamental structures of any society. We strongly believe that successful economies are predicated on good education. Unfortunately, the Zimbabwean education system, which has been the country's greatest achievement since gaining political independence in 1980, is today in a deep crisis as reflected by poor academic outcomes, inadequate instructional and learning materials, dilapidated school infrastructure, deteriorating working conditions, low credibility of the national examination system, and lack of qualified teachers. The education system is severely underfunded, under-resourced and functioning way below its capacity. Poor management, ill-advised policies, and economic and political instability are among some of the challenges derailing the once-vibrant education system. In this chapter we will discuss some of the challenges facing the Zimbabwean education system. But most importantly, we will discuss how the education system can help the country to meet the unique needs of a 21st century economy. Specifically, we will identify and recommend ways to improve the education system so that it addresses the needs of the country by equipping its population with the skills needed to support a 21st century economy.

THE CHALLENGES

Land Reform

Agriculture is the backbone of the country's economy contributing about 20% of gross domestic output (Hellum & Derman, 2004). However, the agricultural system has been on the decline since 2000 when the government started the controversial land reform program. The land reform program was a government initiative which was meant to redress the historical inequalities in land ownership. The necessity of land reform in Zimbabwe cannot be overemphasized. However, the initiative attracted attention in Africa and beyond due to its celerity, impact, forced displacement of landowners and farm workers, and human rights abuses (Hellum & Derman, 2004). One of the criticisms was that the new landowners lacked large-scale agricultural skills and equipment and as a result production plummeted making the country depend on other countries in the region for food (Potts, 2006). Also, as a result of the human rights abuses associated with the program, the country got isolated from the international community and was blocked from any form of international trade and any opportunities for financial assistance (Hellum & Derman, 2006). This paralyzed the economy such that the government could not afford to provide quality education in a number of ways.

Firstly, the government could not pay schoolteachers well enough to keep up with the ever increasing cost of living; hence, a lot of teachers either left the profession and or the country for better opportunities elsewhere. This left the sector severely deprived of trained personnel to teach the students and also to execute other duties like administering examinations. In addition, the mass exodus of teachers to other countries created a disproportionate teacher student ratio.

Secondly, because the economy was crippled, the education sector was severely underfunded such that it could not provide funds for instructional materials such as textbooks, science equipment, and other instructional resources. Several reports were made of children sitting on the floor because of shortage of furniture in the classrooms. In addition, there was also a disproportionate student book ratio with some students not having textbooks at all.

Thirdly, the land reform plunged the country into a deep economic crisis, which is discussed in the next section. The economic crisis led to a rise in the cost of living such that some students could not afford to pay school fees, buy school uniforms and other school resources. As a result, some students were forced to drop out of school and find employment to support their daily needs. In addition, there were reports of students failing to sit for Ordinary level and Advanced level examinations because of failure to pay school and examination fees. According to the Zimbabwe Herald Newspaper (2011), in 2010 approximately 15,000 pupils in Matabeleland failed to register for national examinations because of financial problems.

Lastly, the land reform program also led to the closure of some schools in farming areas which were established and primarily controlled in terms of infrastructure by commercial farmers (Shizha & Kariwo, 2012). As the commercial farmers and farm workers were evicted from farms, thousands of children were forced out of school. Wherever the former farm workers relocated, shortage of school fees and long distances to the nearest schools became the main challenge for their children to attend school and as a result they dropped out. According to Shizha and Kariwo (2012), approximately 500 schools on previously white owned farms were closed and about 250,000 children were forced out of school.

Economic Crises

There are a number of factors, which plunged Zimbabwe into an economic quagmire. As discussed in Chapter 1, these factors include the Economic Structural Adjustment Program (ESAP), the unbudgeted payment of veterans of the liberation war, the country's military involvement in the Democratic Republic of Congo, the land reform program, and the most recent Operation Murambatsvina. UNDP (2008) traces the onset of Zimbabwe's economic crisis to the time when the government decided to pay war veterans hefty gratuities as compensation for their involvement in the liberation war. This move left the economy cash-starved. Subsequent to this move, the Zimbabwean government decided to participate in the Democratic Republic of Congo's civil war, a move which also drained millions of dollars from the already cash-starved economy thereby fuelling a ballooning fiscal deficit (Chagonda, 2012). Both these issues had adverse impact on an already fragile economy. Although the issues discussed above had catastrophic effects on the Zimbabwean economy, a sharp decline in the economy was experienced when the country implemented the controversial land reform program discussed earlier. This program, coupled with other ill-advised policies discussed above plunged the country into the worst economic crisis since gaining political independence (Chitiyo & Chitiyo, 2010). In 2007, the country had a negative GDP growth of 4.4% and the economy declined by 40%; by the end of 2008 unemployment was reported to be 94% (UN office for the coordination of humanitarian affairs, 2009). In addition, the country went through a hyperinflationary period registering inflation rates of about 231 million percent – the highest in any country in the world outside of a war zone. The impact of this hyperinflation on the education system cannot be overemphasized.

The hyperinflation made teacher salaries and other professionals worthless because of the ever-increasing cost of living. These deteriorating conditions led to a massive brain drain among professionals in search of better employment opportunities in other countries for example South Africa, Botswana, Namibia, United Kingdom and New Zealand (Chitiyo & Chitiyo, 2009). Among these professionals, schoolteachers constituted the greatest number of emigrants. It was estimated that approximately about 45,000 teachers left the country between 2007 and 2010 in search of better opportunities abroad (UNICEF, 2009). The emigration of schoolteachers has continued in recent years because the teachers' salaries cannot keep up with the ever-rising cost of living. As a result, many schools were staffed by unqualified personnel hired to teach and administer examinations at both primary and secondary levels. UNICEF (2011) reported that approximately 25% of teachers who were in schools did not meet the minimum teaching requirements of the Ministry of Education, Sports and Culture. In addition there was lack of motivation among the remaining schoolteachers because of their meager salaries. As a result, there were frequent strikes by teachers demanding better working conditions; these strikes disrupted the provision of quality education. The ultimate outcome was poor academic performance of students on national examinations. The Zimbabwean Herald newspaper reported that of the 172,698 students who registered to sit for Ordinary level exams in 2012, only 31,767 (18.4%) attained passing grades in five subjects.

The economic meltdown also left the education sector severely underfunded. As a result of poor funding from the government, the education sector could not provide basic instructional materials. To support this, Mavundutse et al. (2012) conducted a study to explore some of the needs of teachers in rural areas and found that there were severe shortages of materials such as textbooks, chalk, manila-paper for making charts, furniture for both students and teachers and most classrooms were not conducive for learning.

Education is not free in Zimbabwe at all levels, i.e., primary, secondary and high school, and because families were struggling to meet the daily needs of food, shelter, and transportation, many parents were not able to enroll their children in school because they could not afford school fees. In addition, many parents could not afford school supplies such as school uniforms. As a result, many were forced to withdraw their children from school leading to a decline in school enrollment. A survey conducted by UNICEF (2011) revealed that between 2000 and 2009, high school completion rates dropped from 74% to 68%, with secondary school enrolment reporting a 7% decline; only 50% of primary school children were reported to have proceeded to secondary school.

Political Instability

The political temperature in Zimbabwe has been rising since the formation of the opposition Movement for Democratic Change in 1999. In 2000 the government lost to the opposition in a referendum campaign for a new national constitution. Since that time, the political climate in Zimbabwe has not been favorable to the ailing education system. In May

2005, the government of Zimbabwe implemented a program called Operation Murambatsvina which translates to "drive out trash" (Avert, 2010). The program was aimed at abolishing all forms of illegal informal sector activities which included vending, and relocating people from urban areas to rural areas. Some political analysts argued that this was designed to dilute the support of the opposition by driving thousands out of the urban areas where the opposition enjoyed majority support. With an unemployment rate of about 94%, spiraling inflation rates and an ailing economy that had shrunk by 40%, many people had turned to the informal sector as a source of livelihood (Bratton & Masungungure, 2006; UN office for the coordination of humanitarian affairs, 2009). However, as a result of the unplanned and chaotic operation Murambatsvina program, several people were displaced from their homes after houses were demolished and many children were forced to drop out of school. According to the United Nations (2005), it is estimated that approximately 30,000 children in the urban areas were forced out of school. Several schools were closed and the few schools that were functioning were refusing to recruit new students because of overcrowding (United Nations, 2005). As a result, educational services for children were severely disrupted. Teachers were also among the victims of this program. A study by Mhangami (2005) revealed that hundreds of teachers were left homeless after Murambatsvina, and it took many of them several days to find and settle in new homes. In addition, according to the same report, some teachers failed to report for work because they feared losing their property which was left in the open after their houses were destroyed. This resulted in massive loss of instructional time, which was a disadvantage to schoolchildren, especially those who were to sit for their final exams at the end of the year.

Apart from the unprecedented school dropout rates and displacement of teachers in urban areas, political violence also directly affected schoolteachers in the rural areas; there were numerous reports of politically motivated violence against teachers because they were believed to be supporters of the opposition. According to a research report by Pswarayi and Reeler (2012), between 2007 and 2009, approximately 10,000 teachers fled to neighboring countries because of politically motivated violence. Not surprisingly, many schools in rural areas were closed because of the shortage of teachers further compromising children's access to a quality education.

Corruption within the Examination System

Having inherited the British Education system at independence in 1980, the country started to localize the education system in the 1990s. This led to the setting up of the Zimbabwean Schools Examination Council (ZIMSEC), which assumed the responsibilities of considering and approving subjects suitable for examination, grading exams, approving and the conferment of certificates and diplomas, maintaining the integrity of examinations at primary and secondary levels, and registering examination centers. Although this move was designed to be a cost-saving strategy, the system faced several challenges. Firstly, the board was underfunded such that it struggled to fund examinations. Secondly, due to shortage of funds, examination results were not published on time and the board could not produce certificates on time thereby disrupting the academic calendar of students who needed to proceed to the next grade level. Thirdly, the credibility of the board has been questioned. There have been several reports of examination papers leaking, examination scripts getting lost during transportation, and mixing-up of examinations results (Kanyongo, 2005). Kanyongo adds that reports of corrupt school officials opening examinations and selling them on the black market have been reported. Faced with gross incompetence the board has lost credibility and people have lost confidence in its ability to efficiently run the system (Musarurwa & Chimhenga, 2011).

HIV/AIDS

With around 14% of the population living with HIV/AIDS, Zimbabwe is currently experiencing one of the worst HIV/AIDS epidemics in the world. Responding to the task has been an uphill struggle as the country continues to experience a tense political, economic and social climate. Chitiyo and Chitiyo (2010) indicated that the pandemic has overwhelmed the health sector where it was estimated that 75% of bed occupancy was HIV/AIDS related. A majority of the patients affected are adults and youths in their productive years (i.e., 15–49 years); hence, economic production has been seriously affected by the shortage of manpower (Rena, 2008). In 2007, the HIV/AIDS prevalence rate among adults between the ages of 15 and 49 years was reported to be 15.3%.

The scourge has created a host of problems that have threatened and overwhelmed the organization, management, and provision of education. According to Goliber (2000), the increase in morbidity and death of teachers to this pandemic has caused a massive shortage of teachers in schools.

Goliber (2000) also adds that Zimbabwe was likely to lose 2.1% of teachers due to the HIV/AIDS pandemic annually over a ten-year period beginning in 2000. With such huge loses, a disproportionate teacher student ratio is created and there is the replacement of qualified teachers with unqualified temporary teachers who are mostly high school graduates with no teacher training. In addition, with more teachers being infected with HIV/AIDS there has been loss of instructional time because teachers would be too sick to execute their duties or they would be absent from school in order to seek medical attention. This absenteeism of teachers has led to poor quality education.

HIV/AIDS has also resulted in a substantial increase in the number of orphans internationally and UNICEF projects that by the year 2020, 40 million youth may have lost one or both parents to the pandemic (Maughan-Brown, 2010). In Zimbabwe, with life expectancy as low as 43 years (WHO, UNICEF, & UNAIDS, 2008), many parents die young leaving their children at an elevated risk of emotional and behavioral disorders such as anxiety and depression. Without adequate support mechanisms such children go through emotional turmoil on their own which in turn leads to post traumatic stress. These conditions can affect education in a number of ways. According to Gunderson, Kelly and Jemison (2004) orphans have poor school attendance.

Children are forced to drop out of school in order to assume responsibilities of heading and providing for households and supplementing income. For those students fortunate enough to enroll in school, some of them will be so traumatized by the pain of losing their parents or guardians such that they are unable to concentrate and learn in the classroom.

HOW TO OVERCOME THE CHALLENGES

Considering all the challenges discussed, it is apparent that the Zimbabwean education system is in a dire state and requires urgent attention. The revitalization of the country's education system is important for Zimbabwe's social and economic growth because education gives opportunities for individuals to realize their full potential. With regards to the economic problems, there is need for the country to engage the international community in an effort to maximize foreign aid flow and other forms of international assistance. The country has to revise its trade policies so as to attract foreign investment. The availability of international aid and foreign investment can boost economic growth, which may allow the country to fund key sectors of the economy like education.

Considering the current state of the education system, there is need for enormous financial resources to improve the working conditions of schoolteachers. The quality of education is dependent on the availability of qualified and motivated teachers. Good working conditions, such as attractive salaries, will encourage teachers to stay in their respective professions and also lure the human capital lost during the brain drain back into the education system. Therefore, the government has to boost professionals' confidence on the stability of the economy.

As previously mentioned, the Zimbabwe examination council has lost its credibility due to corruption and mismanagement. In order to restore ZIMSEC's credibility, the government has to implement systems which improve the efficiency of the examination board. Musarurwa and Chimhenga (2011), suggest that the government can find a local validating board like the University of Zimbabwe to endorse school certificates and diplomas. Certificates and diplomas issued by the University of Zimbabwe are recognized worldwide hence having them validate school certificates may restore credence to the local educational qualifications.

Reviving the Education System

Part of the Nziramasanga Commission (1999) recommended that the curricula should suit the essential skills and employment needs. Another recommendation was that there must be harmony between what is taught in school and what is required in terms of employment. Children should be accorded with an enabling learning environment and appropriate curricula to equip them with skills necessary to meet their employment needs. However, 14 years down the line, the recommendations of this commission are still to be implemented.

The Zimbabwean education system has to provide the fundamental skills that will empower all students to be active contributors in the country's social, economic, cultural and political advancement. To achieve this objective we recommend the development of a comprehensive education plan. The lack of a long-term comprehensive plan deprives the country of consistent policies as the policies appear to change depending on who is the minister of education at the time.

The country also needs to reach out to experienced teachers who left the country and are serving in the diaspora back into the profession. The multifaceted challenges of the globally networked 21st century demands critical and reflective thinking school curricula. Concerted effort should be made to bring back experienced teachers serving in different countries; these teachers will bring invaluable expertise and new perspectives. Therefore, we recommend a campaign, in collaboration with teachers' unions, to attract teachers back into the profession and into schools.

There should be intentional effort to engage the private sector, parents, civic groups, regionally and internationally-based Zimbabweans to provide adequate resources. Most schools do not have learning and teaching resources; therefore, we recommend that the government should prioritize funding educational programs through its budget. Civic groups such as churches and non-governmental organizations that work with child development programs must play active roles in the provision of materials. If education is to be a vehicle for economic development there is need to equip all schools with up-to-date materials. It is through empowering education that attitudes, which promote patriotism, are sustained.

Teacher Preparation

Teacher education programs need to ensure that they use rigorous assessment tools to ensure that every teacher is adequately prepared to teach. The top-performing countries invest considerable amount of time and financial resources in designing and developing teacher preparation programs but the same cannot be said of Zimbabwe. We encourage the government to engage the international community, donors, and civic organizations to fund institutions of higher education.

In a country experiencing a high unemployment rate and a soaring HIV/AIDS epidemic, there is need to network and collaborate among teacher preparation programs. To that end, we recommend that all parties involved in preparing teachers should collaborate to make sure that the standards, programs and outcomes are aligned to reflect the current economic, social, cultural and political realities on the ground. Teacher preparation programs must ensure that all teacher candidates have the essential skills to empower all students. The dissemination of accurate HIV/AIDS information is a crucial aspect that can mitigate the further spread of this deadly disease.

The media can be a tremendous force in the war against HIV/AIDS by raising the public's awareness about the pandemic through promoting prevention of the virus and reducing the stigma associated with those suffering from it. In addition, teachers can also contribute to the fight against HIV/AIDS. The government can implement professional development workshops in schools and require teachers to continually participate in professional development. Having the teachers participate in these workshops will give them better understanding of the current aspects of the pandemic and also make them aware of the importance of adopting effective ways of teaching students who are infected with the virus.

Teachers also need to be familiar with new technology and incorporate it in classroom instruction. The use of technology in learning helps the students interact with the content, programmed interface, the instructor, and other learners both individually and in groups. Teacher preparation colleges need to change from traditional models of teacher education that do not socially, economically, culturally, and politically empower students.

Educational Assessment and Research

Assessment is central to education. The only way that educators can measure the effectiveness of their efforts and strategies is through the use of carefully designed assessment tools. We recommend that teacher preparation programs devote a portion of their curricula to issues of measurement and assessment so that the graduates of such programs will be well-equipped to measure student performance in order to improve student outcomes.

Having tried to demystify the subject of educational research, it is our hope that teachers will be able to appreciate the value of classroom research more than before. We encourage classroom teachers to make use of extant research in making decisions about teaching strategies. This can be accomplished through the use of research tools, the basic tenets of which have been addressed in this book.

Finally, the Learning Metrics Task Force (2013) recommends that the education system needs to track indicators of child development and learning at different levels. Such data will inform practices at the classroom and school levels (such as developing appropriate interventions for all students), and policy at the macro levels. The measurement of educational performance indicators can be one of the best tools that school systems can use to improve practice. Zimbabwe can fortify its educational system by strengthening its capacity to measure learning outcomes, and to use such evidence to improve practice.

Early Childhood Education

In order for early childhood education in Zimbabwe to be more effective and beneficial to children, parents and schools, there are several factors that need to be addressed. Firstly, all Early Childhood Centers should be registered and monitored by the Ministry of Education, Sport and Culture. The centers should also have suitable facilities and provide conducive environments for child development. This would promote consistency and quality control. Secondly, the teachers and teacher aides should be qualified; in addition to being certified, they should be required to participate in continuing education and professional development through workshops and seminars. Thirdly, there should be universal screening and assessment to identify children who may have or may be at risk of having disabilities or developmental delays. Finally there should be efforts to promote parental and community involvement, which can help consolidate programs offered by different early childhood education centers. Early childhood education is the foundation of every nation's education and economy. It must therefore, be given all the necessary support to make it effective.

Special Education

There is need to develop special education in order to maximize educational outcomes for all children with disabilities in Zimbabwe. Even though we embrace the need for full inclusion of children with disabilities in the general education classroom, we also acknowledge the reality that Zimbabwe, among other African countries, may not be ready for it at the moment. The country does not have enough special education teachers and other support personnel to promote full inclusion of all students with disabilities in the general education classroom. There is need to train more special educational professionals who can provide support to the general education teachers across schools. Also, we suggest that the government should consider revising the teacher preparation curricula in the country and make it mandatory for all pre-service teachers to have basic special education training. Such curricula could include special education courses where all teachers will be introduced to basic special education issues such as different types of disabilities and their characteristics, identification and assessment of children with disabilities, instructional accommodations and modifications, assistive technology, and special education pedagogy. Such training would equip all teachers, both general and special education, with the necessary skills to effectively teach students with disabilities in the general education classroom.

Furthermore, the government should promote early identification of children with disabilities. Research has indicated that children with disabilities, who are identified early and therefore, go on to receive necessary supports early, have better functional and educational outcomes compared to those who are not identified early. Early identification requires awareness among, and cooperation of, parents and families as they may be the first to notice any developmental differences among their children. Besides helping with early identification, parents of children with disabilities need to be involved in the education of their children and work closely with schoolteachers in identifying and implementing effective interventions and supports necessary for the educational success of the children. We strongly believe that given the right support, children with disabilities can experience educational success and become contributing members of the society.

Counselor Education

Counseling is one of the most important areas in the education of every country. Qualified counselors should be registered and licensed in order for the government to monitor and control the services given to clients whether in a school setting or in the community. However, for school programs to be beneficial to students there is need for qualified counselors in all schools. Counselors should have suitable facilities and rooms that allow students to access counseling comfortably and with assurance of confidentiality. Counseling programs should be evaluated regularly in order to make the necessary adjustments for continuous improvement. There should be collaboration between guidance teachers, regular class teachers and the administration for the programs to run smoothly.

The practice of counseling should be carried out professionally to allow students to express their problems and frustrations. If the process is carried out well, the students will reflect on their situations and resolve their problems rationally. Counselors should be relieved of teaching other subjects and focus on counseling students who experience problems. It is vital for counselors to work with parents and employ a variety of counseling techniques. Multicultural counseling should be applied in situations where schools have students from different countries and have different cultural practices.

EDUCATING STUDENTS FOR UNIQUE ROLES OF A 21ST CENTURY ECONOMY

As society evolves, so too do its societal needs. Zimbabwe entered the 21st century on a low political, economic and social platform. In the previous two sections of this chapter, and elsewhere in this book, we have highlighted some of the challenges bedeviling the country as it entered the 21st century. In this section we discuss what we consider fundamental educational needs of a 21st century economy. We believe that one of the ways by which Zimbabwe can reverse the decadence of the past two decades and revitalize its economy is through education. As such the education system needs to be revitalized in alignment with current trends.

Preparing Innovative Thinkers

The world today has become more interconnected than ever before. Hence, others have called it a global village. In order to successfully compete in such an interconnected world countries have to be innovative. This new reality requires that our education system has to change. For example, our education system has to change from what Freire (1972) calls the "banking" concept where learners are considered to be empty vessels that have to be filled with knowledge by the teacher – an enduring legacy of the colonial system. Instead, we have to view all learners as being capable and therefore, promote creativity by stimulating their intellectual development through socially engaging curricula. Such curricula would promote innovative thinkers.

According to Torun and Cicekci (2007) innovation is the engine for economic growth. Like Torun and Cicecki, we believe, for a number of reasons, that innovation is what will drive successful economies in the 21st century. Torun and Cicecki identified the following, among others, as reasons why innovation may help to spur economic growth: i) it creates employment which will then promote production and increase a country's GDP; ii) it creates knowledge, which is essential to the creation of highly skilled labor-force; iii) it promotes cooperation among universities and corporations; and it promotes development and adoption of novel technology. Innovation is the reason why some Asian countries such as China, South Korea and India have achieved remarkable growth in the past few years. Against this backdrop, we urge the government of Zimbabwe to promote innovation across all levels of school from primary to high school and especially in higher education. The relevant ministries should invest in programs that are designed to encourage innovation at all levels of school.

Use of Technology

The world today is inundated with technology. In most developed and some developing countries technology is changing the way children learn. Even though there is not much research on this subject, preliminary evidence suggests that "technologies can expand the range of opportunities for children to learn about the world around them, to develop their communicative abilities, and to learn" (Plowman & McPake, 2013, p. 32). The school curricula should therefore, prepare students for future success in careers that will be so infused with technology. Unfortunately, most Zimbabwean schools today are not equipped even with the most basic learning materials such as books and computers. We suggest that the government should equip all schools with instructional and educational technologies that are prerequisite to the production of technologically literate students. For example, all students should have access to and learn how to use computers at school because almost everything we do today is connected to the computer. This includes communication, learning, and almost every work environment or business sector. Besides, technology can also assist students with disabilities to access the curriculum thereby maximizing the potential of all students as we suggested in Chapters 4 and 5.

Promoting Research

Our educational system should also value and promote scientific inquiry and research, which could help to generate solutions to the societal problems that our country faces. Children are naturally curious and inquisitive (Martin, Jean-Sigur & Schmidt, 2005). According to Martin and colleagues, teachers should capitalize on this natural curiosity and let children explore their interests and construct what is meaningful to them. Instead of the traditional educational approach where students are forced to reproduce what has already been done in the past, for example in terms of scientific experiments, we should let children construct new knowledge based on their own inquiry. Our science laboratories – which every school should have – should not only be semi empty rooms where students come to repeat previously conducted experiments, but they should be places where students can come and explore their world, experiment and reach conclusions that are meaningful to them (Martin et al., 2005). We believe that if this approach is implemented across the education system from primary school to higher education, the country will be able to develop great talent capable of generating solutions to fix the many problems, most of which have become perennial, that our country continues to experience. With seemingly recalcitrant problems like such as disease, hunger, starvation, poor and dilapidated infrastructure, this appears to be a more sustainable solution to the country's problems than relying on donor countries to solve our problems.

Jobs Training

Our tertiary education system needs to be reviewed constantly in order to identify possible areas in need of improvement. One such area is preparing students for the job market. The skills required to sustain a 21st century economy are different from the skills that were required when the country first gained political independence three decades ago. We think the country should identify the most pressing current needs in terms of workforce and then take an inventory of current tertiary educational programs to see if what our colleges are producing match the country's needs. Our guess is that if this is done, we will possibly find a huge mismatch. But again, this is simply a guess and since we do not have data to support it, it should be taken just as that – a guess. Whatever the outcome, inventorying our programs and needs allows us to plan better so that we can focus on training students on the skills that are necessary for the development of our country.

Educating Students to Be Life-long Learners

Our final suggestion is that our education system should prepare students to be life-long learners. Lifelong learning can be defined as "basically promoting active citizenship and the necessary knowledge, skills, values, attitudes toward employment and work" (UNESCO, 2002, p 4). Life-long learners constantly seek to update their knowledge and competencies in relation to personal or career goals (Klamma, Chatti, Duval, Hummel, Hvannberg, Kravcik et al., 2007). The government, through relevant ministries, should promote lifelong learning by creating a supportive learning environment. For example, the government can make the internet readily available and accessible in communities, schools, and other public places. The internet allows easy access to a variety of learning materials which can be motivational to learners. Countries that fail to harness the power of the internet in this web-based era will only do so to their own disadvantage.

CONCLUSION

The purpose of this chapter was to provide the reader with an insight into the challenges faced by the Zimbabwean system and to provide a set of recommendations that we think are necessary to revive the country's education system. As a result of economic instability, political turmoil, poor policies, and the scathing impacts of HIV/AIDS, the once acclaimed education system is in a fragile state. However, according to a report by the United Nations Office for the Coordination of Humanitarian Affairs (2013) there were signs of recovery since the formation of an inclusive government in 2009. However, there is still need for a serious commitment on the part of the government to revive the country's education system. Specific recommendations on how to revive the education system in line with the demands of a 21st century economy have been discussed. We believe that these suggestions can help to revitalize the country into a successful 21st century economy for indeed, as Mr. Nelson Mandela said, "education is the most powerful weapon which you can use to change the world."

Reflection Questions

1) Discuss how each of the following factors have negatively affected the education system in Zimbabwe:

   - HIV/AIDS pandemic
   - Land reform program
   - Economic crisis
   - Political instability

2) Discuss possible solutions to the crisis affecting the country's education system
3) Generate a list of recommendations, which you think might help in the revival of the country's education system

REFERENCES

Adams, C. M., & Pierce, R. L. (2004). Tiered lessons: One way to differentiate mathematics instruction. *Gifted Child Today, 27*(2), 58-65.

Adler, A. (1959) *Understanding human nature*. New York: Premier Books.

Africa University Handbook. (2010). Mutare: Africa University Publication.

Africa University Curriculum Guide. (2011). Mutare: Africa University Publication.

Alao, I. (2009). Counseling and Nigeria National Policy on Education: The question of relevance and competence. *The Nigerian Journal of Guidance and Counseling,* 14(1), 134-141.

Allen, J. & Allen, M. (1989). Discovering and accepting hearing impairment: Initial reactions of parents. *Volta Review*, 81(5).

Allen, H. A. & Sawyer, H. W. (1984). Individuals with life-threatening disabilities: A rehabilitation counseling approach. *Journal of Applied Rehabilitation Counseling*, 15(2), 26-29.

Amen, D. (2012). Theories of Counseling. Retrieved from www.askmikethecounselor2.com/theories-of-counselinghtl Retrieved 8 November 2013

American Educational Research Association (2013). American Educational Research Association Website (www.aera.net).

American Educational Research Association. (2008). Definition of scientifically based research. Alternate Definition of Scientifically Based Research (SBR) Supported by AERA Council, July 11, 2008. Retrieved July 15, 2013 from http://www.aera.net /Portals /38/docs/About_AERA/KeyPrograms/DefinitionofScientificallyBasedResearch.pdf

Annual Report of the Secretary for African Education (1971). Harare: Government Printers.

Annual Report of the Secretary for Education and Culture (1995) *All enrolment statistics from 1980 to 1995.* National Report of the Republic of Zimbabwe. Atkinson, N. (1972). *Teaching Rhodesians: A history of educational policy in Rhodesia.* London: Longman Group LTD.

Avert, (2010, January 14). Introduction to HIV and AIDS in Zimbabwe. Retrieved from http://www.avert.org/aids-zimbabwe.htm

Baeza, M. C. (2002). *Inclusive education in southern Africa: Responding to diversity in education.* Harare: UNESCO.

Barnart, S. M., & Kabzems, V. (1992). Zimbabwe teachers' attitudes towards the integration of pupils with disabilities into regular education. *International Journal of Disability, Development and Education, 39*, 135-146.

Bass, R.E. (2002) *Hope for Today's Problems.* Greenville: Book Surge Publishing.

Beers, C. (1908) *A Mind that Found Itself.* Yale; Yale University.

Beirne-Smith, M., Patton, J. R. & Kim, S. H. (2006). *Mental retardation: An introduction to intellectual disabilities (7th Ed).* Upper Saddle River: Pearson

Best, J. W. & Kahn, J. V. (2006). *Research in Education* (10th ed). Boston: Pearson,

Bindura University of Science Education Curriculum Guide (2014). Bindura: Bindura University of Science Education Publication.

Black, P., & Wiliam, D. (1998). Assessment and classroom learning. *Assessment in Education, 5*(1), 7-74.

Black, S. (1999). Building a better teacher. *American School Board Journal, 186*(4), 50-53.

Boafo-Arthur, K. (1991). Ghana: Structural adjustment, democratization, and the politics of continuity. *African Studies Review, 42*(2), 41–72.

Borgman, D. (1988). *Counseling African Youth. Encyclopedia of Urban Ministry.* Center for Youth Studies Urban Youth Workers Institute.

Brammer, L.M. Shostrom, E.L. & Abrego, P.J. (1989). *Therapeutic psychology: Fundamentals of counseling and psychotherapy.* Englewood Cliffs, New Jersey: Prentice-Hall.

Bratton, M. and E.Masunungure (2006) 'Popular reactions to state repression: Operation Murambatsvina in Zimbabwe', *African Affairs 106* (422), 21–45.

Brewer, J. A. (1998). (3rd Ed.) Introduction to Early Childhood Education. Boston, Allyn & Bacon.

Cagne, R.M. (1985). *The conditions of learning and theory of instruction.* Fort Worth: Holt, Rinehart, and Winston.

Campbell, J., Gilmore, L., & Cuskelly, M. (2003). Changing student teachers' attitudes towards disability and inclusion. *Journal of Intellectual & Developmental Disability, 28*(4), 369-379

Campbell, D. T., & Stanley, J. C. (1963). Experimental and quasi-experimental designs for research on teaching. In N. L. Gage (Ed.), Handbook of research on teaching (pp. 171–246). Chicago, IL: Rand McNally.

Capuzzi, D. & Gross, D. (1997). *Introduction to counseling profession*, (2nd ed.). London: Allyn and Bacon.

CARA/IOM Zimbabwe Higher Education Initiative 'Consultation Findings' (2010). Leadership Dialogue on Rebuilding Higher Education in Zimbabwe.

CEO Forum on Education and Technology. (1999). *Professional development: A link to better learning?* Washington, DC: Author. Retrieved from www.ceoforum.org/downloads/99report.pdf

Chagonda, T., (2012). Teachers' and bank workers' responses to Zimbabwe's crisis: uneven effects, different strategies. *Journal of Contemporary African Studies, 30*(1), 83-97.

Charema, J. (2004). *Explaining the ways in which parents of children with hearing impairments in Zimbabwe accessed counseling services.* Unpublished PhD. Thesis, University of Pretoria, Pretoria; South Africa

Charema, J. (2007). From special schools to inclusive education: The way forward for developing countries south of the Sahara. *The Journal of the International Association of Special Education, 8*(1), 88-96.

Charema, J. (2009a). Counseling in Educational Institutions in Sub-Saran African Countries: Is there anything new? Strategies for the 21st Century. *The Rehabilitation Professional, 17*(1), 17-24

Charema, J. (2009b). Preference for sources of counseling among parents of children with hearing impairments in Zimbabwe. *The Nigerian Journal of Guidance and Counseling 14*(1), 1-14

Charema, J. (2010). Inclusive education in developing countries in the sub Saharan Africa: From theory to practice. *International Journal of Special Education, 25*(1), 87-93.

Charema, J. (2012). Early Intervention for Children with Disabilities in Countries South of the Sahara: How do Family and Community Involvement and Cultural Values benefit Intervention Programs? *Journal of Linguistics, Culture and Education, 1*(2), 54 - 65.

Charema, J. & Eloff, I. (2011). Parents of children with hearing impairment accessing counseling in Zimbabwe. *The Journal of the International Association of Special Education, 12(1), 17-27.*

Charema, J. & Shizha, E. (2008). Counseling Indigenous Shona People in Zimbabwe: Traditional Practices Versus Western Eurocentric Perspectives. *ALTERNATIVE; AN International Journal of Indigenous Peoples, 4*(2), 123-139.

Chase, C. I. (1999). *Contemporary assessment for educators.* New York: Longman.

Chimedza, R. (2001). *A study on children and adolescents with disabilities in Zimbabwe.* Harare: UNICEF. Retrieved from http://catalogue.safaids.net/publications/study-children-and-adolescents-disabilities-zimbabwe-pp-73-88

Chimedza, R. (2008). Disability and inclusive education in Zimbabwe. In Len Barton, Felicity Armstrong (editors). *Policy, experience and change: Cross-cultural reflections on inclusive education (pp. 123-132).* Springer

Chireshe, R. (2008). The Evaluation of School Guidance and Counseling Services in Zimbabwe. *The Nigerian Journal of Guidance and Counseling, 13*(1), 54-68.

Chireshe, R. (2011). Special needs education in-service teacher trainees' views on inclusive education in Zimbabwe. *Journal of Social Science, 27*(3), 157-164.

Chiromo, A. S. (2007). *A history of teacher education in Zimbabwe: 1939-1999.* Harare: University of Zimbabwe Publications.

Chiromo, A. S. (1990). Teacher education courses in relation to preparation for teaching practice: Views from student teachers. *Zimbabwe Journal of Educational Research.* Pp. 62-75.

Chitiyo, M. (2008). Special education law in Zimbabwe. *The Journal of the International Association of Special Education, 9*(1), 5-12.

Chitiyo, M. (2013). *A pedagogical approach to special education in Africa.* New York: Nova Science Publishers.

Chitiyo, M., Changara, D. M., & Chitiyo, G. (2008). Providing psychosocial support to special needs children: A case of orphans and vulnerable children in Zimbabwe. *International Journal of Educational Development, 28,*384–392

Chitiyo, G. & Chitiyo, M. (2009). The impact of the HIV/AIDS and economic crises on orphans and other vulnerable children in Zimbabwe. *Childhood Education, 85*(6), 348-351.

Chitiyo, M., Chitiyo, G., Chitiyo, J., Oyedele, V. I., Makoni, R., Fonnah, D. J., & Chipangure, L. (2014). Understanding the nature and causes of problem behavior in

Zimbabwean schools: Teacher perceptions. *International Journal of Inclusive Education.* DOI:10.1080/13603116.2013.875068

Chitiyo, G., Chitiyo, M, Rumano, M. B., Ametepee, L. K., & Chitiyo, J. (2010). Zimbabwe education system: emerging challenges and the implications for policy and research, *Journal of Global Intelligence & Policy, 3*(3), 35-43.

Chivore, B. R. S. (1990) *Teacher Education in Post-Independent Zimbabwe.* Harare: Longman Press.

Chivore, B. R. S. (1991). *Curriculum Evaluation in Zimbabwe: An appraisal of case studies.* Harare: Books for Publishing Africa House.

Colledge, R. (2002). *Mastering counseling theory.* Hampshire Palgrave: MacMillan Press.

Cooley, R. J., Cradler, J., & Engel, P.K. (1997). *Computers and classrooms: The status of technology in U.S. schools.* Princeton, NJ: Policy Education Center, Educational Testing Service.

Corey, G. (1990). *Theory and practice of group counseling*, (3rd ed.). Pacific Groove, California: Brooks/Cole.

Corey, G. (1986). *Theory and practice of counseling and psychotherapy*, (3rd ed.). Monterey, California: Brookes/Cole.

Crone, D. A., & Horner, R.H. (2003). *Building positive behavior support systems in schools: functional behavior assessment.* New York, Guilford Press.

Csapo, M. (1986). Zimbabwe: Emerging problems of education and special education. *International Journal of Special Education, 1*(2), 141-60.

Curriculum Development Unit (CDU) (1983). *The developments in education: The education system for the new Zimbabwe.* National Report of the Republic of Zimbabwe. Retrieved from http://www.ibe.unesco.org/International/ICE/natrap/Zimbabwe.pdf

Dale, D. M. C. (1984). *Individualized Integration.* London: Hodder & Stoughtton.

Darling-Hammond, L. (Ed.). (2005). *Professional development schools: Schools for developing a profession* (2nd ed.). New York: Teachers College Press.

Darling-Hammond, L. (1996). *What matters most: A competent teacher for every child.* Phi Delta Kappan, 78(3), 193-201.

Devlieger, P.J. (1998). Physical 'disability' in Bantu languages: Understanding the relativity of classification and meaning. *International Journal of Rehabilitation Research, 21*, 63–70.

Devlieger, P. J. (1999). Frames of reference in African proverbs on disability. *International Journal of Disability, Development and Education, 46*(4), 439-451.

Dolan, R. P. & Hall, T. E. (2001). Universal Design for Learning: Implications for large-scale assessment. *IDA Perspectives* 27(4), 22-25.

Donaldson, M. (1978). Children's Minds. London, Croom Helm.

Dugger, W.E., Jr. (2001). Standards for technological literacy. *Phi Delta Kappan, 82*(7), 513-517.

Dzvimbo, K. P. (1989). The dilemmas of teacher education reform in Zimbabwe. *Interchange, 20*(4), 16-31.

Farquhar, J. (1987). *Jairos Jiri: The man and his work.* Gweru, Zimbabwe: Mambo Press.

Fraenkel, J. R., Wallend, N. E., & Hyun, H. H. (2012). *How to design and evaluate research in education* (8th ed.). New York: McGraw Hill.

Freire P. (1972). *Pedagogy of the oppressed.* Harmondsworth: Penguin.

Friend, M. (2006). *Special education: contemporary perspectives for schools professionals.* Boston: Allyn and Bacon.

Gargiulo, R. M. (2012). *Special education in contemporary society: An introduction to exceptionality (4th Ed).* Los Angeles: Sage.

Gazda, G.M., Ginter, E.J. & Horne, A.M. (2001). *Group Counseling and Group Psychotherapy.* Columbus: Prentice Hall.

Geer, P. (2000). What happens when teachers design educational technology? The development of technological pedagogical content knowledge. *Journal of Educational Computing Research, 32*(2), 131-152.

Gesinde, A.M. (2009). Guidance and Counseling in the Universal Basic education Scheme: Relevance and Challenges. *The Nigerian Journal of Guidance and Counseling, 14*(1), 112-121

Gilliland, B.E., James, R.K. & Bowman, J.T. (1989). *Theories and strategies in counseling and psychotherapy.* Englewood Cliffs, New Jersey: Prentice-Hall.

Gladding, S. T. (1996) *Counseling: A comprehensive profession* (3rd edition). London; Macmillan Publication Co.

Goliber, T. J. (2000). *Exploring the implications of the HIV/AIDS epidemic for educational planning in selected African countries. The demographic question.* Washington, DC: The World Bank.

Goswami, D., & Stillman, P. R. (Eds.). (1987). Reclaiming the classroom: Teacher research as an agency for change. Upper Montclair, NJ: Boynton/Cook.

Gay, L. R., (1996) *Educational research: competencies for analysis and application* (5th ed.). new Jersey: Merrill-Prentice Hall.

Gunter, P. L., Coutinho, M. J., & Cade, T. (2002). Classroom factors linked with academic gains among students with emotional and behavioral problems. *Preventing School Failure, 46*(3), 126-133.

Hallahan, D. P. & Kauffman, J. M. (2006). *Exceptional learners: an introduction special education (10th Ed.).* Boston: Allyn and Bacon.

Hammersmith, J. A. (2007). Converging indigenous and Western knowledge systems: Implications for tertiary education. Unpublished Doctoral Thesis. Pretoria: University of South Africa (UNISA).

Hansen, J.C., Stevic, R.R. & Warner, R.W. (1986). *Counseling: Theory and process.* Boston: Allyn & Bacon.

Hapanyengwi, O. (2009). A synoptic view of the history of special needs education in Zimbabwe. Retrieved from http://www.thefreelibrary.com/ASynopticViewoftheHistoryof SpecialNeedsEducationinZimbabwe-a01073960231

Healey, A. C., & Hays, D. G. (2011). Defining counseling professional identity from a gendered perspective: Role conflict and development. *Professional Issues in Counseling Journal*, Spring. Retrieved from http://www.shsu.edu/~piic/DefiningCounseling ProfessionalIdentityfromaGenderedPerspective.htm

Hellum, A., & Derman, B., (2004). Land reform and human rights in contemporary Zimbabwe: Balancing individual and social justice through an integrated human rights framework. *World Development, 32*(10), 1785-1805.

Henley, M., Ramsey, R.S., & Algozzine, R. F. (2006). *Characteristics of and strategies for teaching students with mild disabilities (5th Ed).* Boston: Allyn and Bacon.

Hegarty, S. (1986). *Special needs in ordinary schools.* London: Cassell.

Heward, W. (2009). Exceptional children: An introduction to special education. Upper Saddle River, NJ: Pearson. Retrieved on 23 September 2013

Ivey, A.E. (1987). Counseling 2000: Time to take charge! *The Counseling Psychologist, 8*(4), 12-16.

Ivey, A.E. & Ivey, M.B. (1993). *Counseling and psychotherapy: A multicultural perspective.* Boston, Allyn & Bacon.

James, V., Makuto, D. & Maponga, C. C. (2009) *PROJECT: Identifying and developing best practices in the utilization of Zimbabwe Diaspora health professionals to support the health sector in Zimbabwe.* Harare: Zimbabwe

Jongwe, A, (2009, August 7). "Ministry gears up to tackle brain drain", *The Financial Gazette.* Retrieved from http://www.financialgazette.co/zw/companies-a-markets/1543-ministry-gears-up-to-tackle-brain-drain.html

Justice, L. M. (2007). Early intervention training in Ukraine: Building capacity one step at a time. *The ASHA Leader, 12*(10), 30-31.

Kabzems, V. & Chimedza, R. (2002). Development assistance: Disability and education in Southern Africa. Disability & Society, 17(2), 147-157.

Kanyongo, G. Y. (2005). Zimbabwe public education system reforms: Successes and challenges. *International Educational Journal, 6*(1), 65-74.

Kariwo, M. T. (2007).Widening Access in Higher Education in Zimbabwe. *Higher Education Policy, (20),* 45–59.

Karoly, L.A., Kilburn, M.R. & Cannon, J.S. (2005). *Early Childhood Interventions; Proven Results, Future Promise.* RAND Labour and Population Corporation.

Klamma, R., Chatti, M. A., Duval, E., Hummel, H., Hvannberg, E. H., Kravcik, M., Law, E., Naeve, A., & Scott, P. (2007). Social Software for Life-long Learning. *Educational Technology & Society, 10*(3), 72-83.

Kuster, S. (1999). *African education in colonial Zimbabwe, Zambia and Malawi: Government control, settler antagonism and African Agency, 1890 – 1964.* New Jersey: Transactions Publishers.

Lacey, A. (2001). *Stumbling blocks and stepping stones of teachers' use of Web-based strategies to enhance teaching.* Unpublished master's thesis, University of Wisconsin-Green Bay.

LaCombe, S. (2012). Counseling Theories – Making therapy work. Retrieved from www.myshrink.com/counseling-theory.php?t-id=87

Leu, D.J., Jr. (2000b). Developing new literacies: Using the Internet in content area instruction. In M. McLaughlin & M.E. Vogt (Eds.), *Creativity and innovation in content area instruction.* Norwood, MA: Christopher-Gordon.

Learning Metrics Task Force. 2013. *Toward Universal Learning: Recommendations from the Learning Metrics Task Force.* Montreal and Washington, D.C.: UNESCO Institute for Statistics and Center for Universal Education at the Brookings Institution.

Makinde, O. (1978). Historical Foundations of Counseling in Africa. *The Journal of the Negro Education, 47*(3), 303-311

Mandina, S. (2012). Bachelor of education in service teacher trainees' perceptions and attitudes on inclusive education in Zimbabwe. *Asian Social Science, 8*(13). Retrieved from doi:10.5539/ass.v8n13p227 URL: http://dx.doi.org/10.5539/ass.v8n13p227

Mapara, J. (2009). Indigenous knowledge systems in Zimbabwe: Juxtaposing postcolonial theory. *The Journal of Pan African Studies, 3*(1), 139-155.

Maphosa, F. Kujinga, K. & Chingarande, S. D. (2007). *Zimbabwe's development experiences since 1980: Challenges and prospects for the future.* Harare: Zimbabwe: OSSREA-ZIMBABWE.

Martin, D.J., Jean-Sigur, R. & Schmidt, E. (2005). Process-oriented inquiry—a constructivist approach to early childhood science education: teaching teachers to do science, *Journal of Elementary Science Education, 17*(2), 13-26.

Maughan-Brown, B. (2010). Stigma rises despite antiretroviral roll-out: A longitudinal analysis in South Africa. *Social Science and Medicine, 70,* 368–374

Mavundutse, O., Munetsi, C., Mamvuto, A., Mavhunga, P. J., Kangai, K., Gatsi, R. (2012). Emerging teacher education needs as a result of land reform in Zimbabwe: A focus on new resettlement areas. *Academic Research International, 3*(2),298-305.

Mawire, T.L. (2011). *Evaluating the implementation of guidance and counseling in a Zimbabwean secondary school*, MEd dissertation, University of Pretoria.

McLeod, J. (2003). *An Introduction to Counseling.* Buckingham, Philadelphia: Open University Press.

McLeod, J. (2013). Person-Centered Counseling in Action (4th Edn.)Dundee: SAGE Publications Ltd.

McLeod, J. (2013). An Introduction to Research in Counseling and Psychotherapy. Dundee: SAGE Publications Ltd.

Mcleskey, L., Rosenberg, M. S., & Westling, D. L. (2013). *Inclusion: effective practices for all students (2nd Ed).* Boston: Pearson.

McWhirter, J.J. & McWhirter, B.T. (1991). A framework of theories in counseling. Boston: Allyn & Bacon.

Mearns, D. & Thorne, B. (2000). *Person-centered therapy today.* London: SAGE.

Meese, R.L. (2001). Teaching learners with mild disabilities: integrating research and practice (2nd ed.). Australia: Wadsworth Thomson Learning.

Merkley, D.J., Schmidt, D.A., & Allen, G. (2001). Addressing the English language arts standards in a secondary reading methodology course. *Journal of Adolescent & Adult Literacy, 45*(3), 220-231.

Mhangami, M. (2005). The impact of Zimbabwe's urban cleanup operation on education: A case of plan program areas. Retrieved from http://www.rocare.org/Mhangami.pdf

Mielke, J., Adamolekun, B., Ball, D., Mundanda, T. (1997). Knowledge and attitudes of teachers towards epilepsy in Zimbabwe. *Acta Neurologica Scandanavica, 96,* 133-137.

Ministry of Education and Culture. (1987). *Policy goals and new directions in special education.* Harare: Ministry of Education.

Ministry of Education and Culture. (1990). *Education Circular no. P.36.* Harare: Ministry of Education and Culture.

Ministry of Education Sports and Culture Circular NO. 23 of 2005 (2005). *Implementation Guidelines for the Institutionalisation of The Guidance and Counselling Programme in All Primary and Secondary Schools.* Ministry of Education Sports and Culture.

Ministry of Education, Sports, and Culture (2009). Education in Zimbabwe: *Facts and information.* Harare: Zimbabwe.

Ministry of Education, Sports, and Culture (2011). Education in Zimbabwe: *Facts and information.* Harare: Zimbabwe.

References

Ministry of Higher and Tertiary Education (2009). Baseline study on the status of human capital development and training institutions in Zimbabwe. *Baseline data and statistical information, situation analysis.* Harare: Zimbabwe.

Ministry of Higher and Tertiary Education. (2013). *The expansion of higher and tertiary education in Zimbabwe.* Retrieved from http://www.mhet.gov.zw/homepage/ministry-structure.

Ministry of Higher and Tertiary Education Report. (1997). *The Zimbabwe science and technology policy.* Harare: Government Printers.

Ministry of Higher Education and Technology (2000). Education in Zimbabwe: *Facts and information.* Harare: Zimbabwe.

Ministry of Higher Education and Technology (2009). Education in Zimbabwe: *Facts and information.* Harare: Zimbabwe.

Ministry of Higher Education and Technology (2013). Education in Zimbabwe: *Facts and information.* Harare: Zimbabwe.

MIT Study Report. (2005). *Early Childhood Education for All: A Wise Investment.* MIT Workplace Center.

Monthly Digest of Statistics (1982). *Primary and secondary enrollments.* The Ministry of Education, Sports and Culture. Harare, Zimbabwe.

Musarurwa, C. (2011). Teaching with and learning through icts in Zimbabwe's teacher education colleges. *US-China Education Review, 20*(2), 113-129.

Musarurwa, C. & Chimhenga, S. (2011). Credibility of school examinations in Zimbabwe: A reflective analysis. *Academic Research International, 1*(1), 173-179

Mutepfa, M. M., Mpofu, E., & Chataika, T. (2007). Inclusive education in Zimbabwe: Policy, curriculum, practice, family, and teacher education issues. *Childhood Education, 83*(6), 342-346.

Mutumbuka, D. (1984). *Minister, in the Ministry of Education Policy Statement.* Harare, Zimbabwe.

National AIDS council: Coordinating the multi-sectoral response to HIV and AIDS in Zimbabwe (n.d.). Retrieved from http://nac.org.zw/

National Council for the Accreditation of Teacher Education, Task Force on Technology and Teacher Education. (1997). *Technology and the new professional teacher: Preparing for the 21st century classroom.* Washington, DC: Author. Retrieved from www.ncate.org/accred/projects/tech/tech-21.htm

Nyanga, L. W. (2009). Early childhood education programmes in Kenya: challenges and solutions. *Early Years: An International Research Journal, 29*(3), 227-236

Nystul, M. S. (1999). *Introduction to counseling: An art and science perspective.* London: Allyn & Bacon.

Oakland, T., Mpofu, E., Glasgow, K., & Jumel, B. (2003). Diagnosis and administrative interventions for students with mental retardation in Australia, France, and Zimbabwe 98 years after Binet's first intelligence test. *International Journal of Testing, 3*(1), 59-75.

O'Shea, D. J. & Drayden, M. (2008). Legal aspects of preventing problem behavior, *Exceptionality, 16,* 105-118.

Parker-Rees, R. & William, J. (2006). *Early Years Education.* London, Taylor & Francis Group.

Peresuh, M. & Barcham, L. (1998). Special education provision in Zimbabwe. *British Journal of Special Education, 25*(2), 75-80.

Peresuh, M., Mushoriwa, T. D., Chireshe, R. (2006). A review of research findings on the inclusive education movement: Perspectives from developed and developing countries. *Educamate, 2*(2), 50-62.

Ploch, L. (2009). *Zimbabwe The power sharing agreement and implications for U.S. policy. Congressional Research Service.* CRS Report for Congress, Washington, DC.

Plowman, L. & McPake, J. (2013). Seven myths about children and technology. *Childhood Education, 89*(1), 27-33.

Popham, W. J. (2014). *Classroom assessment: What teachers need to know.* New Jersey: Pearson Education, Inc.

Portfolio Committee on Education, Sport, Arts and Culture (2010). Second Report to Parliament on *Provision and Development of Early Childhood Development in Zimbabwe*. Zimbabwe Parliament.

Potts, D. (2006). "All my hopes and dreams are shattered": Urbanization and migrancy in an imploding African economy-the case of Zimbabwe. *Geoforum, 37*, 537-551.

Pridmore, P., Yates, C. (2005). Combating AIDS in South Africa and Mozambique: the role of open, distance, and flexible learning (ODFL). *Comparative Education Review, 49*(4), 490–511.

Pwasirayi, L. & Reeler, T. (2012). Fragility and education in Zimbabwe: Assessing the impact of violence on education. Research and Advocacy Unit

Ramey, C. (2013). *Closes achievement gap, brings societal benefits.* Virginia, Virginia Tech Carilion Research Institute.

Raymond, E. B. (2008). *Learners with mild disabilities: A characteristics approach*(3rd Ed.). Pearson: Boston.

Reifel, S. & Brown, M.H. (2001). *Early Education and Care, and Re-conceptualizing Play.* London, Elsevier Science.

Richards, K. (2012). Counseling in Zimbabwe: History, Current Status, and Future Trends. Journal of Counseling and Development. Retrived from htt://www.readperiodicals.com /201201/258847741.html.

Riddel, A. R. (1998). Reforms of educational efficiency and equity in developing countries: An Overview. *Compare, 28*(3), 227-292.

Rumano, M. B. (2008). Hope replenished: Education and transformative leadership for dealing with HIV/AIDS epidemic in the Zimbabwean schools. *The International Journal of Knowledge, Culture, and Change Management, 8*(5), 76-85.

Salend, S. J. (2005). *Creating inclusive classrooms: Effective and reflective practices for all students* (5th Ed.). Upper Saddle River, New Jersey: Pearson.

Shavo, E. (2011*). Origin and Development of Guidance and Counseling Practice in Tanzanian Schools. Retrieved from* http://EzineArticles.com/5766594.

Shaw, R. (1992). *Teacher training in secondary schools.* London: Kogan Page Ltd.

Shizha, E. & Koriwo, M.T. (2012). *Education and Development in Zimbabwe: A Social, Political and Economic Analysis.* Rotterdam: Sense publishers

Shoko, J. (2013). *The Africa Report: Zimbabwe war veterans demand compensation.* Retrieved from http://www.theafricareport.com/Southern-Africa/zimbabwe-war-veterans-demand-compensation.html

Smith, H. Chiroro, P. & Musker, P. (2012). *Process and impact evaluation of the basic education assistance module final evaluation report to the Government of Zimbabwe.* Harare: Government Publication.

Sokwanele (2013). *Education in Zimbabwe.* Retrieved from http://www.sokwanele.com/thisis zimbabwe/archives/4601.

Stiggins, R. J. (2008). *An introduction to student-involved assessment FOR learning* (5th ed.). New Jersey: Pearson Prentice Hall.

Sugai, G., Horner, R.H., Dunlap, G., Hieneman, M., Lewis, T.J., Nelson, C. et al. (1999). Applying positive behavior support and functional behavioral assessment in schools. *Technical assistance guide*, version 1.4.3. Washington DC.

Sweeney, T.J. (1989). *Adlerian counseling: A practical approach for a new decade.* Muncie, In: Accelerated Development, Inc.

Taylor, R. (1970). *African education: The historical development and organization of the system.* Salisbury, Rhodesia: Government Printer.

The Central Statistical Office (2000). *The Zimbabwean education progress report.* Harare: Zimbabwe.

Tiene, D., & Luft, P. (2002). The technology-rich classroom. *American School Board Journal, 189*(8), 37-39.

Tomlinson, C. A. (August, 2000). Differentiation of instruction in the elementary grades. ERIC Digest. ERIC Clearinghouse on Elementary and Early Childhood Education.

Torun, H. & Cicekci, C. (2007). *Innovation: Is the engine for the economic growth?* Ege University. Retrieved from http://www.tcmb.gov.tr/yeni/iletisimgm/Innovation.pdf

Tuckman, B. W., & Harper B. E. (2012). *Conducting educational research* (6th ed.). United Kingdom, Rowman & Littlefield Publishers, Incorporated.

Turnbull, A., Turnbull, R., Wehmeyer, M. L. & Shogren, K. A. (2013). *Exceptional lives: special education in today's schools (7th Ed).* Pearson: Boston.

UC Berkeley Early Childhood Education Committee (2011-2012). *UC Berkeley Early Childhood Education Program: PARENT HANDBOOK.* Sacramento, California.

UNAIDS. (2011). HIV and AIDS estimates: 2011. Retrieved from http://www.unaids.org/en /regionscountries/countries/zimbabwe/

UNDP (1999). Verbal report to Sub-Saharan Africa education for all. 2000 Conference, Johannesburg 7th December.

UNDP, 2008. Comprehensive economic recovery in Zimbabwe. A discussion document. Harare: UNDP.

UNESCO (1994). The Salamanca statement and framework for action on special needs education. Retrieved from http://www.unesco.org/education/pdf/SALAMA_E.PDF

UNESCO (2002). *Early Childhood Care and Education.* Dakar, Global Context.

UNESCO (2002). *Integrating lifelong learning perspectives.* Philippines: UNESCO Institute for Education

UNESCO, (2001). The Zimbabwe national commission for UNESCO, *the ministry of higher education and technology report.* Harare: Zimbabwe.

UNESCO (2009). EFA Global monitoring report. Paris: UNESCO.

UNESCO (n.d.). Early childhood care and education. Retrieved from http://www.unesco.org /new/en/education/themes/strengthening-education-systems/early-childhood/

UNICEF (2004*). Report on the Zimbabwe country programme end of cycle review 2000-2004.* Retrieved from http://www.unicef.org/evaldatabase/index_29582.html

UNICEF (1998). Children in especially difficult circumstances in Zimbabwe. Final report of UNICEF consultancy to the Government of Zimbabwe Ministry of Public service, labor and Social Welfare.

References

UNICEF (2011). Education in emergencies and post-crisis transition. Retrieved from http://www.educationandtransition.org/wpcontent/uploads/2007/04/Zimbabwe_EEPCT_2010_Report.pdf

United Nations, (2005). Report on the fact finding mission to Zimbabwe to assess scope and impact of Operation Murambatsvina. Retrieved from http://www.hpcrresearch.org/mrf-database/mission.php?id=51

UN Office for the Coordination of Humanitarian Affairs. (2009). Zimbabwe, consolidated appeal.

UN Office for the Coordination of Humanitarian Affairs. (2013). Is Zimbabwe's education sector on the road to recovery. Retrieved from http://www.irinnews.org/report/97324/is-

University World News (2010). From a special correspondent, 14 March 2010, Issue: 0049, ZIMBABWE: *Pay hike ends lecturer strike.* Harare: Zimbabwe.

Van Blerkom, M. L. (2009). *Measurement and statistics for teachers.* New York: Taylor and Francis.

Wadsworth, N. (1990) *Theories of Counseling and Psychotherapy: A basic issues approach.* Newton, MA: Allyn Bacon.

Wallace, W.A. (1986). *Theories of counseling and psychotherapy: A basic issues approach.* Newton, Massachusetts: Allyn & Bacon.

Webb, S.B. (2000). Debugging counseling for the new millennium: A counselor's view from Mount Hikurangi. *International Journal for the Advancement of Counseling*, 22:301-315.

WHO (2012). HIV and AIDS in Zimbabwe. Retrieved from http://www.avert.org/hiv-aids-zimbabwe.htm

www.childforum.com/options/258-early-childhood-education-in-new-zealand-ece. What is Early Childhood Education? And Do All Children Benefit Equally from it? Retrieved on 14 September 2013.

www.mywage.org/Zimbabwe Child care in Zimbabwe. Retrieved on 15 September 2013.

www.wisegeek.com/what-what-is-so-important-about-early-childhood-education.htm. Retrieved on 28 September 2013.

Zimbabwe Central Statistics Office. (1997). *Intercensal Demographic Survey*. Zimbabwe: Author.

Zimbabwean Herald (2013). 2012 O' level results out. *The Herald online.* February 5 2013

Zimbabwe Independent, (2010). *Tertiary students fail to write exams over fees*, written by Nqobile Bhebhe and Ashley Marimo article published 3rd June 2010. Harare: Zimbabwe.

Zimbabwe Millennium Development Goals Progress Report (2012). *Ministry of economic planning and investment.* Harare: Zimbabwe Government Publications.

Zindi, F. (1997). *Special education in Africa.* Mogoditshane, Botswana: Tasalls Publishing.

Zvobgo, R. J. (1986). *Transforming Education: The Zimbabwean experience.* Harare, Zimbabwe: Harare College Press.

Zvobgo, R. J. (1999). *The post-colonial state and educational reform (Zimbabwe, Zambia and Botswana).* Harare, Zimbabwe: Zimbabwe Publishing House.

AUTHORS' CONTACT INFORMATION

Dr. Morgan Chitiyo,
Associate Professor
Duquesne University
600 Forbes Avenue
Pittsburgh, PA 15282
Tel: 412 3964036
Email: chitiyom@duq.edu

Dr. John Charema,
Director of Education
Mophato Education Center
Botswana

Dr. Moses B. Rumano,
Assistant Professor
Malone University
Canton, OH

Mr. Jonathan Chitiyo,
Ph.D. Candidate
Southern Illinois University
Carbondale, IL

Dr. George Chitiyo,
Assistant Professor
Tennessee Tech. University
Cookeville, TN

INDEX

#

20th century, 6
21st century, vii, 66, 97, 143, 144, 149, 153, 154, 155, 164

A

abuse, 85, 91, 92, 117
academic learning, 61, 64
academic performance, 11, 16, 21, 56, 138, 146
academic problems, 112
academic progress, 12, 117
academic success, 128
academic tasks, 62
access, 2, 5, 7, 8, 9, 10, 11, 17, 23, 24, 25, 32, 33, 46, 47, 49, 51, 52, 66, 68, 70, 71, 72, 102, 107, 110, 147, 152, 154, 155
accessibility, 12
accommodations, 66, 67, 70, 72, 104, 152
accountability, 38, 117, 129
accounting, 26
accreditation, 16
action research, 131, 132
adaptations, 65, 66
adjustment, 86, 87, 88, 158
administrators, 2, 26, 115, 116, 117
adolescents, 159
adult literacy, 102
adulthood, 92
adults, 7, 22, 29, 32, 34, 42, 92, 148
advancement, 6, 106, 110, 149
advocacy, 77
Africa, vii, 2, 3, 6, 9, 17, 25, 59, 77, 94, 97, 98, 104, 105, 106, 126, 143, 144, 157, 159, 160, 162, 165, 166, 167, 171, 172
age, 6, 7, 8, 9, 14, 15, 20, 32, 35, 36, 39, 41, 42, 47, 59, 76, 105, 108, 109, 112, 116, 120, 125, 136

agencies, 24, 25, 33
aggression, 37, 57, 68, 112
agriculture, 48
AIDS, 46, 47, 61, 97, 108, 109, 110, 133, 148, 150, 157, 164, 165, 166, 167
albinism, 59
alcohol abuse, 112, 114
alertness, 61
alienation, 81
alternative treatments, 137
American Educational Research Association, 132, 157
ancestors, 48, 92
anger, 37
Angola, 105
antagonism, 162
anthropology, 48, 77
anxiety, 57, 77, 79, 83, 89, 148
appropriate technology, 108
aptitude, 80, 123
arithmetic, 4
articulation, 60
Asian countries, 153
assessment, 52, 76, 85, 119, 120, 122, 125, 126, 127, 128, 130, 150, 151, 152, 159, 160, 165, 166
assessment tools, 119, 120, 125, 127, 150, 151
assimilation, 84
assistive technology, 52, 72, 152
asthma, 47, 61
atmosphere, 68, 84
Attention Deficit Hyperactivity Disorder (ADHD), 56, 58, 64
attitudes, 25, 39, 49, 50, 71, 72, 80, 81, 87, 88, 112, 133, 139, 150, 155, 157, 158, 162, 163
authority, 5, 38, 52, 67, 85, 98, 138
autism, 46, 56, 58, 59, 127, 171
autonomy, 82, 94, 98
awareness, 34, 57, 72, 78, 80, 83, 84, 150, 152

B

bad behavior, 77
banking, 153
barriers, 1, 8
base, 16, 63
basic education, 165
basic needs, 12, 82, 87
basic research, 131
basic services, 67
behavior modification, 87, 114, 137
behavioral assessment, 71, 166
behavioral change, 86
behavioral disorders, 47, 56, 58, 64, 71, 148
behavioral problems, 161
behavioral theory, 81
behaviors, 57, 62, 71, 81, 83, 89, 112, 114, 117, 133, 137
belief systems, 114
beneficiaries, 25
benefits, 10, 28, 31, 34, 35, 40, 41, 42, 90, 118, 165
bias, 13, 17
birds, 38
black market, 148
Blacks, 6
blindness, 59
blueprint, 117
boils, 38
Botswana, vii, 116, 146, 167, 171
Braille, 46, 69
brain, 27, 28, 29, 32, 56, 57, 58, 60, 146, 149, 162
brain damage, 56, 60
brain drain, 27, 28, 29, 146, 149, 162
brain growth, 32
breakdown, 117
Britain, 46, 49, 143
brokered ceasefire, 5
browsing, 121
building blocks, 32
bullying, 57, 62, 68, 112, 114, 117, 138
business management, 82
businesses, 27

C

campaigns, 72
cancer, 113
candidates, 13, 14, 21, 46, 47, 114, 150
caregivers, 41
case studies, 160
cash, 24, 145
catalyst, 101
causal inference, 135
ceasefire, 5
certificate, 21, 91, 99, 102, 104, 106
certification, 97, 98, 101
challenges, 1, 5, 8, 10, 11, 16, 17, 18, 19, 23, 24, 27, 28, 29, 31, 32, 33, 34, 40, 46, 58, 61, 75, 77, 83, 91, 92, 93, 95, 97, 103, 107, 108, 109, 110, 111, 112, 114, 115, 116, 118, 143, 144, 147, 149, 153, 155, 160, 162, 164
checks and balances, 10
Chicago, 158
child abuse, 57, 58, 92
child benefit, 40
child development, 39, 40, 41, 130, 150, 151
childcare, 33, 35, 47
childhood, 9, 13, 31, 32, 33, 34, 35, 36, 37, 38, 39, 40, 41, 42, 43, 129, 151, 163, 164, 166, 167
children, 1, 2, 5, 7, 8, 10, 11, 13, 14, 20, 22, 24, 25, 29, 31, 32, 33, 34, 35, 36, 37, 38, 39, 40, 41, 42, 46, 47, 48, 49, 50, 51, 52, 53, 55, 57, 58, 59, 61, 66, 67, 68, 71, 72, 85, 90, 91, 92, 99, 108, 109, 113, 115, 127, 129, 131, 133, 137, 145, 146, 147, 148, 151, 152, 153, 154, 158, 159, 162, 165
China, 153, 164
chronic illness, 133
citizens, 5, 6, 29, 101, 107, 130
citizenship, 155
civil servants, 8
civil war, 113, 145
civilization, 2, 77
classes, 7, 12, 33, 39, 50, 52, 99, 108, 115, 116, 134, 136
classification, 160
classroom, 37, 61, 66, 67, 68, 69, 70, 72, 73, 88, 105, 107, 108, 114, 115, 116, 119, 125, 130, 131, 132, 140, 141, 148, 150, 151, 158, 161, 164, 166
classroom environment, 115
classroom management, 105, 108
classroom teacher, 61, 67, 72, 73, 125, 131, 151
cleanup, 163
cleft palate, 60
clients, 22, 76, 78, 79, 80, 81, 82, 83, 84, 85, 86, 87, 88, 89, 90, 92, 95, 114, 152
climate, 12, 79, 81, 146, 148
closure, 16, 145
cognition, 34, 61, 62, 129
cognitive development, 32, 38
cognitive function, 34, 35
cognitive process, 69
cognitive skills, 35, 62
cognitive tasks, 62
coherence, 78
collaboration, 21, 33, 115, 150, 152

college students, 23
colleges, 15, 16, 17, 18, 20, 23, 25, 26, 27, 97, 98, 100, 101, 102, 103, 104, 107, 108, 109, 110, 113, 150, 154, 164
colonial rule, 6
colonization, 3, 126
color, 49
commercial, 145
communication, 56, 58, 60, 61, 93, 115, 129, 154
communication skills, 61
community, 2, 3, 6, 12, 13, 18, 25, 27, 33, 38, 39, 41, 42, 48, 50, 76, 77, 86, 92, 93, 94, 102, 105, 108, 109, 112, 113, 116, 118, 135, 144, 149, 150, 151, 152, 155
compensation, 145, 165
competition, 114
competitiveness, 16, 130
complement, 87, 103, 114
complexity, 95
compliance, 57
complications, 46, 58, 113
comprehension, 62
compulsory education, 14
computer, 129, 154
conditioning, 81, 85
confidentiality, 115, 117, 152
conflict, 46, 47, 79, 115, 161
confrontation, 85
congenital malformations, 60
Congo, 145
congress, 165
consciousness, 79, 86
construct validity, 121, 123
consulting, 93, 171, 172
consumers, 132
continuous data, 70
control condition, 136
control group, 136
controlled trials, 135
controversial, 144, 145
conviction, 38
cooperation, 152, 153
cooperative learning, 72, 108
coordination, 16, 32, 146, 147
coping strategies, 93
correlation, 32, 123, 124, 134, 138
correlation analysis, 134
correlation coefficient, 123, 124, 138
corruption, 113, 149
cosmos, 48
cost, 2, 33, 103, 144, 145, 146, 147
cost of living, 144, 145, 146

counseling, 46, 75, 76, 77, 78, 79, 80, 81, 82, 83, 84, 85, 86, 87, 88, 89, 90, 91, 92, 93, 94, 95, 108, 111, 112, 113, 114, 115, 116, 117, 118, 133, 138, 152, 157, 158, 159, 160, 161, 162, 163, 164, 166, 167
craving, 135
creativity, 153
crises, 16, 47, 66, 114, 116, 159
critical thinking, 22
Cuba, 106
cues, 62
cultural differences, 78, 116
cultural practices, 21, 152
cultural values, 92, 116
culture, 2, 12, 47, 76, 82, 92, 93, 94, 116, 129
currency, 27
curricula, 11, 12, 13, 14, 16, 25, 27, 33, 46, 49, 50, 66, 67, 104, 149, 151, 152, 153, 154
curriculum, 3, 4, 10, 11, 12, 13, 14, 15, 19, 20, 29, 46, 47, 49, 50, 52, 66, 69, 70, 99, 100, 104, 108, 109, 117, 118, 121, 122, 154, 164

D

damages, 59
data analysis, 127, 134, 135, 137
database, 167
deaths, 113
decay, 93
deficiencies, 62, 85
deficit, 56
delinquency, 42
Delta, 160
democracy, 5, 13
Democratic Republic of Congo, 9, 10, 145
democratization, 158
demonstrations, 9, 16
denial, 91, 110
Department of Education, 102, 172
dependent variable, 134, 135, 136
depression, 57, 91, 112, 114, 148
deprivation, 47
depth, 130
derivatives, 88
destiny, 83
destruction, 92
devaluation, 9, 10
developing countries, 66, 113, 153, 158, 159, 165, 171
developmental change, 102
developmental disorder, 56, 58
diabetes, 59, 61
direct observation, 133

disability, 46, 47, 48, 50, 52, 56, 57, 58, 61, 62, 69, 70, 71, 72, 116, 158, 160
disaster, 9
disclosure, 79
discomfort, 80
discrimination, 2, 10
diseases, 59
disorder, 56, 57, 58, 60
displacement, 144, 147
disposition, 48
distance education, 103
distortions, 90
distribution, 139
diversity, 12, 42, 67, 95, 105, 116, 157
doctors, 77
domestic violence, 91
donor countries, 154
donors, 25, 108, 150
drawing, 36, 68, 84
dream, 107, 122
drought, 113
drugs, 60, 92
dysgraphia, 56
dyslexia, 56, 57

E

eating disorders, 114
economic crisis, 145
economic cycle, 110
economic development, 5, 7, 10, 150
economic empowerment, 112
economic growth, 149, 153, 166
economic meltdown, 9, 27, 146
economic performance, 93
economic problem, 29, 149
economic reform, 9
economic status, 89
economics, 172
editors, 159
educated manpower, 8
education industry, 42
education reform, 160
educational background, 33, 35
educational experience, 72
educational opportunities, 1, 2, 6, 11, 17
educational policy, 2, 8, 16, 157
educational practices, 65, 66
educational programs, 2, 32, 150, 154
educational qualifications, 149
educational research, 132, 141, 151, 166
educational services, 33, 50, 52, 147
educational settings, 32, 66, 72, 134, 135, 136

educational system, 3, 4, 49, 66, 151, 154
educators, 38, 39, 46, 51, 52, 55, 56, 58, 59, 67, 106, 110, 120, 130, 151, 159
elders, 76, 77, 91, 92, 93
electricity, 11, 108
emigration, 27, 146
emotional disorder, 112
emotional distress, 113
emotional experience, 79
emotional problems, 82, 111
emotional stability, 114
empathy, 81, 85
employees, 22, 29
employers, 16, 29
employment, 4, 13, 15, 16, 20, 23, 24, 42, 112, 113, 145, 146, 149, 153, 155
employment opportunities, 23, 146
empowerment, 77, 101
encounter groups, 82, 89
encouragement, 39, 40, 80
energy, 35, 84
engineering, 26
enrollment, 5, 6, 7, 10, 17, 48, 104
entrepreneurship, 26
environment, 3, 13, 24, 27, 32, 33, 34, 39, 40, 41, 42, 50, 58, 65, 68, 69, 70, 82, 85, 87, 88, 90, 92, 93, 112, 114, 115, 116, 117, 133, 134, 151
environmental change, 86
environmental factors, 56, 58
epidemic, 97, 108, 109, 110, 150, 161, 165
epilepsy, 47, 61, 163
equality, 11
equipment, 8, 10, 27, 28, 36, 67, 70, 107, 144, 145
equity, 165
ERA, 132
erosion, 9
essay question, 128, 129
ethical issues, 137
ethics, 94, 118
ethnic groups, 95
ethnicity, 13
Europe, 2
European Commission, 24
everyday life, 89
evidence, 12, 34, 35, 41, 58, 63, 120, 122, 124, 125, 126, 127, 129, 131, 141, 151, 153
examinations, 11, 12, 14, 15, 16, 20, 21, 102, 121, 145, 146, 147, 164
exercise, 76, 85, 94, 140
experimental design, 135, 136, 158
expertise, 25, 108, 150
exploitation, 7
exposure, 46, 56, 58

external locus of control, 63
external validity, 136
extreme poverty, 9, 24, 46, 47
extrinsic motivation, 63

F

face validity, 121, 123
faith, 134
false belief, 40
families, 9, 10, 25, 39, 41, 42, 76, 82, 91, 94, 116, 146, 152
family factors, 111
family members, 39, 77
family relationships, 79
family support, 78, 91, 114, 117
family therapy, 82, 91
fantasy, 12
farmers, 145
farms, 145
feelings, 37, 76, 79, 81, 90, 100
financial, 3, 5, 14, 15, 24, 25, 27, 28, 33, 144, 145, 149, 150
financial resources, 15, 27, 149, 150
financial stability, 28
financial support, 28
fiscal deficit, 145
flaws, 11
foams, 36
food, 38, 113, 144, 146
force, 22, 63, 83, 91, 129, 150, 153
foreign aid, 149
foreign investment, 149
formal education, 40, 47, 48
formal sector, 8
formation, 24, 25, 146, 155
formula, 124
foundations, vii, 2, 45, 52, 101, 102
France, 164
free will, 76
freedom, 6, 34, 84, 86, 88, 90, 112, 144
freedom of choice, 86
Freud, 79
friendship, 80, 114
funding, 4, 5, 6, 13, 16, 23, 25, 27, 29, 40, 50, 52, 146, 150
funds, 8, 27, 52, 67, 145, 147

G

gait, 60
gangs, 117

GDP, 145, 153
gender equality, 8
gender equity, 34
General Certificate of Education (GCE), 15, 21
general education, 39, 46, 49, 50, 66, 67, 70, 72, 151
genetics, 56, 57, 58, 59
geometry, 108, 121
Gestalt, 78, 84
gifted, 46
glasses, 38, 46
glaucoma, 59
global demand, 110
global village, 110, 116, 153
globalization, 93
goal setting, 76
God, 48
goods and services, 24
governance, 6
government expenditure, 6
government policy, 14, 15, 113
governments, 31, 42, 65
grades, 11, 14, 15, 16, 19, 22, 40, 42, 99, 138, 146, 166
grading, 14, 21, 147
graduate students, 23, 26
grants, 3, 6
Great Britain, 2
group activities, 87, 89
group size, 41
group therapy, 82, 88
group work, 88
grouping, 100
growth, 6, 24, 26, 34, 35, 56, 68, 80, 81, 82, 84, 85, 86, 87, 88, 104, 145, 149, 153
guardian, 133
guidance, 34, 38, 39, 50, 76, 86, 87, 92, 112, 113, 114, 115, 117, 118, 138, 152, 163
guidance counselors, 112
guidelines, 12, 21, 41, 78, 115
guilt, 77, 79

H

handwriting, 56, 57
harmony, 114, 115, 149
healing, 90, 92, 115
health, 9, 24, 28, 34, 46, 47, 61, 77, 92, 112, 148, 162, 172
health condition, 46, 47, 61
hearing impairment, 46, 59, 157, 158, 159
hearing loss, 59, 60
height, 24, 120

high school, 11, 12, 13, 14, 20, 21, 39, 40, 41, 107, 113, 114, 115, 116, 117, 146, 148, 153
higher education, 8, 16, 17, 18, 23, 25, 26, 27, 28, 29, 40, 42, 150, 153, 154, 166, 172
historical overview, 45
history, 7, 12, 77, 81, 82, 97, 157, 159, 161
HIV, 9, 47, 61, 91, 97, 108, 109, 110, 113, 133, 143, 148, 150, 155, 157, 159, 161, 164, 165, 166, 167, 171, 172
HIV/AIDS, 9, 47, 61, 91, 97, 108, 109, 110, 113, 143, 148, 150, 155, 159, 161, 165, 171, 172
home culture, 40
homes, 32, 39, 92, 147
homework, 122
honesty, 81
host, 112, 148
hostilities, 5
house, 5, 160, 167
human, 6, 12, 13, 15, 16, 17, 23, 24, 25, 76, 80, 81, 83, 87, 92, 101, 105, 112, 132, 144, 149, 157, 161, 164
human behavior, 81
human capital, 149, 164
human condition, 132
human development, 17, 24, 101, 105
human dignity, 92
human nature, 83, 157
human resource development, 16
human resources, 13, 23
human right, 6, 12, 17, 24, 105, 144, 161
human values, 92
husband, 93
hydrocephalus, 60
hygiene, 93
hyperactivity, 56, 58, 112
hyperinflation, vii, 24, 27, 146
hypothesis, 134, 140

I

ICE, 160
ideal, 136
identification, 52, 152
identity, 12, 37, 82, 83, 161
illiteracy, 101
immigrants, 2
impairments, 59, 61
imperialism, 2
impulses, 37
impulsivity, 58
inattention, 58
income, 28, 33, 41, 120, 129, 148

independence, vii, 1, 2, 5, 6, 7, 8, 9, 10, 12, 13, 16, 17, 18, 20, 21, 24, 26, 28, 36, 38, 46, 48, 49, 51, 85, 90, 97, 98, 100, 101, 102, 104, 106, 110, 143, 144, 145, 147, 154
independent variable, 134, 135, 136
India, 153
indigenous knowledge, 48
indirect effect, 10, 34
individual character, 72
individual differences, 35, 115, 116
individual students, 56, 70, 114, 115, 116, 120
individual traditional families, 76
individuality, 80
individuals, 22, 23, 26, 29, 36, 45, 46, 48, 49, 51, 52, 53, 59, 63, 69, 76, 82, 83, 86, 87, 89, 90, 94, 113, 132, 137, 149
indoctrination, 82
industry, 2
inequality, 2, 5, 11
infants, 33, 34, 36, 47
inferiority, 6, 79
inflation, 10, 146, 147
informal sector, 147
infrastructure, 9, 16, 24, 27, 50, 107, 144, 145, 154
ingredients, 77, 101
injury, 57, 58, 60
inner world, 79
insects, 38
instinct, 35
institutions, 15, 16, 17, 18, 20, 23, 26, 27, 28, 29, 35, 43, 49, 75, 77, 78, 82, 95, 98, 99, 100, 101, 107, 109, 110, 111, 112, 113, 118, 120, 150, 164
instructional activities, 70
instructional materials, 145, 146
instructional practice, 66
instructional procedures, 126
instructional time, 62, 147, 148
integration, 12, 50, 52, 78, 84, 85, 107, 133, 157
integrity, 147
intellectual disabilities, 56, 57, 158
intelligence, 57, 120, 123, 164
intelligence tests, 57
interface, 108, 150
internal consistency, 124
internalizing, 57
international trade, 144
interpersonal relations, 57, 88
interpersonal skills, 40
intervention, 24, 25, 42, 48, 87, 120, 125, 126, 127, 130, 137, 162
intimidation, 68
intrinsic motivation, 63
investment, 3, 5, 42, 143, 149, 167

isolation, 57
issues, 5, 18, 19, 52, 58, 76, 77, 88, 92, 93, 114, 115, 116, 120, 133, 145, 151, 152, 164, 167, 171

J

job skills, 26

K

Kenya, 33, 164
kindergarten, 35
kinship, 48

L

labeling, 120
labor force, 2, 4
labor market, 13, 42
Lancaster House, 5
landscape, 2
languages, 13, 160
laws, 45, 46, 49, 52, 53, 93
lead, 3, 35, 56, 82, 91, 101, 112, 116, 132
leadership, 89, 109, 165, 171
learners, 31, 53, 58, 61, 62, 63, 69, 75, 108, 150, 153, 155, 161, 163
learning, 11, 15, 16, 17, 22, 23, 25, 27, 28, 29, 32, 33, 34, 35, 36, 37, 38, 39, 40, 46, 47, 55, 56, 58, 59, 60, 61, 62, 63, 64, 65, 66, 67, 68, 69, 70, 71, 72, 75, 78, 83, 88, 95, 103, 105, 106, 107, 108, 109, 110, 111, 112, 113, 114, 115, 120, 122, 125, 126, 127, 128, 129, 130, 132, 144, 146, 149, 150, 151, 154, 155, 158, 164, 165, 166
learning disabilities, 46, 56, 127
learning environment, 40, 67, 68, 69, 71, 149, 155
learning outcomes, 61, 129, 151
learning process, 39, 56, 61, 63, 68, 107, 114, 115, 132
learning skills, 62
learning styles, 68
learning task, 58
legislation, 31, 42, 51, 52, 111, 117
legs, 60
lesson plan, 121
liberation, 5, 8, 9, 10, 90, 100, 102, 145
Liberia, 105
life cycle, 132
life expectancy, 9, 109, 148
lifelong learning, 155, 166
light, 4, 77, 97
linguistics, 48

literacy, 8, 9, 12, 25, 38, 46, 47, 107, 129, 143, 160
literacy rates, 46
living conditions, 91, 93, 112
local community, 32
locus, 63
love, 77, 79, 80
LTD, 157
lying, 112

M

magazines, 93
majority, 2, 6, 7, 11, 14, 23, 47, 70, 93, 102, 103, 116, 139, 147, 148
malnutrition, 46, 56, 57
man, 49, 93, 123, 160
management, 23, 26, 70, 81, 95, 144, 148
manipulation, 86, 136
manpower, 5, 7, 8, 16, 21, 28, 108, 148
marriage, 80, 82, 91, 93
mass, 12, 72, 145
mass media, 72
materials, 16, 27, 28, 31, 32, 33, 36, 39, 40, 42, 46, 101, 102, 108, 109, 144, 146, 150, 154, 155
mathematics, 11, 62, 126, 129, 157
matter, 3, 34, 108
measurement, 119, 120, 125, 129, 130, 133, 151
meat, 38
media, 22, 29, 93, 150
medical, 15, 148
medication, 90
medicine, 23, 26, 48, 77
membership, 89
memory, 61, 62
mental health, 76, 77, 78, 113
mental illness, 77
mental retardation, 46, 56, 164
mentoring, 133
mercury, 56
methodology, 100, 163
Miami, 171
migration, 91, 93
military, 9, 10, 145
miniature, 88
Ministry of Education, 13, 14, 20, 21, 22, 23, 33, 50, 52, 67, 109, 113, 121, 146, 151, 163, 164
mission, 3, 4, 6, 14, 16, 21, 22, 23, 105, 115, 167
mixing, 40, 148
models, 78, 84, 150
modifications, 46, 70, 77, 90, 152
modules, 102
momentum, 35
moral behavior, 92, 113

moral code, 79
morale, 39
morbidity, 148
mortality, 9
mortality rate, 9
Moses, v, 1, 19, 97, 171
motivation, 63, 67, 87, 146
motor activity, 34
motor control, 60
motor skills, 32, 36, 38, 57
Mozambique, 102, 165
muscles, 60
muscular dystrophy, 60
music, 20, 35, 49
mutual respect, 68
mutuality, 84

N

Namibia, 146
NAP, 24
national policy, 14, 20
needy, 25
negative attitudes, 71, 109
neglect, 48
Nelson Mandela, 144, 155, 171
New Zealand, 24, 78, 146
Nigeria, 94, 157
no voice, 91
North America, vii
nuclear family, 92, 93, 95
nurses, 15, 20
nutrition, 33, 34

O

obstacles, 1, 71, 109
officials, 148
openness, 79, 81
operating system, 115
opportunities, 6, 9, 23, 38, 42, 52, 63, 107, 113, 144, 145, 146, 149, 153
oppression, 7
optimism, 110
oral presentations, 69
organize, 38, 62
ownership, 128, 144

P

Pacific, 160
pain, 79, 148

parental involvement, 40, 42
parenting, 58, 92
parents, 5, 7, 10, 11, 13, 32, 33, 34, 35, 36, 39, 40, 41, 42, 43, 48, 79, 85, 89, 90, 91, 105, 109, 112, 114, 115, 116, 118, 133, 140, 146, 148, 150, 151, 152, 157, 158, 159
Parliament, 165
participants, 80, 88, 89, 90, 138
pastures, 27
patriotism, vii, 150
peace, 114
pedagogy, 104, 152
performance indicator, 130, 151
peri-urban, 93
permit, 67, 135
personal development, 87
personal problems, 114
personal relations, 82, 87, 94
personal responsibility, 4, 82
personality, 79
Philadelphia, 98, 163
Philippines, 166
physical health, 34
physical well-being, 39, 61, 129
platform, 153
Plato, 76
pleasure, vii, 79
pleasure principle, 79
police, 91
policy, vii, 1, 4, 6, 7, 8, 11, 12, 13, 21, 28, 31, 33, 34, 42, 49, 50, 51, 52, 101, 108, 109, 113, 130, 151, 160, 164
policy makers, vii, 52
political independence, 2, 5, 9, 46, 49, 98, 101, 143, 144, 145, 154
political instability, 143, 144
political power, 3
politics, 158
population, 2, 4, 6, 8, 9, 18, 61, 66, 71, 109, 135, 144, 148
positive attitudes, 71, 72, 115
positive correlation, 42
post-traumatic stress disorder, 47
poverty, 23, 24, 34, 41, 42, 102, 107, 112, 113
poverty reduction, 24, 112
power sharing, 165
powered wheelchairs, 70
predictive validity, 122
pregnancy, 114
preparation, 33, 52, 97, 98, 102, 104, 107, 108, 110, 125, 150, 159
preparedness, 36
preschool, 33, 35, 36, 40, 42, 133

president, 10, 144
prevalence rate, 61, 148
prevention, 58, 70, 77, 116, 150
primary school, 5, 6, 7, 8, 13, 14, 20, 24, 31, 32, 33, 36, 39, 42, 43, 98, 99, 100, 103, 112, 113, 115, 117, 138, 146, 154, 171
principles, 69, 85, 94, 101, 105, 132
private enterprises, 33
private schools, 14, 21
private sector, 26, 27, 150
problem behavior, 62, 70, 71, 159, 164
problem solving, 31, 36, 38, 57, 76, 81
procurement, 67
professional development, 50, 72, 150, 151
professional qualifications, 98
professional teacher, 105, 164
professionalism, 23
professionals, vii, 9, 27, 28, 50, 146, 149, 152, 161, 162
profound disabilities, 52
project, 68, 129
proliferation, 49
promote innovation, 153
pronunciation, 57
prosperity, 2, 9
protection, 92, 115
psychiatrist, 76
psychiatry, 77
psychoanalysis, 80
psychological development, 34, 79
psychological problems, 92, 114
psychologist, 76, 87
psychology, 76, 77, 79, 93, 158
psychosocial support, 159
psychotherapy, 85, 158, 160, 161, 162, 167
public awareness, 72
public debt, 27
public education, 162
public policy, 42
public sector, 26
punishment, 70, 87

Q

qualifications, 23, 40, 41, 98, 99, 100, 110, 113
quality control, 151
quality education, 5, 10, 18, 24, 25, 38, 97, 102, 129, 144
quantitative research, 134
questioning, 62
quizzes, 120

R

race, 13, 37, 49, 116
racism, 114
random assignment, 135
rape, 91
reactions, 39, 157, 158
reading, 4, 5, 31, 35, 56, 57, 62, 68, 75, 136, 138, 163
reading disorder, 57
reading problems, 56
realism, 79
reality, 8, 79, 80, 81, 82, 89, 151, 153
reasoning, 56, 61
recession, 112
recognition, 34, 49, 70, 91
recommendations, 97, 99, 127, 130, 149, 155, 156
reconciliation, 6, 83
reconstruction, 17
recovery, 155, 166, 167
reflective practice, 165
reform, vii, 1, 2, 5, 6, 7, 8, 9, 10, 12, 13, 77, 97, 110, 143, 144, 145, 155, 161, 162, 163, 167
refugees, 6, 102
regeneration, 12
regression, 123
regression analysis, 123
regulations, 3
regulatory bodies, 118
rehabilitation, 17, 49, 116, 157
reinforcement, 71
relatives, 77, 90, 91, 93
relativity, 160
relaxation, 35
relevance, 25, 77, 157
reliability, 123, 124, 125, 128, 129, 133
relief, 24, 25, 29
religion, 77
religious beliefs, 116, 134
remediation, 28, 48, 116
repression, 7, 158
reputation, 21
requirements, 14, 17, 23, 84, 104, 107, 146
researchers, vii, 39, 48, 56, 58, 71, 72, 130, 132, 135, 138, 141
resettlement, 163
resistance, 11
resources, 8, 11, 12, 18, 21, 23, 25, 27, 33, 39, 41, 42, 50, 66, 67, 72, 94, 100, 103, 117, 145, 150
response, 67, 76, 100, 121, 164
restrictions, 1, 7, 8
retardation, 158
rewards, 63, 79

rights, 92, 115, 144, 161
risk, 34, 46, 47, 53, 59, 89, 117, 120, 148, 151
role playing, 69
root, 17, 76, 92
rubber, 36
rugby, 20
rules, 34, 117, 120
rural areas, 6, 7, 21, 92, 100, 101, 102, 146, 147
rural development, 12
rural schools, 11, 24

S

safety, 127
savings, 42
school, 3, 4, 5, 6, 7, 8, 9, 10, 11, 13, 14, 15, 16, 18, 19, 20, 21, 22, 24, 25, 26, 27, 28, 29, 32, 33, 34, 35, 36, 38, 39, 40, 41, 42, 43, 47, 48, 49, 50, 52, 57, 58, 62, 63, 64, 66, 67, 70, 71, 72, 75, 76, 79, 82, 83, 90, 91, 94, 95, 99, 100, 101, 102, 103, 104, 105, 106, 108, 109, 110, 111, 112, 113, 114, 115, 116, 117, 118, 121, 125, 126, 130, 131, 133, 138, 141, 144, 145, 146, 147, 148, 149, 150, 151, 152, 153, 154, 155, 158, 160, 161, 163, 164, 165, 166, 172
school achievement, 34
school community, 66
school enrollment, 49, 146
school fees, 7, 14, 21, 29, 145
school work, 117
schooling, 32, 34
science, 11, 12, 14, 17, 23, 26, 106, 123, 129, 138, 145, 154, 163, 164
scientific method, 134
scope, 167
scripts, 83, 147
secondary education, 6, 7, 10, 11, 13, 14, 20, 29, 99, 102
secondary school students, 21, 25
secondary schools, 7, 11, 14, 15, 17, 20, 21, 26, 91, 99, 115, 165
secondary students, 20
secondary teachers, 98, 103, 106
security, 34, 48
segregation, 2, 7, 133
selective attention, 61
self-actualization, 23, 80
self-assessment, 128
self-awareness, 37, 84, 86, 89
self-confidence, 37, 128
self-control, 36
self-discipline, 22, 113
self-esteem, 92, 114, 133
self-expression, 84
self-image, 112
self-interest, 3
self-study, 85
self-understanding, 81, 85
self-worth, 92
seminars, 151
senate, 101
sensation, 60
sensitivity, 88, 89
separateness, 82
service provider, 32, 33, 39
services, 31, 32, 33, 34, 40, 41, 42, 46, 50, 51, 52, 90, 91, 94, 113, 115, 116, 118, 152, 158
sex, 76, 112, 116
sexual abuse, 114
sexual orientation, 116
sexuality, 87
shape, 34, 117, 144
shelter, 146
short term memory, 62
shortage, 5, 8, 11, 16, 27, 33, 102, 106, 113, 145, 147, 148
siblings, 39
signals, 123
signs, 57, 78, 79, 155
single test, 126
skill acquisition, 42
skilled workers, 2
skills training, 16, 104
skin, 60
slavery, 6
smoking, 112
soccer, 20, 38
social behavior, 37, 86
social control, 83
social development, 34, 37, 112
social environment, 37
social exclusion, 114
social fabric, 35
social group, 37
social interactions, 68, 92
social justice, 161
social life, 114
social network, 90, 93
social norms, 62
social relations, 62, 114
social sciences, 23, 26
social services, 9, 10, 24
social skills, 35, 37, 39, 40, 42, 57, 59, 61, 62, 113
social support, 72, 93
social welfare, 28
socialism, 102

socialization, 93
socially acceptable behavior, 37
society, 12, 21, 42, 47, 48, 49, 52, 58, 76, 77, 79, 80, 82, 85, 87, 88, 90, 92, 93, 94, 97, 109, 116, 130, 132, 144, 152, 153, 161
software, 108
solution, 154
South Africa, 4, 48, 116, 144, 146, 158, 161, 163, 165
South Korea, 153
Spearman-Brown, 124
special education, 40, 42, 45, 46, 47, 49, 50, 51, 52, 53, 66, 67, 71, 124, 127, 137, 151, 159, 160, 161, 162, 163, 166, 171
specialization, 23, 26
speech, 8, 46, 60, 70
spending, 6, 102
spina bifida, 60
spinal cord, 60
spine, 60
spirituality, 77
spontaneity, 81
spreadsheets, 108
Spring, 161
stability, 9, 24, 125, 149
staff development, 108
staff members, 117
stakeholders, 115, 118
standard deviation, 57
standard of living, 23
standardization, 101
starvation, 154
state, 13, 16, 21, 22, 23, 31, 36, 45, 52, 82, 83, 84, 90, 98, 104, 106, 107, 108, 110, 114, 124, 125, 134, 136, 149, 155, 158, 167
statistics, 7, 47, 134, 139, 157, 167
stereotypes, 133
stereotyping, 68
stigma, 110, 133, 150
stigmatized, 120
stimulation, 62
stimulus, 81, 134
stomach, 60
stress, 112, 114, 135, 148
stressors, 34
structural reforms, 9
structure, 13, 19, 20, 79, 88, 93, 99, 164
student achievement, 134
student enrollment, 4, 16
student teacher, 98, 101, 102, 103, 104, 106, 107, 108, 109, 110, 158, 159
style, 58, 80, 86
subdomains, 129

sub-Saharan Africa, 93, 126
subsidy, 9
substance abuse, 92, 114
subtraction, 126
suicide, 117
superego, 79
supernatural, 48
supervision, 26
supervisor, 171
support services, 32
surplus, 35
survival, 92, 103, 114
suspensions, 70
sustainability, 16, 112
sustainable development, 105
symptoms, 78
syndrome, 93, 137
systematic desensitization, 90

T

tactics, 126
talent, 154
Tanzania, 116
target, 24, 66, 71, 92, 130
Task Force, 129, 130, 151, 162, 164
taxation, 4
taxes, 36, 42
taxonomy, 68
teacher preparation, 97, 101, 102, 103, 104, 106, 107, 109, 110, 150, 151, 152
teacher training, 23, 98, 99, 100, 104, 106, 108, 110, 148
teachers, vii, 8, 9, 11, 12, 13, 15, 16, 17, 20, 22, 25, 26, 28, 33, 35, 38, 41, 42, 43, 50, 52, 58, 61, 62, 63, 64, 66, 67, 68, 69, 70, 71, 72, 97, 98, 99, 100, 101, 102, 103, 104, 105, 106, 107, 108, 109, 110, 112, 115, 116, 117, 118, 120, 122, 124, 126, 127, 130, 131, 132, 133, 136, 138, 140, 141, 144, 146, 147, 148, 149, 150, 151, 152, 154, 157, 161, 162, 163, 165, 167
teaching strategies, 108, 151
technical assistance, 50
techniques, 37, 82, 85, 86, 87, 89, 93, 105, 152
technological advancement, 107
technological advances, 107
technological change, 97
technology, 12, 17, 26, 27, 28, 29, 70, 97, 107, 108, 110, 129, 150, 153, 160, 161, 164, 165, 166
temperament, 58
temperature, 146
tension, 79
terminal patients, 113

tertiary education, 16, 17, 19, 20, 23, 25, 26, 27, 29, 111, 117, 154, 161, 164
test items, 121, 124
test scores, 120, 125, 134, 138
testing, 108, 122, 123
test-retest reliability, 123, 125
textbooks, 8, 138, 141, 145, 146
theft, 62
theoretical approaches, 85
therapeutic relationship, 80
therapist, 80, 81, 82, 84, 85, 86
therapy, 46, 78, 80, 82, 83, 84, 85, 86, 87, 88, 162, 163
thoughts, 76, 82, 85
threatened abortion, 91
threats, 68, 136, 137
time allocation, 118
time periods, 136
time series, 135
toys, 32, 36, 38
trachoma, 59
trade, 9, 149
trade liberalization, 9
traditions, 12
trainees, 71, 102, 104, 159, 162
training, 3, 4, 15, 16, 17, 20, 22, 23, 25, 33, 34, 72, 81, 82, 88, 91, 98, 99, 100, 101, 102, 103, 104, 106, 107, 108, 109, 110, 111, 112, 113, 118, 152, 155, 162, 164, 165
training programs, 16
traits, 79
transactions, 83
transmission, 108
transparency, 23
transportation, 146, 148
trauma, 59, 91, 133
treatment, 14, 76, 77, 78, 84, 85, 89, 90, 133, 136, 137
triggers, 76, 112
tuition, 25, 27

U

U.S. policy, 165
Ukraine, 162
UNDP, 109, 145, 166
unemployment rate, 25, 93, 147, 150
UNESCO, 32, 34, 35, 40, 41, 65, 129, 155, 157, 162, 166
unhappiness, 81
unions, 150
united, 17, 24, 25, 34, 77, 98, 100, 101, 104, 146, 147, 155, 166, 167

United Kingdom, 146, 166
United Nations (UN), 24, 25, 34, 146, 147, 155, 167
United States, 77, 98
universal access, 5
universe, 121
universities, 16, 17, 18, 20, 23, 25, 26, 27, 28, 98, 104, 108, 110, 153
university education, 20, 113
urban, 7, 21, 24, 41, 93, 147, 163
urban areas, 7, 21, 93, 147
urban schools, 24
urbanization, 4, 91, 93

V

vacuum, 27
validation, 77
variables, 76, 125, 133, 134, 138, 139
variations, 86, 137
vegetables, 38
vein, 76, 89
vessels, 153
victims, 66, 91, 117, 147
violence, 47, 62, 68, 91, 117, 147, 165
vision, 25, 59
visual acuity, 59
visual stimuli, 59
visual system, 59
vocational education, 26
vocational training, 16

W

war, 4, 5, 7, 8, 9, 10, 46, 91, 100, 101, 108, 145, 150, 165
war years, 4
Washington, 158, 161, 162, 164, 165, 166
water, 28, 38, 41
watershed, 5
weakness, 52, 107
wealth, 112
web, 85, 155
welfare, 2, 49, 111, 113, 115, 117
well-being, 82, 112
wellness, 77
western culture, 94
WHO, 148, 167
wholesale, 95
William James, 87
Wisconsin, 162
witchcraft, 48
withdrawal, 9, 66, 82, 137

work environment, 117, 154
workers, 9, 26, 144, 145, 158
workforce, 17, 26, 154
working conditions, 16, 144, 146, 149
World Bank, 9, 24, 161
worldwide, 105, 149
writing process, 56, 57

Y

Yale University, 158
yield, 12, 42, 95, 135
young adults, 7
young people, 93, 109, 112, 113
young women, 91

Z

Zimbabwe, v, vii, 1, 2, 3, 5, 6, 7, 9, 10, 12, 14, 15, 16, 17, 18, 19, 20, 21, 22, 23, 24, 25, 26, 27, 28, 29, 32, 33, 35, 42, 45, 46, 47, 48, 49, 50, 51, 52, 53, 65, 66, 71, 72, 73, 75, 76, 90, 91, 92, 93, 94, 95, 97, 98, 99, 100, 101, 102, 104, 106, 107,108, 109, 110, 111, 113, 115, 116, 130, 143, 144, 145, 146, 148, 149, 150, 151, 153, 155, 157, 158, 159, 160, 161, 162, 163, 164, 165, 166, 167, 171, 172
Zimbabwean education, 1, 5, 6, 12, 13, 19, 29, 130, 143, 144, 149, 166
zoology, 48